Command Responsibility: Holding Military Leaders Accountable For Their Troops

James B. Whisker
and
Kevin R. Spiker, Jr.

Command Responsibility: Holding Military Leaders Accountable For Their Troops

James B. Whisker
and
Kevin R. Spiker, Jr.

Academica Press
Washington~London

Library of Congress Cataloging-in-Publication Data
Names: Whisker, James B., author | Spiker, Kevin R., author
Title: Command responsibility : holding military leaders accountable for their troops / James B. Whisker
and Kevin R. Spiker
Description: Washington : Academica Press, 2020. | Includes references and index.
Identifiers: LCCN 2020932993 | ISBN 9781680531336 (hardcover)

Dedicated to the memory of
Jeffrey Lucien Radell, Ph.D.
Professor, Political Science
University of Wisconsin-Oshkosh

James Biser Whisker, Sr. is professor emeritus from West Virginia University. He is a graduate of Bedford High School, Mount St. Mary's College, Niagara University and the University of Maryland where he received his Ph.D in 1969. He is the author of The Right to Hunt; The Rise and Decline of the American Militia System; The Citizen-Soldier and U. S. Military Policy; and studies of arms makers in sixteen states. His five volume study of the American colonial militias won the Adele Mellen Prize. At WVU he was longtime adviser to the College Republicans and Young Americans for Freedom. Professor Whisker has won several teaching awards, including one from the WVU Honors Program.

Kevin Ray Spiker, Jr. Is a graduate of Bedford High School, the Pennsylvania State University, and West Virginia University where he earned his Ph.D. He has taught political science at West Virginia University, Frostburg State University and is currently associate professor at Ohio University. With Professor Whisker he has co-authored a series on Bedford County, Pennsylvania, history; The Alien Tort Statute, and Command Responsibility. They are currently working on additional publications on the death penalty. His teaching areas include areas of American political institutions.

Contents

Introduction

Is there such an event as a civilized war? How does a nation make certain that basic rules of civilization shall be applied in a conflict? If a nation is losing a war may it resort to illicit means to turn defeat into victory? Is it possible that nations of the world can agree on certain ethical principles and then enforce compliance? Once certain basic rules are adopted can these rules be applied retroactively? If we can answer these questions in a meaningful and positive way who shall enforce compliance?

At one time, early on, the Jews thought to obey God's commandments, among which were rules for waging war. After the rise of Christianity the nations of Europe thought to allow popes to referee conflicts only to find that popes were often parties to conflicts rather than acting as impartial judges. The creation of international treaties that sought to remove some of the worst of wars came into being without any existing authority to guarantee compliance. Creation of international organizations did not improve matters as they had no teeth of their own and the nations that should have acted a police failed to do so when confronted by real conflicts.

During the First War for Independence the British complained bitterly that American sharpshooters were decimating the British officer corps. Not only did they object to the American preference for killing the upper class, the British argued that only could officers restrain the most evil impulses of the common soldiers. Kill the officers and the most uncivilized expressions of human behavior will follow. Americans disagreed, having been the victims of the unrestrained warfare practiced by Banastre Tarleton and Hair Buyer Hamilton.

It appeared that no sooner had nations agreed upon some basic regulations than the signatories of resultant treaties were looking for loopholes to violate at least the spirit, if not the letter, of the international instruments. Outlaw expanding or expanding so-called "dum dum" rifle bullets than the British developed full-patch bullets with a natural tendency to tumble upon impact, thus having exactly the same effect of tearing massive wound holes. As we shall see, Japan claimed that treaties outlawing deployment of poison gas were violated by the use of atomic bombs that produced radioactive black rain and similar results.

As it was, there was precious little international law applicable to wars fought before 1920. Among the early legislation were provisions that sought to protect prisoners of war, allow for honorable surrender, and require humane treatment of captured enemy soldiers. In earlier decades officers were often spared, but enlisted men were enslaved, sold, or simply slaughtered. International law also sought to protect civilians and allow for declarations of "open city" to prevent the destruction of urban areas. Likewise, hospitals, orphanages, churches and other houses of worship, schools and colleges, and museums were to be declared off-limits to fighting and destruction. Physicians, nurses, clergy, and certain other non-combatants, even if in uniform, had certain legal protection.

Essentially no legal protections existed for a nation's own citizens and soldiers. There was nary a thought given to establishing rights of traitors, conscientious objectors, and those whose behavior was morally or legally wrong. Military courts-martial operated under rules quite alien to the civilian courts. Judges, prosecutors and such defense counsel as might be offered need not be attorneys.

Enemy spies could expect no protections. Enemy agents who operated without standard uniforms or in the uniforms of their opponents had no recourse and could be executed. No rights so familiar in civil courts were in effect here.

Likewise there were few protections for civilians who lived in occupied territories. No law prevented the taking, even execution, of hostages. Technically, invading armies could confiscate only materials directly connected to the war effort, including foodstuff. But looting and pillage seemed to be under no clear control, even after new international law was adopted after World War I. The Nazis looted the art of occupied Europe, but returning Allied soldiers brought home many "souvenirs" from occupied Germany.

World War II focused much attention of genocide as a most undesirable companion of war. Many Germans argued, with some considerable justice, that there was no existing international law regarding genocide, and what became known later as ethnic cleansing. Seen especially in the reduction of European Jewry, Gypsies, and others in what has become known universally as the Holocaust, there is no question as to genocide being immoral by all known standards. The question is: was it illegal under existing law of nations? Ethnic destruction occurred in Jugoslavia as Croats, long oppressed by Serbs, struck back with fury. And much ethnic destruction occurred in the Soviet Union, especially among nationalities that initially welcomed the invading German Army. Julius Streicher was one of history's most unpleasant characters, leading the onslaught on Judaism in his newspaper and paperback books and pamphlets. He would be guilty today of ethnic intimidation under the United Nations sponsored Genocide Treaty, but what he wrote would be constitutionally protected free speech in the United States.[1] Indeed many of his rantings have been translated and published in the United States, as has been the modern foundation document of anti-Jewish publications, the *Protocols of the Learned Men of Zion.*[2]

The capture, subsequent trial, and resultant execution of Adolf Eichmann has evoked debate since the event occurred. Presumably, Eichmann's capture by agents of the State of Israel was a violation of international law. While genocide is now considered a crime under the law of nations, many assert that was not so when Eichmann engineered the destruction of so many. As the law now is, genocide is a universally condemned violation of law that can be punished by any nation, presumably even one that did not exist until well after the crimes had been executed.[3]

Japan had not been a signatory to the major treaties that European nations had forged immediately before and following World War I. In World War II the Japanese authorities had expressed a desire to act under these laws and to have their own soldiers protected by them. The truth and

---

[1]Bytwerk, Randall L. *Julius Streicher: Nazi Editor of the Notorious Anti-semitic Newspaper Der Sturmer.* Cooper Square Press, 2001.

[2]Herman Bernstein, Herman. *The Protocols of the Wise Men of Zion: The History of a Lie*. Createspace, 2015.

[3]Ardent, Hannah. *Eichmann in Jerusalem: A Report on the Banality of Evil.* Penguin Classics, 1994.

reality were far different.

In the modern world of the 21st century, attention is focused on Third World, especially sub-Saharan African, nations. Ethnic intimidation, genocide, incredibly barbarous warfare, and every other possible aberration of human behavior are to be found. The last portion of our manuscript treats of such damning behavior and the attempt of international organizations and courts to prevent, or at least punish, such events.

1
Command Responsibility Defined

The modern usage of command responsibility can be defined as the responsibility of commanders for war crimes committed by subordinate members of their armed forces or other persons subject to their control. This responsibility is based on a failure to prevent or punish subordinates for their unlawful actions. One of the controversial aspects surrounding recent developments of the doctrine has been the level of knowledge that commanders must possess before they become criminally responsible. While it is widely accepted that actual knowledge of subordinates' crimes is sufficient, debate has centred on the appropriate level of "constructive" knowledge required to warrant individual criminal responsibility. Modern scholarship has seen two different formulations of constructive knowledge emerge. The stricter standard considers whether the commander should have known, in the given circumstances, of the unlawful actions of his subordinates, thereby placing him under a proactive duty to keep informed of the actions of his troops. Under the less stringent standard of constructive knowledge, the commander is held responsible only where he fails to discover his subordinates' actions from information already available to him. Both tests have received support in post-World War II jurisprudence concerned with command responsibility.[4]

International crimes, however, are often committed during armed conflicts or other unstable situations being a component of large scale atrocities that involve many different perpetrators on various levels. As a result, it is often very complicated to determine the personal criminal liability of each individual who contributed to the commission of specific international crimes. Herein lies the paradox: although international criminal law is essentially individual oriented, it usually must be

---

[4]Meloni, Chantal, *Command Responsibility in International Criminal Law*. Cambridge University Press, 2010, 3-23.

concerned with collective criminal phenomena as well. For these reasons, international criminal law has developed some additional forms of liability, namely joint criminal enterprise and superior responsibility. Superior responsibility is a form of indirect liability as the superior is not held criminally liable for the criminal acts in which he participated, e.g. planned, gave orders, assisted, but in connection with the criminal acts committed by subordinates.[5]

A simple definition of command responsibility involves "a duty or obligation where someone is held accountable." The *Army Field Manual* notes, "An Army leader is anyone who by virtue of assumed role or assigned responsibility inspires and influences people to accomplish organizational goals. Army leaders motivate people both inside and outside the chain of command to pursue actions, focus thinking, and shape decisions for the greater good of the organization."[6] The superior responsibility principle stems from the conduct of war by organized armed forces. The fact that the functioning of the armed forces is based on a hierarchical relationship between soldiers and superiors means that a subordinate may be punished for a breach or orders or for not following an order from his superiors. At the same time, the reliability of the armed forces depends on the fact that the commander takes responsibility for his subordinates. As stated, this form of superior responsibility forms the foundation of any organized armed forces, and is thereby inherent in the position of a commanding officer. However, the responsibility of a commander in relation to his subordinates in general is different from the modern concept of command responsibility, which refers to the criminal responsibility of a superior for international crimes committed by his/her subordinates, as tried and recognized by international courts and tribunals.

In essence, command responsibility imposes criminal responsibility for a superior's "failure to act when under a duty to do so." A superior will incur command responsibility if he or she knows or has reason to know that his or her subordinates are about to commit or have committed crimes, unless the superior prevents the subordinates' crimes or punishes the

---

[5]http :// www.ksk.edu.ee / wpcontent/uploads / 2012/12 /KVUOA_Toimetised_15_7_ Vark. Rene Vark, "Superior Responsibility

[6]*Army Field Manual*, 6-22.

perpetrators after the crimes are committed. This legal design places a criminally sanctioned burden on superiors to ensure that their subordinates comply with international law. Thus, the purpose of command responsibility is to ensure a broad compliance with international humanitarian law.[7] The doctrine of command responsibility is not just an academic construct, but a real and vital means by which commanders can be held responsible for failing to prevent or punish the misdeeds of their subordinates.[8] A superior's actual knowledge cannot be presumed, but it may be established through circumstantial evidence.[9]

Command or superior responsibility has often been misunderstood. It is not a form of objective liability whereby a superior could be held criminally responsible for crimes committed by subordinates of the accused regardless of his conduct and regardless of what his knowledge of these crimes. Neither is it a form of complicity whereby the superior is held criminally responsible for some sort of assistance that he has given to the principal perpetrators. Superior responsibility is a form of responsibility for omission to act: a superior may be held criminally responsible under that doctrine where, despite his awareness of the crimes of subordinates, he culpably fails to fulfill his duties to prevent and punish these crimes. The commission of one or more crimes attributable to a subordinate is a prerequisite for the application of that doctrine. In addition, the following requirements have been identified as forming part of the doctrine of superior responsibility under customary international law: (A) A relationship of superior-subordinate linking the accused and those who committed the underlying offenses at the time of the commission of the crime; (B) The knowledge on the part of the superior that his subordinates have committed or taken a culpable part in the commission of a crime or are about to do so; and (C) A failure on the part of the superior to take necessary and reasonable measures to prevent or to punish those crimes. This doctrine might apply, in principle, to military commander (at whatever level in the military structure), civilian officials (regardless of

---

[7] Green, Leslie, "Command Responsibility in International Humanitarian Law," *Transnational Law and Contemporary Problems* 5 (1995) 319-371.

[8] Moloto, Bakone, "Command Responsibility in International Criminal Tribunals" *Berkeley Journal of International Law*, 3: [2009] 12-25

[9] *Halilović* Judgment, 66; *Brima et al.* Judgment, 792.

the nature of their function, including heads of state or ministers) or paramilitary leaders. Under customary international law the elements of the doctrine are the same as a matter of law regardless of the nature of the authority which the superior exercised, the International Criminal Court Statute draws certain differences between military and non-military superiors.[10]

The person to whom the doctrine is relevant must be superior, hierarchically, to those who have committed the crimes in the sense that there must have existed between them a hierarchical relationship within a common chain of authority. That relationship may be *de jure,* i. e., it is recognized and sanctioned in the relevant domestic legal regime or it may be *de facto*, that is, where the relationship of authority is one based, not on legal regulations, but on the state of affairs. There is contradictory jurisprudence as to the time that is relevant to establishing the existence of such a link, i.e., the time when the crimes were committed or the time when the superior is said to have failed in his duty. command responsibility could apply, in theory, to any person who is able to exercise effective control over one or more people. The requirement of effective control, which must be met in relation to all and any sort of superior means that he must have had the material ability, at the time relevant to the charges, to prevent or punish the crimes of subordinates. Mere influence or charisma, even if significant, would not meet that standard. In all cases, there must be an expectation of obedience to orders on the part of the superior and a parallel expectation of subjection to his authority on the part of those who are under his authority. The idea that a superior could be held criminally responsible in relation to crimes of subordinates is central to the ability of international law to ensure compliance with standards of humanitarian law, and it remains a most important legal instrument in the fight against impunity.[11]

Since military or paramilitary forces carry out many cases of torture and extra-judicial killings, unique issues of who is responsible for these crimes arise. In most criminal and tort law contexts, a failure to act

---

[10]"Command Responsibility" Peaceandjusticeinitiative.org

[11]Mettraux, Guénaël, *The Law of Command Responsibility*. Oxford University, 2009, 62.

will not subject one to liability absent an agency or other statutorily or judicially recognized relationship. Military commanders, however, hold a unique position of power and authority over their soldiers. By law and tradition, soldiers must follow orders issued by officers superior in rank. Logically, if a commander has effective control of his soldiers, he has the ability to prevent or stop any objectionable actions.[12]

Command responsibility is an *omission* mode of individual criminal liability: the superior is responsible for crimes committed by his subordinates and for failing to prevent or punish, as opposed to crimes he ordered. This definition was established by the Hague Conventions IV (1907) and X (1907) and applied for the first time by the German Supreme Court in Leipzig after World War I. The 4th Hague Convention of 1907 held that in order for an armed force to be lawful it must be "commanded by a person responsible for his subordinates." Further, when an armed force takes possession of enemy territory the responsible officer must "take all measures in his power to restore, and ensure, as far as possible, public order and safety, while respecting, unless absolutely prevented, the laws in force in the country."[13]

Under international humanitarian law [IHL] commanders have been entrusted with the task of ensuring respect for that body of law by their subordinates. This responsibility includes not only the training in IHL of those under their command, but also the taking of necessary measures to prevent or punish subordinates committing violations of IHL. Failure by a commander to do so will give rise to criminal liability, often termed superior responsibility.[14]

By 1977 the doctrine of command responsibility was accepted as customary international law and was thus codified in the Additional Protocol I to the Geneva Conventions, relating to the International Armed Conflicts. Its status as customary law has been confirmed with the explicit

---

[12] Brooker, John W., "Ford v Garcia: A Puzzling Fusion of the Command Responsibility Doctrine with the Torture Victim Protection Act," 28 *N.C. Journal of International Law* [2003] 701.

[13] Annex to 4th Hague Convention, 18 October 1907, articles 1 and 43. 36 Statutes 2277, 2295, 2306.

[14] Williamson, Jamie A., "Some Considerations on Command Responsibility and Criminal Liability" 90 *International Review of the Red Cross* [2008] 303

inclusion of command responsibility. It should be noted that international law recognizes the principle of command responsibility both in *international* and in *internal* armed conflict. Thus, the ICTR Statute explicitly provides for command responsibility, including for grave breaches of common article 3 of the Geneva Conventions, in the context of the conflict in Rwanda.[15]

In 1977 there was a codification of the statutory international law of command responsibility which provides that parties to a conflict should require military commanders to prevent, supervise and report breaches of the Geneva Conventions and Protocol by troops and others under their command and, where appropriate, initiate disciplinary action. The treaty identified three conditions for command responsibility : (A) the person to be held responsible must be the superior of the person or persons committing the breach of the convention; (B) the superior must have known or had information which should have enabled him to conclude that a breach was being committed or was going to be committed; and (C) the superior did not take all feasible measures within his powers to prevent the breach.[16] These requisites were later reflected in the Statute of the International Criminal Tribunal for the former Yugoslavia [ICTY] which provides as follows: "The fact that any of the ... crimes within the jurisdiction of the [Tribunal] was committed by a subordinate does not relieve his superior of criminal responsibility if he knew or had reason to know that the subordinate was about to commit such acts or had done so and the superior failed to take the necessary and reasonable measures to prevent such acts or to punish the perpetrators thereof." The Trial Chamber identified three elements for liability: (A) the existence of a superior-subordinate relationship; (B) that the superior knew or had reason to know that the criminal act was about to be or had been committed; and (C) that the superior failed to take the necessary and reasonable measures to prevent the criminal act or punish the perpetrator.[17]

---

[15]Article 7(3) of the Statute of the International Criminal Tribunal for the former Yugoslavia (ICTY) and article 6(3) of the Statute of the International Criminal Tribunal for Rwanda (ICTR), as well as article 28 of the Rome Statute for an International Criminal Court (ICC)

[16]Protocol I to the Geneva Convention of 1977, Article 87

[17]Article 7(3) Statute of the International Criminal Tribunal for the former Yugoslavia

The Protocol explains the nature and conditions of a superior's responsibility, holding that the fact that a breach of the Geneva Conventions or of the Additional Protocol,

> was *committed by a subordinate* does not absolve his superiors from penal or disciplinary *responsibility*, as the case may be, if they *knew*, or *had information which should have enabled them to conclude* in the circumstances at the time, that he was committing or was going to commit such a breach and if they did not take *all feasible measures within their power* to *prevent* or *repress* the breach.[18]

In *U.S. v Medina*, Judge Latimer wrote, "Military law recognizes no principal which is more firmly fixed than the rule that a military superior is responsible for the proper performance by his subordinates of their duties." For indeed, the responsibility of a commander for controlling and supervising his subordinates is the cornerstone of a responsible armed force. A commander must 'give clear, concise orders' and must 'be sure they are understood.' 'After taking action or issuing an order, 'a commander' must remain alert and make timely adjustments as required by a changing situation." A commander keeps informed on the situation at all times and goes where he can beat influence the action. "Without undue harassment, he supervises his unit by checking on its progress in accomplishment of actions and orders." Stated succinctly, "The successful commander insures mission accomplishment through personal presence, observation, and supervision."[19]

One recent authority wrote, "The privilege of command is a fleeting sensation. Those who are commanded are the beneficiaries of the system, as their lives—their very existences—are placed uniquely in the care of the commanding officer. They have a right to expect that their leader will be held to exacting standards of professionalism and personal accountability. Their parents, husbands, wives, children, and friends should also expect this to be so, as the commander is entrusted with the

---

[ICTY].

[18]Protocol Additional to the Geneva Conventions of 12 August 1949, and relating to the Protection of Victims of International Armed Conflicts (Protocol I), Article 86(2) [emphasis added].

[19]*U.S. Army v. Captain Ernest Medina*, Fort McPherson, Georgia, 1971

treasured life of their loved-ones."[20]

Generally, "A person who planned, instigated, ordered, committed or otherwise aided and abetted in the planning, preparation or execution of a crime . . . shall be individually responsible for the crime." The fact that any of the acts was committed by a subordinate does not relieve the superior of criminal responsibility if he knew or had reason to know that the subordinate was about to commit such acts or had done so and the superior failed to take the necessary and reasonable measures to prevent such acts or to punish the perpetrators thereof. Not only are military commanders but also non-military superiors may incur responsibility under the doctrine of superior responsibility. For civilian superiors the establishment of a superior-subordinate relationship usually cannot be drawn from the official position of the person.[21]

The underlying theory of the doctrine of command responsibility is simple: military commanders are responsible for the acts of their subordinates. If subordinates commit violations of the laws of war, and their commanders fail to prevent or punish these crimes, then the commanders also can be held responsible. command responsibility, although it gained notoriety after World War II, is not a new doctrine in military codes or national law.[22] As early as the 15th century, King Charles VII of Orleans decreed that his military commanders were to be held liable should those under their command commit crimes against the civilian population, irrespective of the commanders' participation in the crimes.

Before the codification of international law nations relied on customary law. The Anglo-American understanding of the customary law

---

[20]Bryan McGrath, *Information Dissemination*, 18 September 2010, quoted in Joe Doty and Chuck Doty, "Command Responsibility and Accountability," *Military Review*, (Jan.-Feb. 2012), 34-37.

[21]"Individuals in positions of authority, whether civilian or within military structures, may incur criminal responsibility under the doctrine of command responsibility on the basis of their *de facto* as well as *de jure* positions as superiors" *Prosecutor* v. *Zejnil Delalić, Zdravko Mucić, Hazim Delić and Esad Land?o*, (*Čelebići*), Judgement, Case No. IT-96-21-T, 16 November 1998, paragraph 354. See also Article 7(1) of the Statute of the International Criminal Tribunal for the former Yugoslavia (ICTY) and Article 6(1) of the Statute of the International Criminal Tribunal for Rwanda (ICTR).

[22]"Command Responsibility for War Crimes," *Yale Law Journal*, 82: 1272-1304 [1973].

regarding execution of command responsibility was well defined in the American courts c.1800. In the case of the *Flying Fish* Chief Justice John Marshall looked at the responsibility of military officers who received illegal orders issued by the American government. The case arose out of an incident that occurred during the engagement with France at the end of the 18th century. The frigate USS *Boston* commanded by captain George Little captured a Danish vessel, the *Flying Fish*, under orders of the Secretary of the Navy on behalf of President John Adams. Adams ordered naval vessels "to intercept any suspected American ship sailing *to* or *from* a French port." The Congress, however, had passed a law authorizing the navy to seize "vessels or cargoes [that] are apparently, as well as really, American" and "bound or sailing to any [French] port" in an attempt to prevent American vessels transporting goods to France. The *Flying Fish* was sailing from and not to a French port. Captain Little was declared to be liable for executing a command that was illegal in nature. In trial Little was found guilty so he appealed the decision to the U. S. Supreme Court. The court's reasoning was simple: the legislative branch is to make laws and the job of the executive branch is to enforce those laws. The legislative act provided only for the capture of vessels traveling to France. "The Flying Fish was on a voyage from, not to, a French port, and was therefore, had she even been an American vessel, not liable to capture on the high seas."[23] The Act limited the president's authority by only allowing the capture of certain vessels. The President acted contrary to these limitations. Marshall wrote the opinion of the court.

> I confess, the first bias of my mind was very strong in favor of the opinion, that though the instructions of the executive could not give a right, they might yet excuse from damages. I was much inclined to think that a distinction ought to be taken between acts of civil and those of military officers; and between proceedings within the body of the country and those on the high seas. That implicit obedience which military men usually pay to the orders of their superiors, which, indeed, is indispensably necessary to every military system, appeared to me strongly to imply the principle, that those orders, if not to

[23] *Little v. Barreme*, 2 Cranch (6 U.S.) 170 (1804). The Court found that the President does not have "inherent authority" or "inherent powers" which allow him to ignore a law passed by the United States Congress.

> perform a prohibited act, ought to justify the person whose general duty it is to obey them, and who is placed by the laws of his country in a situation which, in general, requires that he should obey them. I was strongly inclined to think that where, in consequence of orders from the legitimate authority, a vessel is seized, with pure intention, the claim of the injured party for damages would be against that government from which the orders proceeded, and would be a proper subject for negotiation. But I have been convinced that I was mistaken, and I have receded from this first opinion. I acquiesce in that of my brethren, which is that the instructions cannot change the nature of the transaction, nor legalize an act which, without those instructions, would have been a plain trespass.

A slightly later case considered by the U.S. Supreme Court involved an American military officer who refused to obey a superior order which he judged to be illegal under customary law. In this case the Court ruled that the order was legal and therefore should have been obeyed. Justice Joseph Story wrote this opinion of the court.

> The service is a military service, and the command, of a military nature; and in such cases, every delay, and every obstacle to an efficient and immediate compliance, necessarily tend to jeopardize the public interests. While subordinate officers or soldiers are pausing to consider whether they ought to obey, or are scrupulously weighing the evidence of the facts upon which the commander-in-chief exercises the right to demand their services, the hostile enterprise may be accomplished, without the means of resistance.[24]

Generally, English interpretation of customary international law did not admit of the right of soldiers to decide for themselves whether a superior order was valid or not. The great English constitutional scholar Albert Venn Dicey (1835-1922) held that the issue of mindless obedience to superior orders was far from decided in Victorian England. Nonetheless Dicey quoted from Justice Stephens, *The History of Criminal Law of England*, believing this to be the best statement yet made on the subject.

> The doctrine that a soldier is bound under all circumstances whatever to obey his superior officer would be fatal to military discipline itself, for it would justify the private in shooting the colonel by the orders of the captain, or in deserting to the enemy

[24] *Martin v Mott*, 12 Wheaton 28 (1827).

> on the field of battle on the order of his immediate superior. I think it is not less monstrous to suppose that superior orders would justify a soldier in the massacre of unoffending civilians in time of peace, or in the exercise of inhuman cruelties, such as the slaughter of women and children, during a rebellion. The only line that presents itself to my mind is that a soldier should be protected by orders for which he might reasonably believe his officer to have good grounds. The inconvenience of being subject to two jurisdictions, the sympathies of which are not unlikely to be opposed to each other, is an inevitable consequence of the double necessity of preserving on the one hand the supremacy of the law, and on the other the discipline of the army.[25]

Dicey was concerned with the degree to which "a man of ordinary sense and understanding" would be able to determine when an order given was illegal and criminal in nature. This test was found in a passage of Dicey's in reference to the analogous conflict between a soldier's duty to obey orders and his allegiance to the general law of the land: ". . . a soldier runs no substantial risk of punishment for obedience to orders which a man of common sense may honestly believe to involve no breach of law."[26]

William Edward Birkhimer, in his *Military Government and Martial Law*, considered at great length the question of disobedience to superior orders. He understood that, in civilian life, society must protect its members from the unlawful acts of an evil one. It cannot allow such a person to escape the consequences of his act by pleading obedience to superior orders. In the military counseled disobedience is a much more difficult subject for severe penalties for disobedience may be exacted immediately. It is therefore the duty of courts to ascertain the origins of illicit orders and to punish those who issued such commands and to punish them accordingly. One should not punish the members of a firing squad for following illegal orders in carrying out the execution, or even the officer who gave the order to shoot. Responsibility must rest with the officer who initiated the order. Birkhimer wrote,

> A subordinate stands in a different position from the superior when he obeys, and may be absolved from liability for

---

[25] A. V. Dicey, *Law of the Constitution* [8th ed., 1886], 301-302.
[26] Id. at 302.

> executing an order which it was criminal to give. The question is, Had accused reasonable cause for believing in the necessity of the act which is impugned? and in determining this point a soldier may take the orders of the person in command into view as proceeding from one who is better able to judge and well informed; and, if the circumstances are such that the command may be justifiable, he should not be held guilty for declining to decide that it is wrong, with the responsibility incident to disobedience, unless the case is so plain as not to admit of a reasonable doubt. A soldier consequently runs little risk in obeying any order which a man of common sense so placed would regard as warranted by the circumstances.[27]

In an effort to control the behavior of armies in the field, in the early 1860s the U. S. government worked with Alfred Lieber, a professor at Columbia University, to codify the rules governing warfare. The United States adopted the results, a document, known as the Lieber Code, in 1863 during the Civil War. The Lieber Code represents the first attempt to codify the law of conduct of armies. The Lieber Code of April 24, 1863, also known as *Instructions for the Government of Armies of the United States in the Field, General Order № 100* or Lieber Instructions, was an instruction signed by President Abraham Lincoln to the Union Forces of the United States during the American Civil War that dictated how soldiers should conduct themselves in wartime. It was named after the German-American jurist and political philosopher Francis Lieber. The document mandated humane, ethical treatment of populations in occupied areas. It expressly forbade giving no quarter to the enemy, except in such cases where there was an express threat to the survival of the unit that held these prisoners. It forbade the use of poisons; it prohibited the use of torture to extract confessions; and it delineated the rights and duties of prisoners of war and of capturing forces. The Lieber Code discussed the ends of war and the permissible and impermissible means to attain those ends.[28] It is correctly viewed as the precursor to the Hague Regulations of 1907.[29]

---

[27]Birkhimer, William Edward, *Military Government and Martial Law*, Hudson, 1914, 561-62

[28]Witt, John Fabian. *Lincoln's Code: The Laws of War in American History*. Free Press, 2012

[29]Declaration Renouncing the Use, in Time of War, of Explosive Projectiles Under 400 Grammes Weight is an international treaty agreed in Saint Petersburg, Russian

Following the American Civil War Dr. Henry Wirz (1823-1865), commandant of Andersonville Prison where the Confederacy held thousands of Union Soldiers, was tried for war crimes. Because of the rapid increase in the number of prisoners the Confederate government decided to build Andersonville Prison in Georgia. In April 1864 Winder appointed Wirz as commandant of this new prison camp. By August, 1864, there were 32,000 Union Army prisoners in Andersonville. The Confederate authorities did not provide enough food for the prison and men began to die of starvation. The water became polluted and disease was a constant problem. Of the 49,485 prisoners who entered the camp, nearly 13,000 died from disease and malnutrition. The Union tried Wirz on the charge of "conspiring to injure the health and destroy the lives of United States soldiers held as prisoners by the Confederate States." Wirz appeared before a military commission headed by Major General Lew Wallace on 21st August, 1865. During the trial a letter from Wirz was presented that showed that he had complained to his superiors about the shortage of food being provided for the prisoners. However, former inmates at Andersonville testified that Wirz inspected the prison every day and often warned that if any man escaped he would "starve every damn Yankee for it." The tribunal found Wirz guilty and sentenced to death. He was taken to Washington to be executed on November 10, 1865. The gallows were surrounded by Union Army soldiers who throughout the procedure chanted "Wirz, remember, Andersonville." Accompanied by a Catholic priest, Wirz refused to make a last minute confession, claiming he was not guilty of committing any crime. Major Russell read the death warrant and then told Wirz he "deplored this duty." Wirz replied that: "I know what orders are, Major. And I am being hanged for obeying them." Dr. Wirz claimed that he merely acted as a subordinate in carrying out the orders of the commander of the post. The Judge Advocate General admitted that indeed Dr. Wirz had acted under orders, but responded, "A superior officer cannot order a subordinate to do an illegal act, and if a subordinate obey such an order and disastrous consequences result, both

---

Empire, November 29 / December 11, 1868. It succeeded the First Geneva Convention of 1864. It was a predecessor of the well-known Hague Conventions of 1899 and 1907.

the superior and the subordinate must answer for it. General Winder could no more command the prisoner to violate the laws of war than could the prisoner do so without orders."[30]

The Russian diplomat and statesman Prince Alexander Gorchakov convened an international meeting for the purpose of considering the existing rules of war. This conference of delegates met at Saint Petersburg, Russian Empire in December, 1868 and included representatives of Austria-Hungary, Bavaria, Belgium, Denmark, France, the United Kingdom, Greece, Italy, the Netherlands, Portugal, the North German Confederation, Russia, Sweden and Norway, Switzerland, the Ottoman Empire, and Württemberg. The United States was not considered a major power at the time and thus was not invited. The resulting Declaration of St. Petersburg of 1868 prohibited the "employment of arms which uselessly aggravate the sufferings of disabled men or render their death inevitable."[31] The assumption of course was that only decision makers could order such weapons made and deployed.

The term war crimes is of relatively modern origin. Most authorities related its creation and introduction to Lassa James Oppenheim, a British-Jewish authority on international law, about 1906.[32] It has come into common use and has even spawned its own study.[33] Modern nation-states have found that the definition of war crimes is too frequently altered by political considerations and thus varies according to time and place.[34]

The Hague Regulations of 1907, was the treaty-based restatement of the customary law of war. It borrowed much of the Lieber Code and

---

[30]The Trial of Henry Wirz, A Congressionally Mandated Report Summarizing the Military Commission's Proceedings, United States. 40th Congress, 2d Session. 1867–1868. House Executive Document No. 23, December 7, 1867.

[31]Declaration of St. Petersburg of 1868 in Wikipedia.

[32] Kramer, Alan, "The First Wave of International Trials: Istanbul and Leipzig" *European Review*, 14: 4 [Oct. 2006], 447. Lassa J. Oppenheim, *International Law: War and Neutrality* [1921], 2: 169-70.

[33] Falk, Richard A., Gabriel Kolko, and Robert J. Lifton, eds., *Crimes of War: A Legal, Political-Documentary and Psychological Inquiry into the Responsibility of Leaders, Citizens and Soldiers for Criminal Acts In War.* New York: Vintage Books, 1971; Gutman, Roy and David Rieff, eds., *Crimes of War: What the Publ ic Should Know.* New York: Norton, 1999

[34] Hoffman, Stanley, "War Crimes: Political and Legal Issues," *Dissent*, 18: 530-34 [1971].

wrote it into the international treaty law. Many practices would be considered illegal or extremely questionable by more recent standards. In the event of the violation of the laws of war by an enemy, the Code permitted reprisal by firing squad against the enemy's recently captured POWs; and it permitted the summary execution, again by musketry, of spies, saboteurs, *levees en masse, francs-tireurs*,[35] and guerrilla forces, if caught in the act of carrying out their missions. All these practices were later outlawed by the Third and Fourth Geneva Conventions of 1949. The Second World War, had seen these practices in the hands of totalitarian states used as the rule rather than the exception to such.[36]

The Lieber Code, and consequently the Hague Regulations, envisioned a reciprocal relationship between the population and the Army. As long as the population did not resist military authority, it was to be treated well. Should the inhabitants violate this compact by taking up arms and supporting guerrilla movements, then they were open to sterner measures. Among these were the imposition of fines, the confiscation and/or destruction of property, the imprisonment and/or expulsion of civilians who aided guerrillas, the relocation of populations, the taking of hostages, and the possible execution of guerrillas who failed to abide by the laws of war. It authorized the shooting on sight of all persons not in uniform acting as soldiers and those committing, or seeking to commit, sabotage.

As the world entered World War I most civilized nations subscribed to a statement similar to the following which was taken from the British *Manual of Military Law* promulgated in 1914:

> Article 443: Members of armed forces who commit such violations of the recognized rules of war-fare as are ordered by their government or by their commander are not war criminals and cannot therefore be punished by the enemy. He may punish the officials or commanders responsible for such order if they fall into his hands, but otherwise he may only resort to the other means of obtaining redress.

---

[35] Literally "free shooters." This term was used to describe irregular military formations deployed by France during the early stages of the Franco-Prussian War and also World War II; similar to *levees en masse*

[36] Witt, *op. cit.*, chs 6 & 9.

Germany of course wholeheartedly accepted concept of unquestioning obedience to superior orders. What it alone among Western nations rejected was the concept that military leaders could held responsible and tried in criminal proceedings for violations of both customary and codified international law, especially any international law that came under the heading of humanitarian law. The German concept of *Kriegsräson* justified commanders committing violations of humanitarian law in order to win swift victories. German belief in the absolute superiority of acts of state would not allow for the existence of human positive international law higher than German law. As had been traditional among Western nations, Germany still held that there was no law of greater importance than German municipal law. German legal scholars did not see international customary law of war as having been developed and accepted to the point of universal acceptance that made true international law. German military law was a higher concept that customary or codified international law and thus took precedence. This position found some support in the leading international law text of the times, Professor Lassa Oppenheim's *International Law*, edition of 1912. Oppenheim wrote,

> Violations of rules regarding warfare are war crimes only when committed without an order of the belligerent government concerned. If members of the armed forces commit violations by order of their government, they are not war criminals and may not be punished by the enemy; the latter may, however, resort to reprisals. In case members of forces commit violations ordered by their commanders, the members may not be punished, for the commanders are alone responsible, and the latter may, there-fore, be punished as war criminals on their capture by the enemy.

The vast majority of authorities disagreed with Professor Oppenheim. One strong objection to the German position is to be found in the very first book written specifically on the role of law in war. This tome was published well before the end of the war and thus served as a valuable guide to exposit the Allied view.

> It has been contended in some quarters that a combatant's acts, no matter how heinous, outrageous, and abominable, do not possess a criminal character if they are committed under orders from superior officers. But this argument carried to its logical

> conclusion would lead to ineptitude and absurdity; the successive shifting of responsibility would exculpate every one until we reached the ultimate cause-in the case of Germany let us say, for example, the Kaiser. Can it, then, be seriously held that several millions of men may act contrary to law established, and perpetrate horrors and atrocities, and that they should be considered entirely guiltless on the ground that they carried out the admittedly illegitimate commands of their supreme authority? The safety and stability of a nation or of a family of nations are incompatible with such an exaggerated and preposterous notion of vicarious responsibility.[37]

Royal Naval Commander Graham Bower read a paper before the Grotius Society on 27 May 1915 in which he agreed with the German position. He voiced the opinion that German U-boat commanders could not be punished if captured since they were following orders and the German government had accepted responsibility for these actions. This immunity existed, Bower wrote, even if the submarines should act contrary to the customary international laws of war and of humanity.[38] Dr. Hugh H. L. Bellot immediately challenged Bower's contentions. He argued that both the instigators and the perpetrators of acts contrary to international law could be, and should be, punished. Acts contrary to the commonly accepted usages of war were the legitimate object of courts martial.[39]

The infamous case of Captain Charles A. Fryatt (1872-1916) showed that Germany ignored its own position when dealing with its enemies. On 3 March 1915, Fryatt was in command of the SS *Wrexham*, which was attacked by a German submarine. The sub chased Fryatt's ship was chased for 40 nautical miles. On 28 March 1915, as captain of the SS *Brussels*, Fryatt was ordered to stop by *U-33*. Seeing the U-boat had surfaced in order to torpedo his ship, Fryatt ordered full steam ahead and proceeded to try to ram *U-33*, which was forced to crash dive. This action was in compliance with orders issued by the British Admiralty under

---

[37]MacDonnell, John and Coleman Phillipson, *International Law and the Great War* (1915). Nabu Press reprint, 2012, 47.

[38]"The Laws of War; Prisoners of War and Reprisals," Grotius Society *Papers*, [1915] 1: 23.

[39]"The Laws of War" Grotius Society *Papers* [1916], 2: 54-55.

Winston Churchill to captains of merchant ships. Churchill ordered the British commercial officers treat the crews of U-boats as felons rather than as prisoners of war. Churchill specifically told them to ignore white flags. Churchill's order also stated that survivors from U-boats might be shot if this was more convenient than taking them prisoner. Through captured copies of Churchill's orders the Germans became aware of the contents. On 25 June 1916, *Brussels* left Hoek van Holland bound for Harwich. Five German destroyers surrounded *Brussels* and escorted it Bruges. The Germans sent Fryatt and his crew to the civilian internment camp at Ruhleben, near Berlin. On 16 July 1916 Fryatt was charged with sinking a German submarine, even though *U-33* had not been sunk. Fryatt was tried at a court martial held at Bruges Town Hall on 27 July 1916 . He was found guilty of being a *franc-tireur* and sentenced to death, with confirmation of the sentence having been confirmed by the Kaiser. On 2 April 1919, a German International Law Commission named the Schücking Commission, after its chairman Walther Schücking, reconfirmed Fryatt's sentence, with two members dissenting.[40]

A major war crime under customary international law was the killing of prisoners. At least two of the German defendants in the Leipzig Trials following World War I were charged with this crime. Most authors had previously ignored this issue, but the best author on that question at the time, Henry D. Wheaton (1785-1848), justice in the Marine Court of New York and noted authority on international law, thought that a soldier's right to be spared injury at the hands of his captors was far from absolute. A superior could legitimately issue orders "when the achievement of victory would be hindered and even endangered by stopping to give quarter instead of cutting down the enemy and rushing on." Wheaton also thought that "during fighting it is also impracticable so to secure prisoners as to prevent their return to combat." Military necessity could be used to justify and legitimatize the issuance of superior orders to troops and lower rank officers to kill prisoners or refuse to take enemy belligerents prisoner.[41]

No concept is more controversial that the doctrine of military

---

[40] "Charles Fryatt" Wikipedia.

[41] Banteka, Ilias. The Contemporary Law of Superior Responsibility, *American Journal of International Law*, 93.3, 574(1993).

necessity.[42] Although often admitted by the prosecution, it opens a vast panorama of potential violations of code and customary international law. Prosecution and defense would be unlikely to agree on precisely when military necessity could justify orders to violate international law of warfare. If admitted by the prosecution, this excuse could be used in the exculpation of any and all offenses. A typical example of military necessity might be, as Wheaton Had suggested, the execution of prisoners when there was no one available to take them to an internment camp or to guard them.

The Geneva Convention of 1929 was in large part the result of the war crimes which the Allies had blamed on Germany. It sought to prevent, and if not prevent then punish, specific violations of the law of nations and to codify that customary law. Among other protections, the Convention defined as a war crime the ill treatment of civilians in occupied areas. It also sought to provide additional protection to POWs. Article 46, section 3, made it illegal to "willfully, deliberately, and wrongfully permit, encourage, and abet and participate in the killing, shooting, ill-treatment, abuse, and torture of unarmed prisoners of war and unarmed allied civilians." As in the Lieber document, however, there was the assumption of the civilians acting in an orderly and peaceful fashion.[43]

It was only after the creation of the International Military Tribunal for the Prosecution and Punishment of the Major War Criminals of the European Axis and the International Military Tribunal for the Far East (the Nuremberg and Tokyo Tribunals), the criminal tribunals at the end of World War II, that the doctrine of command responsibility was refined into today's recognized standard.[44] The modern legal standard governing the doctrine of command responsibility in the United States rests upon the precedent established by the United States Supreme Court in the case of General Tomoyuki Yamashita. The Court's holding has become known as the Yamashita Standard.[45] In order to hold a military commander either

---

[42]On military necessity see Gerhard von Glahn, *Law among Nations* [1965], 546-47.

[43]Green, Leslie C., "War Crimes, Crimes against Humanity and Command Responsibility," file://A:\Green.htm

[44] Kuhn, Arthur, "International Law and National Legislation in the Trial of War Criminals" *American Journal of International Law*, July 1950, 559-62.

[45]*In re Yamashita*, 327 U.S. 1 (1946). Quotes are taken from this case. The relevant

criminally or civilly liable under the doctrine of command responsibility , the prosecution must prove three elements: (1) those committing the atrocities/war crimes were under the command of the defendant; (2) the commanders knew or should have known, based on the surrounding circumstances at the time, that their subordinates were engaging in impermissible conduct; and (3) the commanders did nothing to prevent or punish those responsible for the commission of such crimes.[46]

Command responsibility is an omission mode of individual criminal liability, that is, the superior officer is responsible for crimes committed by his subordinates and for failing to prevent or punish as opposed to crimes committed under specific orders. Before a United States Military Commission, General Yamashita became the first to be charged solely on the basis of responsibility for an omission. As commanding officer, he was charged with "unlawfully disregarding and failing to discharge his duty as a commander to control the acts of members of his command by permitting them to commit war crimes." By finding Yamashita guilty, the Commission adopted a new standard, stating that where "vengeful actions are widespread offenses and there is no effective attempt by a commander to discover and control the criminal acts, such a commander may be held responsible, even criminally liable." However, the ambiguous wording resulted in a long-standing debate about the amount of knowledge required to establish command responsibility. The matter was appealed, and was affirmed by the United States Supreme Court. Following *In re Yamashita*, courts clearly accepted that a commander's actual knowledge of unlawful actions is sufficient to impose individual criminal responsibility. After sentencing, Yamashita was executed.[47]

Consistently toward the end of World War II the Allies

---

charge held against General Yamashita was that "the law of war imposes on an army commander a duty to take such appropriate measures as are within his power to control the troops under his command for the prevention of acts which are violations of the law of war and which are likely to attend the occupation of hostile territory by an uncontrolled soldiery; and he may be charged with personal responsibility for his failure to take such measures when violations result."

[46]Cowles, Willard B. "Trial of War Criminals by Military Tribunals" *American Bar Association Journal*, June 1944, 330-33.

[47]Feldhaus, J. G. "The Trial of Yamashita," *Current Legal Thought*, 1946-47, 251-62.

promulgated a rule that was hard, fast, and unequivocal. There would be no protection of soldiers who claimed to be following orders. Order number 10 issued by the Allied Control Council and dated 20 December 1945 stated that the existence of superior orders died not shield subordinates from individual responsibility for following illegal orders.[48] The Council tied this order to the customary law principle that subordinate officers are responsible and thus subject to punishment for obeying superior orders which they can be reasonably expected to judge to be illegal.

Under international law, the doctrine of command responsibility clearly has been extended to civilian authorities exercising control over military forces. In the post-World War II prosecutions in Nuremberg and Tokyo, a number of civilian authorities were convicted of war crimes. One of the most prominent examples is Koki Hirota (1878-1948), the Prime Minister and Foreign Minister of Japan during World War II. Following Japan's surrender, Hirota was arrested as a Class A war criminal and brought before the International Military Tribunal for the Far East. He offered no defense and was found guilty of the following charges: (1) waging wars of aggression, and wars in violation of international law; (2) waging unprovoked war against the Republic of China; and (3) disregard for duty to prevent breaches of the laws of war. He was held criminally liable as a commander for the atrocities committed by Japanese military, despite his position as a civilian leader. The principal charge seems to have been knowledge of the Rape of Nanking which was actually the responsibility of the emperor's uncle. In any event, Hirota was executed at Sugamo Prison along with Tojo and others.[49]

Command responsibility as applied in Nuremberg and Tokyo required that the prosecution show that two elements were present: (1) the commander knew or should have known of the commission of an illegal act; and (2) the command was capable of preventing that crime. In the Far East tribunals the courts generally held that have nominal command of troops was insufficient and that a command had to have control, including

---

[48]Green, Leslie, "Superior Orders and Command Responsibility" *Military Law Review* 75 (2003) 309.

[49]Maga, Timothy P., *Judgment at Tokyo: The Japanese War Crimes Trials*. University of Kentucky, 2001.

ability to disciple, over his troops.[50]

Since the Supreme Court's decision in 1946, the United States Congress and federal courts throughout the country have relied on the *Yamashita* standard. Many important human rights cases cite directly from the Supreme Court decision, as does the legislative history of the Torture Victims Protection Act (TVPA). In citing to the *Yamashita* Standard for support in the interpretation of the TVPA, the United States Senate Committee stated, "under international law, responsibility for torture, summary execution, or disappearances extends beyond the person or persons who actually committed those acts -- anyone with higher authority who authorized, tolerated, or knowingly ignored those acts is liable for them."[51] The Second and Ninth Circuits of the United States Court of Appeals affirmed this standard in their decisions *Kadic v. Karadzic,*[52] and *Hilao v. Estate of Marcos,*[53] and it has been repeatedly recognized as the standard in numerous human rights cases litigated under the TVPA and the Alien Tort Claims Act (ACTA) in federal courts across the country.

The Geneva Conventions of 1949, along with the Additional Protocols, provide for criminal liability based on the accused's position as a commander. While the doctrine of command responsibility at the international level rests on the same principle as the doctrine in the United States, there are a number of important differences. Practice in the United States would not bring civilian leaders under indictment for command responsibility although international practice does so. The 1949 Geneva Convention contained no express provision on superior responsibility which resulted in the decline in the use of the doctrine of superior. The vast majority of the rulings in the Nuremberg and Tokyo trials imposed liabilities on superiors to control the actions of their subordinates.

What must be established is whether the superior had the required knowledge of the atrocities committed by his subordinates. Ordinarily, a superior can be held liable where he 'knew or had reason to know' that the

---

[50]D'Amato, Anthony, "Superior Orders vs Command Responsibility" *AJIL*, 80: 3 (1986), 604-08.

[51]Senate Report 249, 102nd Congress, 1st Session, 9 [1991]; *In re Yamashita* 327 U.S. 1 (1946)

[52]70 F.3d 232 (1995)

[53]103 F. 3d 767 (1998)

subordinates had committed or were about to commit atrocities. 'Knew', or the actual knowledge, can be established through direct or circumstantial evidence. The 'had reason to know' requirement is concerned with a situation where the superior did not know about the crimes, but where information was available to him which would have given him the knowledge had he made some further inquiries. The 'had reason to know' standard has been debated, as it slightly differs from the 'should have known' standard that had been applied before. Taking into account the requisite standard of *mens rea,* [54] the rulings lowered the level of knowledge necessary for conviction. Post-World War II jurisprudence had expanded the parameters of command responsibility, imposing liability on commanders for their failure to prevent the commission of crimes by their subordinates. The cases explicitly discussed the requisite standard of *mens rea*, and were unanimous in the finding that a lesser level of knowledge than actual knowledge may be sufficient. However, the jurisprudence created some confusion about the exact standard of constructive knowledge that is required to impose responsibility. However, the more recent definition of the principle in the context of the International Criminal Court (ICC) reintroduced the 'should have known' standard.[55]

Four Geneva conventions dated 1949 constitute the quintessential *corpus* of international law regarding command responsibility during armed conflicts.

> The High Contracting Parties and other Parties to the conflict shall require military commanders with respect to members of the armed forces under their command, and other persons under their control, to prevent, and where necessary, to suppress and

---

[54] *Mens rea* is an element of criminal responsibility, a guilty mind; a guilty or wrongful purpose; a criminal intent. Guilty knowledge and willfulness. *Mens rea* is a fundamental principle of Criminal Law. A crime consists of both a mental and a physical element. *Mens rea*, a person's awareness of the fact that his or her conduct is criminal, is the mental element, and *actus reus*, the act itself, is the physical element. The concept of *mens rea* developed in England during the latter part of the common-law era , about the year 1600, when judges began to hold that an act alone could not create criminal liability unless it was accompanied by a guilty state of mind.

[55] Womack, Brandy "The Development and Recent Applications of the Doctrine of Command Responsibility: With Particular Reference to the *Mens Rea* Requirement" *International Crime and Punishment, Selected Issues* 1 (2003) 101.

> to report to competent authorities, breaches of the Convention. . . . In order to prevent and suppress breaches, High Contracting Parties and Parties to the conflict shall require that, commensurate with their level of responsibility, commanders ensure that members of the armed forces under their command are aware of their obligations. . . . The High Contracting Parties and Parties to the conflict shall require any commander who is aware that subordinates or other persons under his control are going to commit or have committed a breach of the Conventions . . . to initiate such steps as are necessary to prevent such violations . . . and, where appropriate, to initiate disciplinary or penal action. . . . The fact that a breach of the Convention . . . was committed by a subordinate does not absolve his superiors from penal or disciplinary responsibility. . . . [56]

The Additional Protocol I of 1977 to the Geneva Conventions of 1949 was the first international treaty to comprehensively codify the doctrine of command responsibility. Article 86(2) states that "the fact that a breach of the Conventions or of this Protocol was committed by a subordinate does not absolve his superiors from responsibility if they knew, or had information which should have enabled them to conclude in the circumstances at the time, that he was committing or about to commit such a breach and if they did not take all feasible measures within their power to prevent or repress the breach." Article 87 requires a commander to "prevent and, where necessary, to suppress and report to competent authorities' any breaches of the Conventions. . . ." The Additional Protocol I of the Geneva Convention of 1949 clarified the issues of superior knowledge and failure to act, which had been alluded to in the post-WWII trials. Article 87(3), which states: "...Parties to the conflict shall require any commander who is aware that subordinates or other persons under his control are going to commit or have committed a breach of the Conventions or of this Protocol, to initiate such steps as are necessary to prevent such violations of the Conventions or this Protocol, and, where appropriate, to initiate disciplinary or penal action against violators thereof."[57]

---

[56] Protection of Victims of International Armed Conflicts; Protocol to the Geneva Conventions of 12 August 1949.

[57] Protocol Additional to the Geneva Conventions of 12 August 1949, and Relating to the Protection of Victims of International Armed Conflicts (Protocol I), art. 87(1), June 8, 1997 1125 U.N.T.S. 3

In addition to criminal liability for civilian authorities exercising command over military forces, international law recognizes that military forces in an armed conflict may not be connected to a recognized nation-state. Additional Protocol II of the 1949 Geneva Conventions, promulgated in 1977, codified the application of international humanitarian law to "dissident armed forces or other organized armed groups, which, under responsible command, exercise such control over a part of its territory as to enable them to carry out sustained and concerted military operations."[58] This language broadened the scope of international humanitarian law by recognizing that armed groups operating under sophisticated command structures, need not be affiliated with recognized nation states, for them and their commanders, to be held to the same laws governing armed conflict as commanders in recognized nation- states.

The doctrine of command responsibility was codified in Article 28 of the Rome Statute of the International Criminal Court. Article 28(a) imposes individual responsibility on military commanders for crimes committed by forces under their effective command and control if they either knew or, owing to the circumstances at the time, should have known that the forces were committing or about to commit such crimes. Interpreted literally, Article 28(a) adopted the stricter *should have known* standard. The Trial Chamber in *Celebici* strongly suggested that the language of Article 28(a) may reasonably be interpreted to impose an affirmative duty to remain informed of the activities of subordinates. However, given the example afforded by the ICTY's conflicting interpretations of the knowledge requirement it cannot be assumed that a literal interpretation of Article 28(a) will be universally adopted by the ICC.[59]

The Draft Code of Crimes against the Peace and Security of Mankind, prepared by the International Law Commission in 1991 drew heavily upon the "duty of commanders," sections 86 and 87 of the Additional Protocol to the 1949 Geneva Conventions in one area of interest to us. The Commission recommended this language:

---

[58] Additional Protocol II to the Geneva Conventions of 12 August 1949, Article 1

[59] Lippman, Matthew, "The Evolution and Scope of Command Responsibility" *Leiden Journal of International Law* 13 [2000]: 139 at 164; Keith, Kirsten M., "The *Mens Rea* of Superior Responsibility as Developed by ICTY Jurisprudence" *Leiden Journal of International law* 14 [2001]: 617 at 631.

> The fact that a crime against the peace and security of mankind was committed by a subordinate does not relieve his superiors of criminal responsibility, if they knew, or had information enabling them to conclude, in the circumstances at the time, that the subordinate was committing, or was going to commit, such a crime and if they did not take all feasible measures within their power to prevent or repress the crime.[60]

Wide acceptance of the Yamashita Standard does not render it immune from critique. There have been a number of legal questions raised as to the reach of the Standard and the degree to which it imposes strict liability on a military commander for the actions of his or her subordinates. For example, the International Criminal Tribunal for the Former Yugoslavia has rejected the application of the doctrine of strict liability standard for military commanders. In reality many of those charged under the principle of command responsibility under the jurisdiction of the ICTY were not commanders of armies of recognized states, as was Yamashita. Instead they exerted military command over militarized troops of non-recognized entities such as the Republika Srpska and the Republic of Herzegovina-Bosna. The *Yamashita* Standard, however, no doubt will arise in the trial of Slobodan Miloöevic, and others who were in command positions in recognized nation states and will play a role in the jurisprudence of the International Criminal Court.

The establishment of the International Criminal Tribunal for the Former Yugoslavia [ICTY] by the Security Council has led to further international jurisprudence on the doctrine of command responsibility.[61] The ICTY is limited to applying customary international law, and therefore has implemented the *mens rea* standard applicable to command responsibility as it existed in customary law at the time of commission of alleged offences. Article 7(3) of the ICTY Statute states that the fact that the crimes "were committed by a subordinate does not relieve his superior of criminal responsibility if he knew or had reason to know that the subordinate was about to commit such acts or had done so and the superior

---

[60]U.N. International Law Commission Report on the Draft Articles, adopted at the 43rd session, 1991.

[61]See Eugenia Levine, "Command Responsibility," Global Policy Forum, Fe. 2005, Globalpolicy.org.

failed to take the necessary and reasonable measures to prevent such acts or to punish the perpetrators." There are two standards of knowledge encompassed by Article 7(3): "knew" and "had reason to know." "Knew" refers to actual knowledge, which can be established either directly or through circumstantial evidence. The meaning of "had reason to know" has been perhaps the most contentious aspect of command responsibility before the ICTY, and has received conflicting interpretations in the cases. By "interpreting the *mens rea* standard applicable to command responsibility as it existed in customary law at the time of commission of alleged offenses," 19 the ICTY limited the use of precedent in international customary law. As found in the ICTY statute, Article 7(3) specifies command responsibility and the element of *mens rea* holding that: "[Acts] committed by a subordinate do not relieve his superior of criminal responsibility if he knew or had reason to know that the subordinate was about to commit such acts or had done so and the superior failed to take such necessary and reasonable measures to prevent such acts or to punish the perpetrators thereof.[62]

The International Criminal Tribunal for the Former Yugoslavia (ICTY) and the International Criminal Tribunal for Rwanda (ICTR) have held civilians criminally liable for the actions of militarized forces under their control. On May 25th, 1993, United Nations Security Council Resolution 827 effectively established the International Tribunal for the Former Yugoslavia (ICTY). In February 2001, the ICTY found Dario Kordiç, a Bosnian Croat political leader, guilty under a theory of command responsibility for grave breaches of the Geneva Conventions, crimes against humanity, and violations of the laws and customs of war for the actions of Bosnian Croat militia forces operating in central Bosnia. Dario Kordić was indicted on 30 September 1998 with Mario Čerkez. Dario Kordić surrendered on 6 October 1997 and on the same day was transferred to the International Criminal Tribunal for the former Yugoslavia (ICTY). On 8 October 1997 Mario Kordić appeared before the Tribunal for the first time and pleaded not guilty to the 22 counts with

[62] International Tribunal for the Prosecution of Persons Responsible for Serious Violations of International Humanitarian Law Committed in the Territory of the Former Yugoslavia since 1991 (ICTY), article 7(3).

which he was charged. On 26 February, the Trial Chamber found Dario Kordić guilty on the basis of individual criminal responsibility for grave breaches of the Geneva conventions (willful killing; inhuman treatment; unlawful confinement of civilians),violations of the laws or customs of war (unlawful attack on civilians; unlawful attack on civilian objects; wanton destruction not justified by military necessity; plunder of public or private property; destruction or willful damage to institutions dedicated to religion or education), crimes against humanity (persecutions on political, racial or religious grounds; murder; inhumane acts; imprisonment). Dario Kordić was sentenced to 25 years' imprisonment. On 17 December 2004, the Appeals Chamber reaffirmed the sentence for Dario Kordić. In June 2006, he was transferred to Austria to serve his sentence there.[63]

Čelebići prison camp was in operation during the Bosnian War and was utilized by several units of the Bosnian Ministry of the Interior (MUP), Croatian Defence Council (HVO) and later the Territorial Defense Forces (TO). The camp was located in Čelebići, a village in the central Bosnian municipality of Konjic. The camp was used to detain around hundred Serb prisoners of war arrested during military operation meant for de-blocking of the routes to Sarajevo and Mostar in May 1992, earlier blocked by the Serb forces. Alleged mistreatment of internees led to a trial. The 1997 Celebici case instigated a new identification of direct and indirect command responsibility, as well as a more precise definition of the *mens rea* argument. The ICTY found that direct responsibility was established as a result of a positive action, whereas indirect responsibility would be established by the "failure to undertake a necessary act." Further, the Celebici Trial Chamber judgment considered the issue of culpability of non-militarily involved superiors, offering this opinion, "A superior may be exposed to culpability on the basis of *de facto* authority so long as the individual has the fundamental power to control the acts of subordinates." This judgment was notable because it differed from the stricter Yamashita standard of "should have known." Instead, it based its opinion on the far less stringent "had reason to know" and used the Additional Protocol I of the Geneva Convention as the customary international law.[64]

---

[63]The Hague Justice Portal, "Dario Kordić

[64] Hendin, Stuart E., *Command Responsibility and Superior Orders in the Twentieth*

> A companion and contemporary of the Celebici case, the Tihomir Blaskic case reviewed similar principles of command responsibility , yet reached a different conclusion. In June 1992, Tihomir Blaškić became commander of the regional headquarters of the Armed Forces in central Bosnia. In August 1994, he was named Commander of the Croatian Defense Council (HVO) and given the rank of General. According to the Second Amended Indictment, HVO troops committed grave violations of international humanitarian law through their actions against Muslims in Bosnia and Herzegovina between May 1992 and January 1994. The prosecution charged Blaškić on the basis of his individual and superior criminal responsibility. He was charged with crimes against humanity, serious breaches of the Geneva Conventions, and violations of the laws or customs of war. The Blaskic Trial Chamber found that effective control over subordinates or persons committing the crimes must be established in order to charge for command responsibility. These subordinates did not have to be formally under the control of the superior "or in his chain of command" for him to "be found culpable criminally for crimes committed by them." [65] As defined in the Blaskic Trial Chamber, the *mens rea* standard held that "the ordinary meaning of the provision indicated that the commander must have some information available to him which puts him on notice of the commission of unlawful acts by his subordinates."[66]

What is meant by effective control? In *Celebici* the tribunal held that the concept of "effective control" is mainly perceived as "the material ability [or power] to prevent and punish" the commission of offenses, …"effective control" also refers to the material ability to prevent or repress the commission of the crimes or submit the matter to the competent authorities. To this end, this notion does not seem to accommodate any lower standard of control such as the simple ability to exercise influence over forces or subordinates even if such influence turned out to be substantial…That said, the Chamber concurs with the view adopted by the ad hoc tribunals that indicate for the existence of

Century: A Century of Evolution, 10 Murdoch U. Electronic Journal of Law 191-94 (2003).

[65]"Tihomir Blaskic" Hague Portal.

[66]Hendin, op. cit., 211.

effective control are "more a matter of evidence than of substantive law."[67] There are factors which are probative in this regard, for example, official position, the authority to give orders and ensure their implementation, the capacity to alter command structures and promote or remove people, and the ability to require people to engage or withdraw from hostilities were all relevant factors, that had been identified by the *ad hoc* Tribunals.[68]

The *Celebici* decision was greatly concerned with the mental element of command responsibility. There are two levels of mental element, the first of which is actual knowledge. Such knowledge can be determined with the assistance of direct or circumstantial evidence. The second form of mental element that suffices 'is covered by the term "should have known,"...[and]... is in fact a form of negligence.' Negligence is not the best standard. The mental element is summed up by the Appeals Chamber in *Čelebići*, as not covering negligence in failure to find out about offenses, instead requiring either actual knowledge or that the superior "had in his possession information of a nature, which, at the least, would put him on notice of the risk of such offenses by indicating the need for additional investigation." The ICTY in the *Celebici* case elaborated a threefold requirement for the existence of command responsibility, which has been confirmed by subsequent jurisprudence: (A) the existence of a superior-subordinate relationship; (B) that the superior knew or had reason to know that the criminal act was about to be or had been committed; and (C) that the superior failed to take the reasonable. [69]

In the case of Clement Kayeshima the trial court held that Article 6(3) of the United Nations Security Council Resolution 955 expressed a "clear duty upon those in authority, with the requisite means at their disposal, to prevent or punish the commission of a crime," and applies that to the civilians exerting "requisite authority." The court's allusion to the *de facto* power of a superior was a contentious subject due to the lack of formal definition of his or her explicit power. The court also noted that the *mens rea* standard for non-military superiors with established *de facto*

[67] *inter alia Čelebići* in the ICTY, paragraphs 415-16.

[68] Cryer, Robert, "Command Responsibility at the ICC and ICTY: In Two Minds on the Mental Element?" *European Journal of International Law,* July 20, 2009.

[69] *Prosecutor* v *Delalić, Mucić, Delić and Landžo*, Judgment, IT-96-21-A, 20 February 2001.

power would be held to a lower standard of "had reason to know;" it does not "demand a *prima facie* duty upon a non-military commander to be seized of every activity of all persons under his or her control." The International Criminal Court wrote regarding the command responsibility of civilian superiors, "In light of the objective of Article 6(3) which is to ascertain the individual criminal responsibility for crimes as serious as genocide, crimes against humanity and violations of Common Article 3 to the Geneva Conventions and Additional Protocol II thereto, the Chamber finds that the Prosecution must prove that the accused in this case either knew, or consciously disregarded information which clearly indicated or put him on notice that his subordinates had committed, or were about to commit acts in breach of Articles 2 to 4 of this Tribunal's Statute." The tribunal did find that, "In light of this incontestable control that Kayishema enjoyed, and his overarching duty as a Prefect to maintain public order, the Trial Chamber is of the opinion that a positive duty upon Kayishema existed to prevent the commission of the massacre. . . . No evidence was adduced that he attempted to prevent the atrocities that he knew were about to occur and which were within his power to prevent." Kayeshima was sentenced to life imprisonment by the Trial Chamber, which was upheld by the Appeals Chamber in June 2001.[70]

The *Medina* standard, used in the United States, is based on the 1971 prosecution of Captain Ernest Medina who was charged with war crimes in conjunction with the My Lai Massacre during the Vietnam War. This standard holds that a commanding officer, being aware of a human rights violation or a war crime, can be held criminally liable when he does not take action. It has long been a custom of the service that, in general, a commander is responsible for the actions of his subordinates in the performance of their duties. This service custom was judicially underscored by Judge Latimer in the court martial of Earnest Medina for his role in the My Lai Massacre on 16 March 1968. Latimer wrote in his concurring opinion, "Military law recognizes no principal which is more firmly fixed than the rule that a military superior is responsible for the proper performance by his subordinates of their duties." For indeed, the

[70] *Prosecutor v. Clément Kayishema & Obed Ruzindana*, Case No. ICTR 95-1-T, Judgment and Sentence, 213 (Trib. Pénal Int'l Pour Le Rwanda May 21, 1999).

responsibility of a commander for controlling and supervising his subordinates is the cornerstone of a responsible armed force. A commander must "give clear, concise orders" and must "be sure they are understood. . . ." After taking action or issuing an order, a commander "must remain alert and make timely adjustments as required by a changing situation." Medina later said that his objective that night was to "fire them up and get them ready to go in there; I did not give any instructions as to what to do with women and children in the village." Although some soldiers agreed with that recollection of Medina's, others clearly thought that he had ordered them to kill every person in My Lai 4. It may have been that his orders were intentionally vague for it appeared most likely that Medina intentionally gave the impression that everyone in My Lai would be their enemy.[71] However, Medina was acquitted of all charges.[72]

In May 1999, three Salvadoran nationals filed a civil lawsuit in U.S. District Court in Florida seeking damages for torture, and other grave human rights violations against General Carlos Eugenio Vides Casanova, the Director-General of the Salvadoran National Guard from 1979-1983 who then became Minister of Defense; and General Jose Guillermo García, Minister of Defense from 1979-1983. The lawsuit alleged that García and Vides Casanova, both of whom live in retirement in Florida, exercised command responsibility over members of the Salvadoran Military and Security Forces which engaged in unlawful acts constituting torture; crimes against humanity; cruel, inhuman and degrading treatment; and arbitrary detention.[73] Under the applicable statutes, a military commander may be held responsible for abuses by subordinate forces if the commander knew or should have known about and failed to take all reasonable measures to prevent, investigate or punish the abuses. One of these cases, heard in the eleventh judicial district, was *Romagoza Arce et al. v. Garcia and Vides Casanova,* heard in 2006.

---

[71] Hart, Franklin A., "Yamashita, Nuremberg, and Vietnam: Command Responsibility Reappraised," *Naval War College Review* 25: 19-36 [1972].

[72] Raimondo, Tony: "The My Lai Massacre: A Case Study", Human Rights Program, School of the Americas, Fort Benning, Georgia; Barry McCaffrey, *Human Rights and the Commander,* J.F.Q., Autumn 1995, 10-13

[73] The legal basis for the suit rests on two federal statutes: the Alien Tort Claims Act [ACTA] and the Torture Victim Protection Act [TVPA].

The *Romagoza* case did much to clarify the "knew or should have known" component of the doctrine of command responsibility. International law had not defined the concept well. The jury instructions in *Romagoza* read: "The defendant, a military commander knew, or should have known, owing to the circumstances of the time, that his subordinates had committed, were committing, or were about to commit torture/or extrajudicial killing." According to the instructions to the jury, the plaintiffs did not have to prove that the defendant, a military commander knew or should have known of the plaintiffs' particular instances of torture. Rather, the knowledge element would be satisfied if the plaintiffs proved that the defendant/military commander knew, or should have known, that his subordinates "had committed, were committing, or were about to commit, *any* instances of torture and/or extrajudicial killing." Instructions to the jury in *Romagoza* also helped clarify what "all necessary and reasonable measures" in a time of war meant. The instructions for that prong of the instructions read: "The defendant/military commander failed to take all necessary and reasonable measures to prevent torture and/or extrajudicial killing, or failed to punish subordinates after they had committed torture and/or extrajudicial killing." Failure to punish, according to the instructions, "may be established by proof that the defendant/military commander failed to investigate reliable allegations of torture and/or extrajudicial killing by subordinates, or failed to submit these matters to competent authorities for investigation and prosecution." Most guidance for this component, however, can be found in *Yamashita.*[74]

The Rome Statute which created the International Criminal Court used a different definition of the concept "should have known." Its charter reads "had reason to know." However, despite such a difference, which the Chamber does not deem necessary to address in the present decision, the criteria or indicia developed by the ad hoc tribunals to meet the standard of "had reason to known" may also be useful when applying the "should have known requirement." The relevant evidence will be the same in both instances.[75]

The great difficulty with the principle that the commander is

---

[74]*Romagoza Arce et al. v. Garcia and Vides Casanova*, 434 F.3d 1254 (11th Cir. 2006)
[75]Rome Statute, 28 (a).

responsible for everything the unit does and fails to do is really absurd because in reality commanders cannot lead, supervise, or micromanage their subordinates 24 hours a day, seven days a week, nor should they. Commanders and leaders cannot prevent every possible bad thing from happening in a unit, but commanders who understand, internalize, and command their unit by being responsible but not in control will be thinking, planning, and acting in a way that sets up the unit and its soldiers for success. The My Lai Massacre in 1968 is one of the best known and studied examples. Another example took place in Kosovo in September 2000, in Alpha Company, 3rd Battalion, 504th Parachute Infantry Regiment, 82nd Airborne Division was found, according to the investigation, to have a command climate that contributed to torture and a tragic case of rape and murder. The battalion commander was reprimanded but not relieved of command. Examples from Afghanistan and Iraq show questionable command climates contributed to misconduct or crimes.[76]

---

[76]Doty, Joe and Walt Sowden, "Competency vs. Character: It Must Be Both!" *Military Review* (Nov.-Dec, 2009); Joe Doty and Chuck Doty, "Command Responsibility and Accountability," *Military Review*, (Jan.-Feb. 2012), 34-37.

2
Command Responsibility: The Beginnings

The earliest Biblical example of command responsibility may be found in Deuteronomy chapter 20. The author[s] of this work place the blame for war crimes upon the Lord God. Supposedly He orders the Hebrews to commit genocide against their enemies and takes responsibility. "But of the cities of these people, which the LORD thy God doth give thee for an inheritance, thou shalt save alive nothing that breatheth: But thou shalt utterly destroy them; namely, the Hittites, and the Amorites, the Canaanites, and the Perizzites, the Hivites, and the Jebusites; as the LORD thy God hath commanded thee." When fighting against those nations not named above God set strict orders for treating them. "When thou comest nigh unto a city to fight against it, then proclaim peace unto it. And it shall be, if it make thee answer of peace, and open unto thee, then it shall be, that all the people that is found therein shall be tributaries unto thee, and they shall serve thee. And if it will make no peace with thee, but will make war against thee, then thou shalt besiege it: And when the LORD thy God hath delivered it into thine hands, thou shalt smite every male thereof with the edge of the sword: But the women, and the little ones, and the cattle, and all that is in the city, even all the spoil thereof, shalt thou take unto thyself; and thou shalt eat the spoil of thine enemies, which the LORD thy God hath given thee."[77]

An early example of command responsibility may be found the Bible and the killing of Naboth the Jezreelite. Ahab, son and successor to Omri, was one of the most powerful kings of ancient Israel. He governed from approximately 873 to 851 B.C. He became a major player in regional affairs by marrying the princess Jezebel, daughter of King Ethbaal of Tyre.

---

[77]Deut. 20: 10-18

Ahab constructed a massive casemate fortification which enclosed lavishly appointed royal buildings, including the famous Ivory House. The fact that the final pages of Deuteronomy were written from the perspective of Judah, the antagonism between north and south, the unpopularity of Jezebel, and Ahab's conflicts with the prophet Elijah all contributed the general polemics against Ahab.

One of the major clashes between Ahab and Elijah had its roots in the killing of Naboth. Now Naboth was the owner of a plot on the eastern slope of the hill of Jezreel. Described as a small plot of ground, the vineyard was all he owned and it lay close to the palace of Ahab. King Ahab lusted to acquire to "have it for a garden of herbs." In reality Ahab probably wanted it as a ceremonial garden for a temple to Baal whom his wife Jezebel ardently worshiped. Naboth had inherited his land from his father, and, according to Jewish law, could not transfer it and thus he refused to sell it to the king. Ahab became deeply depressed at not being able to procure the vineyard. Returning to his palace, he swooned with depression, and refused to eat. His wife, Jezebel, upon learning the reason for his depression, promised that she would obtain the vineyard for him. Jezebel said to Ahab, "Are you the king or aren't you?" To show her power she plotted to kill Naboth by mock trial, and then told Ahab to take possession of the vineyard.

Thus, the Bible placed the blame upon Ahab for the killing of Naboth even though he did not actually strike the fatal blow. The fault and responsibility fell on Ahab for killing Naboth because Ahab as the king was responsible for all his subjects in his kingdom, including Jezebel his queen. It was Jezebel who gave the orders to kill Naboth. Although Ahab claimed that he was unaware of the killing, he really did know that it was his wife Jezebel) who had given the orders to kill Naboth. "And Jezebel his wife said unto him: 'Dost thou now govern the kingdom of Israel? arise, and eat bread, and let thy heart be merry; I will give thee the vineyard of Naboth the Jezreelite." As punishment for this action, the prophet Elijah visited Ahab while he was in the vineyard, pronouncing doom on him. It was for that Elijah predicted that the dogs of the street would eat Jezebel's corpse. Ahab humbled himself at Elijah's words, and was spared accordingly, with the prophesied destruction being visited instead on his son Joram.[78] The Bible tells the story of Ahab and the killing of Naboth, as an archetype to what was later called command responsibility.[79]

The story of David also contains elements of command responsibility. Having become king over "all Israel" David's troops defeat their enemies including the Philistines. He established Jerusalem as capital. Then David was tempted by "Bethsabee, daughter of Eliam, the wife of Urias the Hethite." David brought her to the palace and slept with her, impregnating her. Horrified by the fruits of his adultery, David tried to entice Urias to sleep with Bethsabee so that he might think the child his, but Urias refused. So David sent Urias back to the front with a letter for Joab. David told Joab, "Set ye Urias in the front of the battle, where the fight is strongest, and leave ye him, that he may be wounded and die." The Lord God disapproved of this treachery, sending word by Nathan the Prophet, "Thou hast killed Urias the Hethite . . . and has taken his wife to be thy wife, and has slain him with the sword." As punishment for commanding his lieutenant Joab to allow Urias to be killed the house of David was beset by evil doings. Rape and murder now erupt in his own house. David's son Absalom rebels and civil war ensues.[80]

In the Far East the rudiments of command responsibility may be found in the writings of Sun Tzu. His *The Art of War* was written during the 6th century BC. Sun Tzu recognized the emergence of a class of military officers as a distinct and generally permanent part of the nobility with very clearly defined responsibilities. Among these manifold charges was the duty of a military commander to guarantee would that his subordinates conduct themselves in a restrained and civilized manner during an armed conflict. The good commander will avoid massacres and atrocities if only because such behavior can provoke resistance and thus allow the enemy to turn the war in his favor. For the victor, the best policy is to capture the state intact; it should be destroyed only if no other options are available.[81] Clear commands are the responsibility of the commander, "If the words of command are not clear and distinct, if orders are not

---

[78]2 Kings 1: 21

[79]See "Jezebel" and "Ahab" in *The Oxford Companion to the Bible*

[80]2 Kings, chs.11 and 12; 2 Samuel 11-20; and "David" in *Oxford Companion.*

[81]Sun Tzu, *The Art of War.* Trans. and annotation by Samuel B. Griffith. Oxford University Press, 1963

thoroughly understood, the general is to blame. But if his orders are clear, and the soldiers nevertheless disobey, then it is the fault of their officers." Blame and punishment are meted out accordingly. Sun Tzu further wrote that, "When troops flee, are insubordinate, distressed, collapse in disorder, or are routed, it is the fault of the general. None of these disorders can be attributed to natural causes."[82]

During the early middle ages a vassal would commit a major war crimes by failing to fully support his liege lord. A vassal must not allow his lord to go into battle without his assistance and troops. If the lord died while the vassal fled, he would become an outlaw. The narrative poem Beowulf[83] has a perspective regarding this obligation. Wiglaf complains on Beowulf's behalf when he is deserted by the companions he had favored with gifts. As a result following Beowulf's death, his former companions mourn their impending exile.

War crimes in the sense this term is used in contemporary literature were not defined and therefore went largely unpunished. Charlemagne executed thousands of prisoners of war, barely raising an objection from anyone. His biographers praised him when he enslaved his captives and redistributed them throughout his lands or sold them on English or Mediterranean markets. Thus the medieval concept of war crime focused almost exclusively on the duties one had toward one's allies and liege lords rather than upon any limitations of violence toward one's foes.'

There were, however, some acts against certain vulnerable populations that went too far and were indeed broadly condemned. A great example of this is the event known as the "Harrying of the North," in 1069/70, perpetrated by William the Conqueror. This invader went into Northern England, which had risen to support his opponents, and murdered thousands of civilians. He laid waste to farm land which induced

---

[82]Ibid., 125.

[83] Beowulf is an Old English epic story consisting of 3,182 alliterative lines and is probably the oldest surviving long story in Old English and is commonly cited as one of the most important works of Old English literature. The date of composition is a matter of contention among scholars; the only certain dating pertains to the manuscript, which was produced between 975 and 1025. The author was an anonymous Anglo-Saxon poet, referred to by scholars as the "Beowulf author". The story is set in Scandinavia

a famine that reduced the native population of Northumbria. In the Domesday Book,[84] compiled about 15 years later, parts of the land were still valued as worthless. Norman Chroniclers, most of whom favored William, could not forgive him for this. Illustrative of the sentiment is Orderic Vitalis, a monk: "The King stopped at nothing to hunt his enemies. He cut down many people and destroyed homes and land. Nowhere else had he shown such cruelty. This made a real change. To his shame, William made no effort to control his fury, punishing the innocent with the guilty. He ordered that crops and herds, tools and food be burned to ashes. More than 100,000 people perished of starvation."

In the 15th century, King Charles VII of Orleans decreed that his military commanders were to be held liable should those under their command commit crimes against the civilian population, irrespective of the commanders' participation in the crimes. Charles decreed in his *Ordinances for the Armies* of 1439, "The King orders each captain or lieutenant to be held responsible for the abuses, ills, and offenses committed by members of his company, and that as soon as he receives any complaint…he bring the offender to justice….If he fails to do so or covers up the misdeed….the captain shall be deemed responsible for the offense, as if he had committed it himself."[85]

The best known precedent for the punishment of war crimes by an international tribunal was the case of Peter von Hagenbach. Charged with a variety of offenses, Hagenbach was tried for war crimes that he had personally committed as well as crimes perpetrated by troops under his command. The latter assumes that a commander is responsible for the general behavior of men under his command, or what we call command responsibility. Fortunately, Professor Gregory S. Gordon of the University of North Dakota Law School has done extensive research on Hagenbach

---

[84]Domesday Book was commissioned in December 1085 by William the Conqueror, who invaded England in 1066. The first draft was completed in August 1086 and contained records for 13,418 settlements in the English counties south of the rivers Ribble and Tees (the border with Scotland at the time).

[85]Meron, Theodor, *Henry's Wars and Shakespeare's Laws*, Oxford University Press, 1994, 149, note 40 citing Louis Guillaume de Vilevault and Louis Brequigny, *Ordonnances Des Rois De France De La Troisième Race* XII: 306 (1782).

and his subsequent trial.[86] We have followed Professor Gordon's treatise carefully.

Charles the Bold, Duke of Burgundy (1433-1477), known to his enemies as Charles the Terrible, had placed Landvogt Peter von Hagenbach at the helm of the government of the fortified city of Breisach, on the Upper Rhine. Charles had recognized in Hagenbach a talented linguist and diplomat who served him well in those capacities. He was also military leader who was unrestrained by humanitarian considerations. Little is known of Peter's origins. His father Anton was a member of the minor nobility from southern Alsace who served the powerful Hapsburg monarchy. He was educated by monks in an unknown monastery, but chose a military career over service to the Church.[87]

Something of Hagenbach's negative character can be realized by recounting the story of a Swiss citizen, Marquand Baldeck. After dining with Baldeck, Hagenbach kidnapped him and demanded a substantial ransom for his release. Philip the Good (1396-1467), son of John the Fearless, and father of Charles the Bold, immediately ordered Hagenbach to release Baldeck unharmed and with payment of any ransom.[88]

Hagenbach was to collect taxes which he accomplished with wanton brutality. As the governor, Hagenbach over-zealously followed his master's instructions and introduced a regime of arbitrariness, brutality and terror in order to reduce the population of Breisach to total submission. Murder, rape, illegal taxation and the wanton confiscation of private property became generalized practices. All these violent acts were also committed against inhabitants of the neighboring territories. A major large coalition, consisting of Austria, France, Bern and the towns and knights of the Upper Rhine, put an end to the ambitious goals of the powerful Duke. It had been rumored that Charles also wanted to become king and even to gain the imperial crown. The siege of Breisach by the coalition accompanied a revolt by both his German mercenaries and the local

---

[86] Gordon, Gregory, "The Trial of Peter von Hagenbach: Reconciling History, Historiography, and International Criminal Law." Electronic copy at http://ssrn.com/abstract=2006370.

[87] Bassiouni, M. C., "Perspectives on International Criminal Justice," *Virginia Journal of International Law* 5: 298.

[88] Vaughan, Richard, *Philip the Good.* Woodbridge: Boydell Press, 2002, 391

citizens led to Hagenbach's defeat. That merely served as a prelude to Charles' death in the Battle of Nancy in 1477.

The trial of Sir Peter von Hagenbach by an ad hoc tribunal of the Holy Roman Empire in 1474, was the first international recognition of commanders' obligations to act lawfully. Hagenbach was put on trial for atrocities committed during the occupation of Breisach, found guilty of war crimes and beheaded. Since he was convicted for crimes "he as a knight was deemed to have a duty to prevent." Hagenbach's 1474 prosecution in Breisach for atrocities committed while serving the Duke of Burgundy constitutes the first international war crimes trial in history. Hagenbach was tried before an ad hoc tribunal of twenty-eight judges from various regional city-states for misdeeds, including murder and rape, he allegedly perpetrated as governor of the Duke's Alsatian territories from 1469 to 1474. Rape, as opposed to murder, appears to have been Hagenbach's preferred weapon of terror and atrocity. Reportedly Peter and his men raped all the young women they could find, including nuns in convents. Sexual violence was completely unrestrained.[89]

As a recent commentator noted

> His regime of arbitrariness and terror extended to murder, rape, illegal taxation and wanton confiscation of private property, and the victim[s] of his depredations included inhabitants of neighboring territories as well as Swiss merchants on their way to and from the Frankfurt fair … the outrages of Hagenbach, remarkable even by the standards of the late fifteenth century, greatly contributed to forging what, until then, had been considered impossible, that is, alliances against Burgundy by all her neighbors: Austria, Berne, France, and the towns and knights of the Upper Rhine, all formerly at loggerheads with one another.[90]

On 9 May 1474, Peter von Hagenbach was tried in a remarkable judicial proceeding in the Rhine city of Breisach. Various regional political authorities, known as the League of Constance, paid off debts for Archduke Sigismund of Austria, allowing him to assume control once again over the Upper Alsatian territory which he had mortgaged to Charles

[89]Maguire, Jill C., "Rape under the Alien Tort Statute" *George Mason Law Review*, 13:956.

[90]Vaughan, op. cit., 255.

the Bold. A crowd attempted then to lynch Hagenbach on Easter Sunday, 10 April 1474. One Friedrich Kappelar rescued Hagenbach but held him awaiting Sigismund's pleasure. The Archduke decided, for reasons known only to him, to convene an international tribunal to consider Hagenbach's case. He chose twenty-eight men, sixteen of whom were knights, to sit in judgment, each a representative of a concerned sovereign. Eight of the judges were nominated by Breisach, and two by each of the other allied Alsatian and Upper Rhenanian towns, namely Strasbourg, Sélestat, Colmar, Basel, Thann, Kenzingen, Neuburg am Rhein, and Freiburg im Breisgau. In addition there were representatives from Berne, a member of the Swiss Confederation, and Solothurn, allied with Berne. Each juror represented a member of the League of Constance, with Canton Berne being the only representative of the Swiss Confederation.

The trial was a mere formality. Following his arrest Peter had been confined to jail where he was bound in chains, his wrists in handcuffs, and his legs secured in stocks. Sigismund sent for the instruments of torture and at least six times they were used with effect upon the body of Hagenbach. The torture took its toll. Peter had to be transported by wheelbarrow because he was no longer able to walk. Presumably he confessed to any and all charges advanced and named various co-conspirators.[91] After such confession a trial was superfluous.

Thomas Schutz, the chief magistrate of Ensisheim, served as the tribunal's presiding judge. The prosecutor was the new Alsatian bailiff, one Hermann von Eptingen, who had been chosen by Sigismund to replace Hagenbach. Eptingen then chose Heinrich Iselin, one of the commissioners from Basel which was a member of the League of Constance, to present the prosecution's case to the court. The other representative from Basel, Hans Irmy, took on Hagenbach's representation. Hagenbach also requested additional attorneys and the tribunal assigned him two attorneys, one being from Colmar and the other from Selestat. The trial was held in open air before the Breisach mayor's residence and was attended by a multitude of people from Breisach and surrounding towns.[92]

---

[91]Kirk, John Foster, *History of Charles the Bold*. Philadelphia: Lippincott, 1864, 488.
[92]Nerlinger, Charles, *Peter von Hagenbach and the Burgundian Domination*. Persee, 1890. Nerlinger judged that Hagenbach was a visionary and forward looking figure.

The defense immediately charged that the trial was illegal. Peter's counsel, Hans Irmy, declared that only the Duke of Burgundy had the right to question Hagenbach's actions for Peter was responsible to the duke alone. No one had the right to judge Hagenbach's fidelity to the Duke's orders. As far as he was concerned, Hagenbach was following superior orders. No authority was legally competent to suggest that Peter should have refused to execute his master's directives. It was not up to Peter to determine the legality of his orders. His only obligation was to carry out to the best of his ability the duke's orders since he was sworn to do so as a knight. Initially, the tribunal thought there was some validity to Irmy's arguments. The duke had, after all, apparently approved and ratified Peter's actions. Heinrich Iselin resigned because, as the evidence and arguments came in, he felt the case lacked merit. Just before withdrawing he moved a motion to withdraw the charges. Sigismund would not countenance that so Iselin was replaced by Hildebrand Rasp.

Rasp was a brilliant and talented man. He met argument with argument. Neither the duke Charles the Bold nor the Holy Roman Emperor, Frederick III, would have thought to order or condone such actions as Hagenbach had committed. The great lords had taken oaths before God to act as God's vicar on earth. To accuse them falsely opened Peter for a new and additional charge, *lese-majesté*.[93] By claiming that his superiors had allowed conduct unbecoming to a representative of God Peter had slandered them. The tribunal of course held that it was legally constituted and thus competent to sit in judgment on Hagenbach.

Hagenbach was well aware that he faced a trial from which he could not possibly emerge the winner. At least several members of the League of Constance planned his downfall even before Sigismund had assumed control. He and his troops were denied entry into Thann and Ensisheim. He was able to enter into Breisach because his mercenaries were already in control there. One of the counts in the indictment had charged that Hagenbach had intended to commit genocide in Breisach and then turn the depopulated city into his personal fortress. In short, as far as

---

[93]Lese-majesty. Law French, from the Latin *laesa maiestas*, "injured majesty;" in English, also *lese majesté* or *leze majesty*) is the crime of violating majesty, an offence against the dignity of a reigning sovereign or against a state.

the tribunal was concerned Hagenbach had "trampled under foot the laws of God and man." More specifically, the tribunal charged Hagenbach with murder, rape, perjury and other *malefacta*, including orders to his non-German mercenaries to kill the men in the houses where they were quartered so that the women and children would be completely at their mercy.

Charles the Bold of Burgundy was notorious for his practice of laying siege to towns and routinely killing all civilians who resisted. This they had practiced in Liege, Dinant, and Bouillon, rebellious towns in what is today Belgium. These and other polities had been subjected to horrific violence by Burgundian troops. Hagenbach had laid siege to Dinant and as the most dedicated of the commanders in the employ of Charles had played a leading role in the mass executions in the city. Even within that most violent culture, Hagenbach was Charles's fiercest and most loyal lieutenant. Thus, Hagenbach argued that he was doing the work prescribed by his patron among the municipalities of the League of Constance. Many of Hagenbach's activities were undertaken at the express and specific command of Charles the Bold, although often as a result of strong recommendations made to him by Hagenbach.[94]

Hagenbach also interrupted international trade. He was especially zealous in controlling and taxing trade from various Swiss cantons. He extended his committed depredations against Swiss merchants going to and from the Frankfurt Fair. The tribunal perhaps recalled the Baldeck kidnapping and concluded Hagenbach's prejudice against all things Swiss.[95]

The charges mounted. Peter had deprived the nobility of its right to hunt. Farmers were conscripted so they could not raise food sufficient for the population. In such times of resultant food shortages Peter's mercenaries confiscated food. Peter quartered his soldiers in the homes of private citizens, requiring them to feed as well as house them. He had voided and often usurped the powers of various town officials and restructured various offices, all without clear legal authority or permission.

---

[94] Gordon, Gregory S., The Trial of Peter Von Hagenbach: Reconciling History, Historiography, and International Criminal Law (February 16, 2012). Available at SSRN: http://ssrn.com/abstract=2006370

[95] Schwarzenberger, George, "A Forerunner of Nuremberg: The Breisach War Crime Trial of 1474" *Manchester Guardian*, 28 September 1946.

The tribunal held Hagenbach to be responsible for various atrocities committed in the region of the League of Constance, even though he personally did not commit the crimes or even order them. It is almost certain that he was unaware of many of them. Specifically, the Picard and Walloon mercenaries he hired toward the end of his reign had a well-known reputation for being violent and especially hostile toward the Alsatian population. Picard soldiers engaged in a mass rape of the women of Breisach in 1473. These troops may have acted on their own initiative but Hagenbach was their superior and thus he bore command responsibility.[96]

There was no surprise verdict. The knights and others found Hagenbach guilty, and stripped him of his knighthood. They then ordered him to be publicly beheaded him by the end of that fateful day, 9 May 1474. Modern legal scholars perceive the trial as a landmark event because it formulated an embryonic version of crimes against humanity. Many praise it for ostensibly labeling rape as a war crime.

Hagenbach defended himself by arguing that he was merely carrying out the orders of the Duke of Burgundy and Charles the Bold. It is the first recorded case in history to reject the defense of superior orders. Despite the fact there was no explicit use of a doctrine of "command responsibility" it is seen as the first trial based on this principle.[97]

Peter's reputation as one of the true villains of history was insured by French historian Prosper de Barante. The latter wrote that Peter was one of the most violent men ever to have had control over other men. Justice was a concept wholly unknown to Peter. Refusal to cater to his every desire was to invite the death penalty. Barante claimed that Peter killed many without their ever knowing what charge he had laid against them. Barante retold the story of the four representatives of Thann who carried the town's appeal against exorbitant taxation. Without any hesitation and without a trial Hagenbach had them instantly beheaded. Many of those killed had met their fate by Peter's own hand.[98]

---

[96] Gordon, Gregory S., "The Trial of Peter Von Hagenbach: Reconciling History, Historiography, and International Criminal Law"

[97] Grant, Linda, "Exhibit Highlights the First international War Crimes Tribunal," *Harvard Law Bulletin*

[98] *Vaughan*, 429-32.

There was ample evidence to convict Peter purely on the evidence of his own misdeeds. That the tribunal chose also to consider his command responsibility is significant. There is little chance that the tribunal was looking to create a precedent, making the matter of which future cases could be built. It chose to cover all the bases, making certain that future generations knew of all Peter's high crimes.

One final thought. Had the tribunal actually taken an adjournment and checked into Peter's claims that he was just following orders, it would have given great validity to a defense based on a defendant following superior orders. As it was the tribunal never gave consideration to that argument. It is more than probable that, whatever Frederick III as Holy Roman Emperor may have allowed or condemned, Charles the Bold had either given specific orders for what the tribunal considered criminal behavior or had given Peter *carte blanche* to achieve certain ends irrespective of the means he chose to employ. The tribunal did not allow the possibility that any illicit orders or unrestrained permission had come from anyone above Hagenbach. Thus, the tribunal did not have to wrestle with the problem of whether a commander must review the legality and morality of superior orders.

The guilty verdict having been pronounced it remained only to execute sentence. Realistically, capital punishment was the only consideration. For his part, Peter asked only that he be beheaded and the tribunal acquiesced. It might easily have pronounced a much more severe method of execution, such as the usual method of execution for commoners, drawing and quartering. Execution of sentence following immediately.

Charles the Bold sought to punish those who dared try his representative. He appointed Peter's brother Stefan von Hagenbach, to lead a raid into Alsatian territory. Stephen's troops raped, mutilated, looted, burned, and killed without restraint. This raid marked the beginning of the Burgundian Wars between the League of Constance and Charles the Bold. In January 1477 Swiss troops under the Duke of Lorraine decisively defeated Charles who was killed. Stefan was not tried for his rapine even though it was at least as criminal as the acts of his dead brother.

There was a long wait after the Hagenbach trial until more was said of command responsibility. In 1625 Grotius, usually viewed as the father of modern international law, wrote that in war ". . . a community, or its rulers, may be held responsible for the crime of a subject if they knew it and do not prevent it when they could and should prevent it." Also, "As for the ways by which rulers over others may become implicated in their crimes, there are two...tolerance and protection...we must hold that a person who knows of a crime and is able and bound to forbid it and does not do so, himself commits a crime...the people or the king are [not] rigidly bound to surrender the offender, but...they [must] either surrender or punish him."[99]

[99] Grotius, Hugo de Groot, *The Law of War and Peace* [*De Jure Belli ac Pacis*], Louise Loomis, Trans., Walter Black, 1949, 235-237.

3
Accountability of Germany after Two World Wars

In the so-called War Guilt Clause, the victors declared that Germany was solely responsible for the conflict: "The Allied and Associated Governments affirm and Germany accepts the responsibility of Germany and her allies for causing all the loss and damage to which the Allied and Associated Governments and their nationals have been subjected as a consequence of the war imposed upon them by the aggression of Germany and her allies."[100] Total war, such as was fought 1914-1918, the Allies claimed, called for total responsibility, and this must include punishment of nations and individuals in the name of justice, democracy, and morality. Allied bitterness over Germany's conduct of the war precluded the kind of amnesty typical of peace settlements such as were concluded prior to 1919. The treaty sought to supply a legal basis for Germany's responsibility, notably with respect to the violation of Belgian neutrality, and so justify the Allied demand for full reparations. But the Germans were not mistaken in discerning moral condemnation in the treaty, and hence their hatred of the articles of the Treaty of Versailles in general.[101]

It was British Prime Minister David Lloyd George who pressed for these treaty conditions. Georges Clemenceau of France and Vittorio Orlando of Italy quietly acquiesced. Orlando was willing to agree to almost anything in order to secure the territorial additions that had caused Italy to change from its treaty obligations to Germany and Austria. The

---

[100] Article 231 of the Treaty of Versailles

[101] Carnegie Endowment for International Peace. *Violation of the Laws and Customs of War: Reports of Majority and Dissenting Reports of American and Japanese Members of the Commission of Responsibilities, Conference of Paris of 1919.* London , 1919.

greatest difficulty came in establishing a consensus on what international law Germany had violated. In fact there was apparently no existing applicable law.

The Versailles Treaty thus ordered "penalties" for and "reparations" from the named responsible and defeated party, Germany, starting with the German emperor, who had abdicated and taken refuge in the Netherlands: "The Allied and Associated Powers publicly arraign William II of Hohenzollern, formerly German Emperor, for a supreme offense against international morality and the sanctity of treaties. A special tribunal will be constituted to try the accused, thereby assuring him the guarantees essential to the right of defense.... In its decision the tribunal will be guided by the highest motives of international policy, with a view to vindicating the solemn obligations of international undertakings and the validity of international morality. It will be its duty to fix the punishment which it considers should be imposed."[102] The requested extradition of William II had no judicial basis for acceding to it. This caused many problems. Ultimately, the Netherlands refused to extradite, and William II eventually died there in 1941, at a time when the country was once again occupied by Germany. Next, "The German Government recognizes the right of the Allied and Associated Powers to bring before military tribunals persons accused of having committed acts in violation of the laws and customs of war. Such persons shall, if found guilty, be sentenced to punishments laid down by law."[103]

The Treaty required that German military leaders and personnel be held accountable for criminal acts perpetrated during the conflict. "Persons guilty of criminal acts against the nationals of one of the Allied and Associated Powers will be brought before the military tribunals of that Power."[104]

By February 1920 the Allied Powers had drawn up charges naming 888 accused individuals. Among the accused were various German princes and other royalty; officers charged with battlefield or prison camp atrocities; and submarine commanders who were held

[102]Article 227 of the Treaty of Versailles
[103]Article 28 of the Treaty of Versailles
[104]Article 229 of the Treaty of Versailles

responsible for attacks on civilian and hospital ships. Fritz Haber, winner of the 1919 Nobel Prize in Chemistry, was indicted for his part in developing poison gas. Also named were former Chancellor Theodora von Bethmann-Hollweg and Field Marshal Paul von Hindenburg, probably the most popular figure in Germany at the end of the war. Eventually this roster was narrowed down to some forty-five individuals, who were to be tried by the German high court in Leipzig.[105]

Although the Allies apparently had no clear and concrete idea of holding war crimes trials themselves, they initially opposed allowing Germans to try Germans. Various figures active in the very weak Weimar Republic argued that by allowing it to hold the trials the very fabric of the government would be preserved. If the Allies came into Germany and took over the trials the already tottering Republic would surely flounder. Lacking any decisive strategy to try the Germans themselves the Allies agreed to give the Weimar Republic full jurisdiction over the accused.

Proceedings began on 23 May 1921 and rapidly turned into a farce. The German public reacted in a way that was exactly the opposite of what the Allies had anticipated. Germans hailed the accused as war heroes rather than as criminals. All but seven were acquitted and even these seven received light sentences. The trial actually did much to boost nationalist sentiments in Germany, further weakening the already fragile Weimar Republic. That government was trapped between Allied demands and a public that damned the government for accepting Versailles's humiliating conditions, among which was the trial itself. The idea of German guilt, so dear to the Allies, never was part of the German character, save only the communists and others on the far left of the political spectrum.[106]

The Leipzig Trials

The trials were held before the *Reichstag's* in Leipzig from 23 May to 16 July 1921. Hearing the cases were seven German judges. The following were [107] The term "command responsibility" was first applied

---

[105]"Leipzig Trials." *Encyclopedia of Modern Europe: Europe Since 1914: Encyclopedia of the Age of War and Reconstruction.* . Encyclopedia.com. 31

[106]Becker, Jean-Jacques. "Les procès de Leipzig." in *Les procès de Nuremberg et de Tokyo*, edited by Annette Wieviorka. Brussels, 1996.

[107]The following were noted in ICLR report on the Leipzig War Trials with additional

in these trials, with Müller's case seeing the first application of that term. The cases tried were:

Sergeant Karl Heynen was charged with mistreating British prisoners of war. He was sentenced to a brief prison term of ten months which was spent in relative comfort and with great public support. He seems to have disappeared soon after his discharge. Captain Emil Müller was also charged with mistreating POWs. Emil Müller held the rank of captain in the German Army. Müller was a barrister before joining the army. He was the commander of the Flavy de Martel prisoner of war camp where approximately 1000 prisoners were incarcerated. Allies charged him with failure to maintain a decent condition of the camp which led to many deaths as a result of dysentery, failure to prevent the commission of crimes and to punish the perpetrators thereof and, as well as physical violence directed towards prisoners. He was sentenced to six months in prison. Private Robert Neumann was also charged with mistreating prisoners of war. Found guilty he was sentenced to six months in prison. In prison and afterward he was viewed as a war hero.

Most controversial by far was the case of Commander Karl Neumann commander of U-boat UC-67. Neumann's submarine sank the British hospital ship *Dover Castle* which was clearly marked with its sole function and in a pattern distinct from warships. For his part Neumann said that he had made the attack in compliance with direct superior orders. He was found not guilty due to the fact that he was following orders. This was the first clear use of this defense and it was to be employed many times thereafter.[108]

First-lieutenants Ludwig Dithmar and John Boldt, charged with war crimes for actions on the high seas. Both were subordinate officers of the submarine U-86 that had sunk the Canadian hospital ship *Llandovery Castle*. Reportedly, after the order to abandon ship they then machine-gunned survivors who were afloat or in the lifeboats. They were each found guilty of war crimes and sentenced to four years in prison. The

---

materials from Wikipedia.

[108] Solis, Gary D. (1999). "Obedience of Orders and the Law of War: Judicial Application in American Forums." *American University International Law Review.* 15: 481–526.

submarine's commanding officer, Helmut Brümmer-Patzig, fled to the Free City of Danzig and was never extradited or prosecuted.[109]

Max Ramdohr, charged with crimes against the civilian noncombatants in occupied Belgium. He was found not guilty.

Lieutenant-General Karl Stenger and Major Benno Crusius, charged with mistreating French POWs. Stenger was found not guilty, while Crusius was sentenced to two years in prison.

First-Lieutenant Adolph Laule, charged with crimes against the civilian population of occupied France. He was found not guilty. Execution of partisans and those civilians aiding escaped POWs and engaging in sabotage could indeed be punished, even executed. No clear international code law covering civilians in war zones had yet been enacted and no conventional international law existed.

Lieutenant-General Hans von Schack and Major-General Benno Kruska, charged with mistreating POWs. Both were found not guilty. Here the general assumption was that nothing had occurred because of *mens rea*, but rather because of the exigencies of war and consequent shortages of food and other supplies. Too, conditions were little different in POW camps run by Allied nations.

What was perceived as leniency in Germany met with outrage in the Allied nations, notably in Great Britain. Germans thought it was insulting that only German servicemen at all ranks were being charged while various Allied personnel went unpunished for similar crimes. The British, while greatly concerned about real and perceived outrages against its soldiers while prisoners of war saw that this was the main area of prosecution. Likewise, the other area of prosecution was what seemed to be clear war crimes, the sinking of hospital ships and killing of survivors.

On 15 January 1922, a commission of Allied jurists, spurred on primarily by England, appointed to inquire into the German trials,

---

[109]Mullins, Claude. *The Leipzig Trials: An Account of the War Criminals' Trials and Study of German Mentality*. London: Witherby, 1921. This is by far the most useful source of information on the trials and those charged with crimes. It has been reprinted. See also Willis, James F. *Prologue to Nuremberg: The Politics and Diplomacy of Punishing War Criminals of the First World War*. Westport, 2014; and Hankel, Gerd. *The Leipzig Trials: German War Crimes and Their Legal Consequences after World War I.* Westport: Republic of Letters, 1982.

concluded that it was useless to proceed with them any further. The commission recommended that the remaining accused should be handed over to the Allies for trial. This recommendation was not followed, and all the trials were quietly abandoned.

Although the Leipzig Trials were absolutely a failure at the time, they set the stage for prosecution following later wars. The Leipzig trials were the first attempt to devise a comprehensive system for prosecution of violations of international law and like so many first halting steps illuminated the path for later improvements. They also showed victors' justice, for these trials absolutely rejected *tu quoque*[110] as a defense. Victors will punish only illicit acts by defeated enemies without giving a thought to the prosecution of the own for similar transgressions.

Punishing Germany for World War II

On 1 November 1943, the Soviet Union, the United Kingdom and the United States published a Declaration on German Atrocities in Occupied Europe, which provided a grave warning that, when the Nazis were defeated, the Allies would "pursue them to the uttermost ends of the earth . . . in order that justice may be done. . . . " The Allies reiterated their intention to hold war crimes trials while at the Yalta Conference in 1945. As early as December 1944, the British Cabinet had discussed the punishment of the leading Nazis. Prime Minister Winston Churchill had advocated a policy of summary execution in some circumstances, with the use of a bill of attainder to circumvent legal obstacles. American leaders dissuaded Churchill from this only by extensive talks later in the war.

In late 1943, during a tripartite meeting at the Tehran Conference, the Soviet leader, Joseph Stalin, proposed executing 50,000 to 100,000 German staff officers. President Franklin Roosevelt suggested that perhaps 49,000 would do. Churchill denounced the idea of the cold blooded execution of soldiers who fought for their country. He again stated that war criminals must pay for their crimes and that in accordance with the Moscow Document which he himself had written. Churchill proposed that

[110]Tu quoque is readily used by defendants in war crime, crimes against humanity or genocide proceedings, if the facts allow. Tu quoque raises a mirror to the adjudicator or accuser to view similar acts committed by nationals of that adjudicating or prosecuting state.

the leaders should be tried at the places where the crimes were committed. Roosevelt was astounded at the extent of the destruction in the Crimea. Therefore he was more amenable to the idea of executing many Germans than he had been a year earlier.

Secretary of the Treasury, Henry Morgenthau, Jr., had suggested a plan for the total demilitarization of Germany which became known as the Morgenthau Plan. The plan advocated the forced de-industrialization of Germany and the summary execution of many Germans. The Allies would work toward converting Germany into a country that would be primarily agricultural and pastoral in its character. The plan would be realized in three steps. First, Germany was to be partitioned into two independent states. Second, Germany's main centers of mining and industry, including the Saar, the Ruhr area, and Upper Silesia were to be internationalized or annexed by Germany's neighbors. All heavy industry was to be dismantled or otherwise destroyed. Roosevelt initially supported Morgenthau's plan, and managed to convince Churchill to support it in a less drastic form. In October 1945 Harper and Brother published Morgenthau's book *Germany is Our Problem*, where Morgenthau described his plan and the rationale for it in greater detail. President Franklin D. Roosevelt had granted permission for the publication of the book the evening before his death, when dining with Morgenthau at Warm Springs.[111]

The secret directive from the Joint Chief of Staff 1067 for the future government of Germany, the final version of which was presented in April 1945, specified that Germany was "occupied not for the purpose of liberation but as a conquered enemy state," that heavy industry was to be dismantled, that cartels were to be dismantled, that the military was to be abolished and that comprehensive denazification measures were to be

[111]The text, and a facsimile image, can be viewed online. Morgenthau, Henry (1944). "Suggested Post-Surrender Program for Germany [The original memorandum from 1944, signed by Morgenthau. [Box 31, Folder Germany: Jan.-Sept. 1944]. Franklin D. Roosevelt Presidential Library and Museum. "Demilitarization of Germany: It should be the aim of the Allied Forces to accomplish the complete demilitarization of Germany in the shortest possible period of time after surrender. This means completely disarming the German Army and people (including the removal or destruction of all war material), the total destruction of the whole German armament industry, and the removal or destruction of other key industries which are basic to military strength."

conducted. Nonetheless, JCS 1067 also contained numerous loopholes, which the U. S. military governor was able to exploit in order to implement a more lenient occupation policy.[112]

When details were leaked to the public there was widespread protest. Roosevelt, aware of the consequences of strong public disapproval, abandoned the plan. Secretary of War Henry L. Stimson and the War Department then drafted a plan for the Trial of European War Criminals. Following Roosevelt's death in April 1945, the new president, Harry S. Truman, gave his approval for judicial proceedings to try Nazi war criminals. After a series of negotiations between Britain, the U. S., Soviet Union and France, details of the trial were worked out. The trials were to commence on 20 November 1945, in Nuremberg.

The question of the legality of the tribunal had been considered during the debates in *ex parte Quirin.*[113] Justice Robert H. Jackson had written a lengthy concurring opinion in *Quirin* which was to become highly important as the war crimes trials against the Axis leaders loomed on the horizon. In his draft, begun in Quirin and expanded in later cases, Jackson attributed sweeping powers to the President. He concluded that (1) the President has the inherent authority to create military tribunals, (2) this authority could not be regulated by Congress, and (3) this power was by virtue of his power as Commander-in-Chief. Jackson stated, "I think the Court's decision of the question whether it complied with the Articles of War is uncalled for. The history and the language of the Articles are to me a plain demonstration that they are clearly inapplicable to this case and it is abundantly clear to me that it is well within the war powers of the President to create a non-statutory military tribunal of the sort here in question." He further wrote "The right to convene such an advisory committee of his staff as a 'military commission' for the discharge of his duties toward prisoners of war is one that follows from his position as commander in chief." Nonetheless, Jackson maintained that the President's power should be "discharged, of course, in the light of any obligation undertaken by our country under treaties or conventions or

---

[112]Federal Agency for Civic Education [Germany]. *Der Zweite Weltkrieg: Von Pearl Harbor bis Hiroshima* [*The Second World War: From Pearl Harbor to Hiroshima*].
[113]317 U.S. 1; 63 S. Ct. 2; 87 L. Ed. 3 (1942)

under customs and usages so generally accepted as to constitute the laws of warfare." Jackson questioned the Court's ability to review the President's actions. He concluded that dealing with enemy prisoners of war was a foreign policy issue that touched upon issues of national security and political questions that were wholly beyond the province of the judiciary. Jackson also stated that granting enemy combatants individual rights over and against U.S. military authorities would not likely be reciprocated by other nations. Jackson analyzed both the history and purposes of the Articles of War to conclude that the Articles are not applicable to enemy combatants — rather, they were meant to protect U.S. civilians in times of military government. Jackson ultimately believed it was a mistake for the Court to review military judgments in times of war. While Jackson withdrew his draft concurring opinion in the end, as regards the war crimes tribunals, it became the base of the Supreme Court's position.[114]

On 14 January 1942, representatives from the nine occupying countries met in London to draft the Inter-Allied Resolution on German War Crimes. At the meetings in Tehran (1943), Yalta (1945) and Potsdam (1945), the United Kingdom, United States, and the Soviet Union agreed on the format of punishment for those responsible for war crimes during World War II. France was eventually awarded a place on the tribunal. The legal basis for the trial was established by the London Charter, which was agreed upon by the four so-called Great Powers on 8 August 1945, and which restricted the trial to "punishment of the major war criminals of the European Axis countries."[115]

The London Agreement & Charter became the basis for the trials before the IMT at Nuremberg. For two months during the summer of 1945, Robert H. Jackson and his team, which included his son William E. Jackson, worked at achieving a consensus among the Allies. Jackson's energy, intelligence and leadership directed the London Conference. The jurisdiction of the Tribunal was outlined in article 6 of the Charter. This article defined the crimes the defendants could be charged with; crimes against peace, war crimes, and crimes against humanity. Justice Robert H. Jackson wrote of the London Charter, "On 8 August 1945 we signed the

---

[114]"Ex parte Quirin." Oyez, 31 Jan. 2019, www.oyez.org/cases/1940-1955/317us1.
[115]https://www.roberthjackson.org/article/london-agreement-charter-august-8-1945/

agreement, as I was authorized to do on behalf of the United States, and it was announced to the world. Up to that time there had been some press rumors that we were having difficulties in arriving at it. We had frankly admitted that we had, but there had been no exploitation of our differences. The document was received with considerable satisfaction in most interested countries."[116]

World War II trials involving German war criminals in which the doctrine of command responsibility were conducted in Nuremberg. The charters governing the Nuremberg and allied trials were silent as to criminal liability under the doctrine of command responsibility. Control Council Law No. 10, the basis for trials of war criminals by the Allies in Germany, did not specifically provide for this form of criminal liability.

Prelude to Nuremberg

Two important cases, one involving Americans, the second concerning Canadians, were heard and decided before any of what are generically called Nuremberg cases were decided. Both involved the execution of soldiers of the respective nationalities.

The first case to be tried as a war crime was General Anton Dostler. As commander of the German Wehrmacht in an Italian region he was called upon to follow orders from Adolf Hitler regarding Allied soldiers caught in civilian clothing and thus acting as spies, saboteurs, or commandoes. Dostler chose to obey superior orders. In the first allied war trial after the war, Dostler was tried and found guilty of war crimes and sentenced to death by firing squad.

Anton Dostler had been born in Munich, May 10, 1891. He achieved the rank of general in the German army during World War II. Anton Dostler joined the German Army in 1910 and served as a junior officer during World War I. From the start of World War II to 1940, he served as Chief of Staff of the 7th Army. Subsequently, he commanded the 57th Infantry Division (1941–1942), the 163rd Infantry Division (1942) and the 42nd Army Corps (1943–1944) in Italy. He was appointed to command the 75th Army Corps in January 1944.

---

[116]*The Reminiscences of Robert H. Jackson*. New York: Columbia University Press, ch. 17.

On March 22, 1944, fifteen American Army soldiers, including two officers, landed on the Italian coast about 15 kilometers north of La Spezia, some 250 miles behind the front lines. The mission was conducted under the auspices of the Office of Strategic Services [OSS]. The operation code-named Ginny II had as its objective the demolition a tunnel at Framura on the railroad line between La Spezia and Genoa. Two days after landing, the group was captured by a party of Italian Fascist soldiers and members of the German Wehrmacht. The prisoners were taken to La Spezia, where they were confined near the headquarters of the 135th Fortress Brigade, which was under the command of German Colonel Almers. The immediate, superior command was that of the 75th Army Corps, commanded by Dostler. The Germans interrogated the captured American soldiers. One of the officers revealed the story of the mission.

This information, noting that it was a commando raid, was then sent to Dostler at the 75th Army Corps. The following day, March 25, Dostler sent a telegram to the 135th Fortress Brigade ordering that the captured soldiers be executed. This was to implement Hitler's Commando Order of 1941 [Führerbefehl] which required the immediate execution without trial of commandos and saboteurs. The text of the Commando order directed that enemy commandos should without quarter "be exterminated to the last man, either in combat or in pursuit" A no quarter order is itself illegal under international law. Any commandos who somehow managed to escape death were to be handed over to the SS.

Officers at the 135th Fortress Brigade contacted Dostler in an attempt to achieve a stay of execution. Dostler then sent another telegram ordering Almers to carry out the execution. Officers in the 135th made two additional attempts to postpone the executions. These efforts being unsuccessful, the fifteen Americans were executed on the morning of March 26, 1944, at Punta Bianca south of La Spezia, in the municipality of Ameglia. Their bodies were buried in a mass grave that was then camouflaged.

Dostler became a prisoner of the Americans on 8 May 1945 and was put before a military tribunal at the seat of the Supreme Allied Commander, the Royal Palace in Caserta. In the first Allied war crimes trial, Dostler was accused of executing an order that was illegal under the Geneva Convention.

The quintessential question the tribunal had to answer: were the fifteen American soldiers dressed in uniform or were they was dressed as Italian civilians? There had been a group of German saboteurs captured in the United States during the war who had themselves been executed after becoming the subject of Supreme Court landmark Ex parte Quirin. Here, a similar act on the German side brought a death sentence. The essential legal difference between the German saboteurs and the OSS men shot at La Spezia was that the Allied court found that the latter were taken in uniform. If uniformed, they were entitled to prisoner of war status; if not, then a summary execution might have been permissible. Dostler's defense team seems to have conceded that the saboteurs were indeed in American uniforms, although the skimpy notes of the trial are rather vague on the point. There is an intriguing indication that the defense disputed the notion that the captive saboteurs' uniforms had the necessary "fixed distinctive sign recognizable at a distance." The New York Times reported that "they wore no insignia, had turned their field jackets inside out."

The importance wearing uniforms of cannot be overstated. Had Wolfe pursued this line of defense carefully he might have gained acquittal, assuming of course that the OSS men were not clad in standard and recognizable American military uniforms. As the Supreme Court wrote in *ex parte Quirin*

> …the law of war draws a distinction between the armed forces and the peaceful populations of belligerent nations and also between those who are lawful and unlawful combatants. Lawful combatants are subject to capture and detention as prisoners of war by opposing military forces. Unlawful combatants are likewise subject to capture and detention, but in addition they are subject to trial and punishment by military tribunals for acts which render their belligerency unlawful. The spy who secretly and without uniform passes the military lines of a belligerent in time of war, seeking to gather military information and communicate it to the enemy, or an enemy combatant who without uniform comes secretly through the lines for the purpose of waging war by destruction of life or property, are familiar examples of belligerents who are generally deemed not to be entitled to the status of prisoners of war, but to be offenders against the law of war subject to trial

and punishment by military tribunals.[117]

In his own defense, Dostler maintained that he had not created the order, but had only passed along an order to Colonel Almers from the German high command. Dostler also contended that Hitler's citation in the Führerbefehl of alleged Allied atrocities made the German policy in reality a reprisal order that was legal under the Geneva Convention. He apparently thought that these two arguments constituted a sufficient defense.

General Dostler's court appointed defense attorney was Col. Claudius Wolfe, U.S. Army. Wolfe was much more interested in pursuing the superior orders defense, presumably because he thought that this was the best way to save his client. Wolfe pursued this line of defense with great vigor and skill. The Allied Powers had not yet decided as a matter of policy not to allow potential war criminals to use that particular defense. The Führerbefehl was the order of the day. General Dostler insisted that he was acting under the orders of General Gustav von Zangen. Dostler had referred this specific decision to the office of General Albert Kesselring, which had insisted upon the executions to the point of directly phoning the fortress which held the Americans to ask why the Americans had not yet been executed. Col. Wolfe's spirited argument appeared to strike a chord with the tribunal's career military officers. In his closing summation, Wolfe impressed upon them the danger to military decorum and order, and to their own positions, of establishing a precedent wherein subordinates can be held accountable for illegal orders from above. Wolfe saw as a great challenge to military precedent and tradition any requirement that officers must judge the morality and legality of superior orders. Wolfe continued, "We won the war this time, but no one knows who will win the next time. We might lose and then you gentlemen might find yourselves sitting where this man is now sitting… If we find this man guilty because of political pressure or because he lost the war and is in our power, we might as well not have won the war."

Alexander zu Dohna-Schlobitten, a member of Dostler's staff, was aware of the Commando Order and thought it to be illegal. He had refused

---

[117]317 U.S. 1 (1942).

to sign the execution order because he thought the Führerbefehl violated the Geneva Convention regarding the treatment of prisoners. He was consequently dismissed from the Wehrmacht for insubordination, but did not prosecute him for standing up for his principles.[118]

Under the 1907 Hague Convention on Land Warfare, it was legal to execute spies and saboteurs disguised in civilian clothes or enemy uniforms, but not those captured in uniforms of their own army and in reality that could have brought about acquittal. In his defense General Dostler maintained that he had not issued the order but had only passed it along to Colonel Almers from Supreme Command, and that the execution of the OSS men was a lawful order. Dostler's plea of superior orders failed before the tribunal, which found that in ordering the mass execution he had acted on his own outside Hitler's orders. The Military Commission also rejected his plea for clemency, declaring that the mass execution of the commando party was in violation of Article 2 of the 1929 Geneva Convention on Prisoners of War, which prohibited acts of reprisals against prisoners of war. In its Judgement the Commission stated that "no soldier, and still less a Commanding General, can be heard to say that he considered the summary shooting of prisoners of war legitimate, even as a reprisal."

The tribunal found General Dostler guilty of war crimes, rejecting the defense of superior orders. He was sentenced to death and shot by a firing squad on December 1, 1945 in Aversa. The execution was photographed by both still and movie cameras.[119]

A second occurrence, this time involving Canadian soldiers, prompted Allied judicial attention. Abbaye Ardenne is the site of a medieval monastery near Caen, France, containing a chapel built in 1121 and other ancient buildings. During the Normandy Campaign, Brigadeführer

---

[118]Associated Press, "Nazi General Executed For Ordering Deaths of G.I.'S [sic] - Dostler Falls Before U. S. Firing Squad," The San Bernardino Daily Sun, San Bernardino, California, Sunday 2 December 1945. See also "Anton Dostler" entry in Wikipedia.

[119]This execution can be found at https://www.bing.com/videos/search?q=execution+of+General+Anton+Dostler&view=detail&mid=80BE07AEFB255BEFC2C2807AEFB255BEFC2C2&FORM=VIRE Three angles of the execution shown also on YouTube.

Kurt Meyer, commander of the 25th Panzer Grenadier Regiment, used the Ardenne Abbey for his regimental headquarters and as an observation post during the Battle of Normandy as the turret allowed for a clear view of the battlefield. Here in June 1944, members of the 12th SS Panzer Division executed 20 Canadian soldiers were executed. During the evening of 7 June, 11 Canadian prisoners of war, were shot in the back of the head.

The Canadian prosecution brought forth three charges: command responsibility and inciting his troops to commit the executions. Commanding his troops to kill 23 POWs at or near the villages of Buron and Authie on 7 June 1944. Commanding his troops, on 8 June 1944, to kill seven prisoners of war at the Abbaye Ardenne, and as a result of such orders the prisoners were shot and killed. Former SS Private Alfred Helzel was the first important witness for the prosecution. While in prison in Quebec, Helzel revealed that in June 1944 Meyer had directed his troops to take no prisoners; on the stand, however, Helzel denied that Meyer made such a declaration. The prosecutor eventually managed to have Helzel verify his original statement. Citizens of the towns of Authie and Buron also testified against the 12th SS and the various atrocities it had committed against Canadian soldiers. Canadian Sergeant Stanley Dudka testified that his column of prisoners arrived at the Abbaye Ardenne on 7 June, after which military police demanded 10 volunteers step forward. Since no one volunteered, 10 men were randomly taken, including Private Moss, later identified as one of the men executed at the Abbaye. The central witness for the prosecution was Jan Jesionek. One of the officers announced: "In the future, no more prisoners are to be taken." Jesionek then saw each prisoner questioned by the officer to whom Meyer had spoken. A name was called out, a prisoner walked up from the passageway leading to the garden in the Abbaye. As soon as the prisoner turned, the officer shot him in the head with a machine pistol; this was repeated for the remaining six prisoners. When the Canadians realized what was happening, each prisoner shook hands with his comrades before walking to the garden to be executed.

The tribunal found Meyer guilty of inciting his troops to commit murder and of command responsibility for the killings at the Abbaye. However, he was acquitted on the second and third charges. Sentenced to death on 28 December 1945, Meyer's sentence was commuted to life imprisonment on 14 January 1946. After serving nearly nine years in prison, Meyer was released on 7 September 1954.

Nuremberg Trials

Some 200 German war crimes defendants were tried at Nuremberg, and 1,600 others were tried under the traditional channels of military justice. The legal basis for the jurisdiction of the court was that defined by the Instrument of Surrender of Germany. Political authority for Germany had been transferred to the Allied Control Council which, having sovereign power over Germany, could choose to punish violations of international law and the laws of war. Because the court was limited to violations of the laws of war, it did not have jurisdiction over crimes that took place before the outbreak of war on 1 September 1939. As concerns us, the trials were remarkable for expanding the reach of command responsibility. They made landmark contributions to the doctrines of joint criminal enterprise and command responsibility. The tribunals expended significant effort in distinguishing between command responsibility, aiding and abetting, "taking a consenting part in," and being connected to criminal "plans or enterprises. The tribunals themselves often either conflated different modes of participation or elided the differences between them." As developed in the trials, the courts made considerable progress in defining both joint criminal enterprise and command responsibility. In the International Military Tribunal for Germany, for example, the Nazi leadership was held directly responsible for its crimes, without need to resort to the principle of superior responsibility. As concerns command responsibility, the trial of those most responsible for war crimes proved little. Virtually all the crimes of the Third Reich are directly traceable to this group. The defendants would have been found guilty of waging an aggressive war and associated crimes because the evidence against them was absolutely overwhelming. It is obvious that none of these defendants could use a defense based upon reception of superior orders. Most of the defendants in this group were, of course, responsible for the issuance of the very criminal orders for which others who obeyed them were punished. For our purposes here there is much more to be gleaned from taking a long look at the subsequent trials.

Many of those most responsible for the main charges at the one international tribunal were dead. Hitler and Himmler had committed suicide. Presumably Martin Borman had been killed trying to escape. Reinhard Heydrich had been assassinated. Josef Mengele and Adolf Eichmann had escaped. Deputy leader Rudolf Hess[120] was placed on trial but was judged mentally incompetent.[121]

Ten prominent members of the political and military leadership of Nazi Germany were executed by hanging: Hans Frank, Wilhelm Frick, Alfred Jodl, Ernst Kaltenbrunner, Wilhelm Keitel, Joachim von Ribbentrop, Alfred Rosenberg, Fritz Sauckel, Arthur Seyss-Inquart, and Julius Streicher. Robert Ley, who might have been executed, had committed suicide early in the trial. The death sentences are carried out on October 16, 1946, with two exceptions: Göring committed suicide shortly before his scheduled execution, and Bormann remained missing.[122] Three were sentenced to life imprisonment: Hess; economics minister Walther Funk; and Grand Admiral Raeder. Four received prison terms ranging from 10 to 20 years: Admiral Doenitz, Baldur von Schirach, Architect Albert Speer, and Baron Konstantin von Neurath. The court acquitted three defendants: Hjalmar Schacht, the economics minister, Franz von Papen, a career German politician, and Hans Fritzsche, the head of press and radio.[123]

Subsequent Nuremberg Trials

There were a number of trials conducted by the individual Allied nations of which twelve post-1946 Nuremberg trials were conducted solely by the United States. These are collectively known as the

---

[120]"Nuremberg Trial Proceedings Vol. 1: Report of Commission to Examine Defendant Hess". Lillian Goldman Law Library, Yale Law School.

[121]Conot, Robert E. Justice at Nuremberg. New York: Harper & Row, 1983; Priemel, Kim C. and Stiller, Alexa, eds. *Reassessing the Nuremberg Military Tribunals: Transitional Justice, Trial Narratives, and Historiography.* Berghahn Books, 2012; and Herbert R. Reginbogin and Christoph J. M. Safferling: *The Nuremberg Trials: International Criminal Law Since 1945*. De Gruyter, 2006.

[122] Denhart, Jeff and Stanley Tilles, *By the Neck Until Dead: The Gallows of Nuremberg*. New York: Jona, 1999.

[123]Heydecker, Joe J. and Leeb, Johannes. *Der Nürnberger Prozeß*. Köln: Kiepenheuer und Witsch, 1979; also Henkel, Matthias, ed. *Memoriam Nuernberger Prozesse.* Nuremberg: Museen der Stadt Nuernberg, 2011.

Subsequent Nuremberg Trials or, more formally, as the Trials of War Criminals before the Nuremberg Military Tribunals (NMT). Most focused on the administration of the Third Reich, internal German politics and government, genocide, crimes against humanity, and similar offenses which are beyond the subject of this treatise. During almost three years, the American Military Tribunals tried 1,672 German war criminals in 489 separate proceedings. In total 1,416 former members of the Nazi regime were convicted. Of these 297 received death sentences and 279 were sentenced to life in prison. These twelve trials were all held before U.S. military courts, not before the International Military Tribunal, but took place in the same rooms at the Palace of Justice.[124]

Post-war tribunals in both Japan and Germany made no attempt to standardize their criteria for conviction. There was no consensus in specifying the mental elements of command responsibility. Where cases adopted the mental object of a specific crime, rejecting expansive interpretations, convictions fell on officers close in rank and geographical location to the commission of crimes. Such tribunals usually dealt only with a few defendants and a limited number of incidents. When the tribunals were charged with larger, and usually more famous cases, they necessarily expanded the mental object. Thus many defendants were often charged with multiple offenses in a single proceeding. In such cases no one really knew whether any particular defendant had knowledge of any specific crime, but rather tried them for a wide variety of acts with an assumption that enough would stick to each defendant to bring about a guilty verdict.

The best known of these trials was held within the former Dachau Concentration Camp because it was the best known of the Nazi concentration camps. These trials considered primarily those who were involved in the administration of the concentration camps and thus the charges were mostly crimes against humanity and genocide. However a few others were tried at Dachau for crimes that are within the scope of this

---

[124]Clapham, Andrew. "Issues of complexity, complicity and complementarity: from the Nuremberg Trials to the dawn of the International Criminal." in Philippe Sands, ed. *From Nuremberg to the Hague: the Future of International Criminal Justice*. Cambridge University Press, 2003.

study. Among those executed for war crimes were the following. Richard Drauz, Nazi Party official, member of the Reichstag (1933-1945), was sentenced to death on 11 December 1945 for his involvement in the summary execution of an Allied prisoner of war on 24 March 1945. Jürgen Stroop, SS Gruppenführer, was sentenced to death on 21 March 1947 for ordering the execution of captured Allied airmen. Before the sentence was carried out he was extradited to Poland to stand trial for his role in the liquidation of the Warsaw ghetto. The Polish court condemned Stroop to death and he was executed in Mokotów Prison in Warsaw on 6 March 1952.[125]

There was one notable acquittal during the Dachau trials. Otto Skorzeny (1908-1975), SS Obersturmbannführer was the commander of SS Panzer Brigade 150 during the Battle of the Bulge. The U. S. authorities brought charges against Skorzeny in August 1947 for violations of the 1907 Hague Convention. He led Operation Greif, a false flag operation in which German troops infiltrated behind Allied lines in the Ardennes Forest wearing British and U. S. Army uniforms and using captured vehicles. German soldiers were to infiltrate through enemy lines, using their opponents' language and customs to spread disinformation and disrupt communications and misdirect military operations and supplies. A handful of his men were captured and spread a rumor that Skorzeny personally was leading a raid on Paris to kill or capture General Eisenhower, who was not amused by having to spend Christmas 1944 isolated for security reasons. Eisenhower retaliated by ordering a manhunt for Skorzeny. He was held as a prisoner of war for more than two years before being tried as a war criminal at the Dachau Trials in 1947 for allegedly violating the laws of war in the Battle of the Bulge. He and other officers were charged with improperly using American uniforms to infiltrate American lines. Skorzeny was brought before a US military court in Dachau on 18 August 1947. The trial lasted over three weeks. One of the original charges, that of stealing Red Cross parcels was dropped for lack of evidence. Skorzeny admitted to ordering his men to wear American uniforms, but he argued that as long as the enemy uniforms were discarded before combat started,

---

[125]Greene, Joshua. *Justice At Dachau: The Trials of an American Prosecutor.* New York: Broadway, 2003.

such a tactic was a legitimate ruse de guerre. On the final day of the trial, 9 September, Wing Commander F. F. E. Yeo-Thomas, a former British Special Operations Executive agent, testified that he had worn German uniforms behind enemy lines. Despite having disallowed the *tu quoque* defense, the tribunal realizing that if it convicted Skorzeny it could expose their own agent to the same charges. The tribunal then acquitted Skorzeny and the other nine defendants. The military tribunal thus drew a distinction between using enemy uniforms during combat and for other purposes including deception. The prosecution could not prove that Skorzeny had given any orders to actually fight in a US uniform. Skorzeny was acquitted of all charges on 9 September 1947. Skorzeny left Germany in 1948, moving first to France, and then to Spain where he died of cancer.[126]

Another unusual acquittal was Heinrich Schmidt. During World War II he was a SS-Hauptsturmführer and medical officer in the Dachau and Mittelbau-Dora concentration camps. Schmidt was indicted by American authorities in August 1947 for suspected war crimes committed during his service as chief physician of the Nordhausen sub-camp of Mittelbau-Dora from March and April 1945. He was acquitted due to insufficient evidence on 30 December 1947. He was subsequently indicted by the District Court of Düsseldorf in November 1975 for alleged crimes against humanity perpetrated during his service as a medical officer in the Majdanek concentration camp in 1942 and 1943). Again the court acquitted him due to lack of evidence on 20 March 1979. His trial was reportedly the longest and most expensive criminal trial in German history. Schmidt died in 2000.[127]

The High Command Trial was the last of the twelve trials for war crimes the U.S. authorities held in their occupation zone in Germany in Nuremberg after the end of World War II. The accused in this trial were all high-ranking generals of the German Wehrmacht (one was a former Admiral); some of them had been members of the High Command of Nazi Germany's military forces. They were charged with having participated in

---

[126]Whiting, Charles, *Skorzeny: "The Most Dangerous Man in Europe,"* DaCapo Press, 1998; and Foley, Charles, *Commando Extraordinary*. England: Arms & Armour, 1987.

[127]https://en.wikipedia.org/wiki/Dachau_trials

or planned or facilitated the execution of the numerous atrocities committed in countries occupied by the German forces during the war. The accused faced four charges of having committed war crimes and crimes against humanity: crimes against peace by waging aggressive war against other nations and violating international treaties; and war crimes by being responsible for murder, ill-treatment and other crimes against prisoners of war and enemy belligerents. Crimes against humanity by participating or ordering the murder, torture, deportation, and hostage-taking, of civilians in occupied countries. They were charged with participating and organizing the formulations and execution of a common plan and conspiracy to commit aforementioned crimes, but the conspiracy charge was soon dropped because it was already covered by the other charges. All defendants were indicted on all counts and all pleaded not guilty. The tribunal considered all accused not guilty of planning a war because they were not the policy-makers and that preparing for war and fighting a war under orders was not a criminal offense under the applicable international law of the time.[128]

The High Command case made pioneering contributions to the doctrine of command responsibility. High Command established that command responsibility includes an obligation to punish crimes committed by subordinates even if those crimes were committed before the commander assumed control; that a staff officer who drafts an illegal order or who takes personal action to see that an illegal order is distributed is liable for the resulting crimes; and that a field commander is criminally liable not only for issuing a criminal order, but even for transmitting an order that was "criminal upon its face." Similarly, the tribunals established that a commanding officer is responsible for the actions of all the forces within his territorial jurisdiction, even if they are not under his direct command, and that a commander is charged with constructive knowledge of all the information available to him, even if he is not personally aware of it. Some aspects of the NMT's jurisprudence, however, has had a negative influence, such as High Command's subjective test for military necessity, which lives on in the Rome Statute.[129]

---

[128]https://www.jewishvirtuallibrary.org/dachau-war-crimes-trials

[129] Appleman, John A. *Military Tribunals and International Crimes.* Westport:

General Kurt Student (1890-1979), commanding German paratroopers, was charged with capturing and subduing the island of Crete during May 1941. As commander of the German forces which captured the island, Student was charged with command responsibility for crimes committed all over the island by various subordinates over a two-month period. There was no clear pattern, let alone plan, of criminality. The tribunal convicted Student of a few charges, but acquitted him of the bulk because there was no policy of criminal behavior. On appeal all convictions were reversed because the court believed that there was no reasonable way that Student could have been aware of any particular crime.[130]

Malmédy Massacre

The Malmédy Massacre occurred on December 17th 1944, during the Battle of the Bulge. It was the worst atrocity committed against prisoners of war in the West European sector during World War Two. In December the U.S. Army sent 17, Battery B, 285th Field Artillery Observation Battalion from Schevenhutte, near Aachen, to St Vith in the Ardennes Forest. Their route took them near the town of Malmédy. Although warned of the German advance in that sector they continued to advance along their designated route. This trip took them to the Baugnez Crossroads, two miles south-east of Malmédy. About half-a-mile from the Baugnez Crossroads, two tanks from the 1st SS Panzer Division led by Joachim Peiper (1915-1976) fired at the column. Clearly outgunned by the Germans, the men from B Battery surrendered. Peiper himself went to the Baugnez Crossroads [known to Americans as Five Points] and brusquely ordered his troops to move on. The 113 American prisoners-of-war who had survived the attack were assembled in a field near the Café Bodarwé at the crossroads.[131]

Greenwood, 1971.

[130]Some Noteworthy War Criminals at the Wayback Machine Source: History of the United Nations War Crimes Commission and the Development of the Laws of War. United Nations War Crimes Commission. London: HMSO, 1948

[131]Weingartner, James J. *Crossroads of Death: The Story of the Malmedy Massacre and Trial.* University of California Press, 1979. This is the best and most fair history of the Malmedy Massacre. We have followed it in the narrative that follows.

According to Belgian and American POW witnesses at about 14.15, soldiers from the 1st SS Panzer Division opened fire on the 113 men in the field. The firing continued until about 14.30. Soldiers then went around the field and shot at close range anyone who seemed to be alive. Later autopsies showed that some men were clubbed to death. Soon after the massacre occurred Peiper had left the area. Reportedly he was not at the field when the shooting started.

The first survivors of the massacre were found by a patrol from the 291st Combat Engineer Battalion at about 2:30 p.m. the same day. A few survivors emerged from hiding and returned through the lines to nearby Malmedy, where American troops held the town. Eventually, 43 survivors found refuge, some with the help of Belgian civilians. Some prisoners did escape after feigning death. It was three of these escapees who encountered Colonel Pergrin who had heard the attack and gone to investigate. Pergrin took the escapees to Malmédy and at 16.40 contacted the First Army's headquarters to inform them that a massacre had taken place at Five Points.[132]

On December 17th, 21 survivors of the massacre made statements to the American authorities in Malmédy. Testimony from the survivors was taken hours after the massacre. All the accounts were similar and corroborated each other, though the men had no opportunity to discuss the events.

As the battle raged neither side could claim the land that the dead men lay in. It was only on 14 January 1945 that the Americans occupied the area around the crossroads and claimed the bodies. The freezing weather had done much to preserve the bodies and that made the autopsies easier. Survey teams found seventy-two snow covered bodies in the field on 14 and 15 January 1945. Twelve more bodies, lying farther from the pasture, were found between February 7 and April 15, 1945.

In May 1946 Peiper and 70 of his men stood trial for partaking in the Malmédy Massacre. The specific charge read, "That they willfully, deliberately and wrongfully permit, encourage, aid, abet and participate in the killing, shooting, ill treatment, abuse and torture of members of the

---

[132]Cole, Hugh M. *The Ardennes: Battle of the Bulge*. U.S. Government Printing Office, 1955.

armed forces of the United States of America." The highest-ranking defendant was General Sepp Dietrich (1892-1966), commander of the 6th SS Panzer Army, to which Peiper's unit belonged.

At the trial the prosecution claimed that on 12 December, Hitler had issued an order which stated that no prisoners were to be taken and that a wave of terror was to descend on the Allies who stood in the way of the offensive. However, at the trial no one presented written evidence at the trial to substantiate this alleged order. Also Peiper's men had taken prisoners in their advance prior to the Malmédy incident.

It was the prosecution's position that the sheer number of prisoners was what sealed the fate of the Americans. The advancing army could not afford to leave 100 prisoners in the field and the Germans had no extra men to guard them. The German army could not send the POWs back to the German lines because Peiper needed the only road to supply his unit. Any men marching in the opposite direction would clog up the road. Peiper's other concern was that he might be attacked by American units known to be in the area.

The prosecution maintained that the German had deliberately murdered the POWs in cold blood. As proof the prosecution noted that the First SS Panzer Division had been responsible for similar and worse atrocities in Russia. Reportedly, they had already shot captured Americans in their advance in the Ardennes Offensive and shot even more POWs after Malmédy. There was no documentary proof showing who gave the order.[133]

The other theory, generally supported by the Germans, was that some Americans tried to escape and were fired on by the Germans. Other Germans heard the firing, but were not aware of how many escapees there were. They then opened fire on the group as a whole. In October 1945, an American soldier made a sworn testimony that he had escaped with two other men who were killed while trying to escape. He had survived and made it back to the American lines. The law would have allowed the Germans to shoot at escaping prisoners although not at the whole group. It is possible that their escape precipitated the shooting of the other men.

---

[133]Kershaw, Alex. The Longest Winter: *The Battle of the Bulge and the Epic Story of World War II's Most Decorated Platoon.* Da Capo Press, 2005

On December 21, during the battle around Gleize, the men of Kampfgruppe Peiper captured an American officer, Major Harold D. McCown, who was leading one of the battalions of the 119th Infantry Regiment. Having heard about the Malmedy massacre, McCown personally asked Peiper about the incident. McCown testified that Peiper told him neither he nor his men were at any risk and that he was not accustomed to killing his prisoners. McCown noted that neither he nor his men were threatened in any manner, so he subsequently testified in Peiper's defense during the 1946 trial in Dachau.

Peiper continued to lead his SS panzer unit. There were reports of other killings of POWs on December 31, 1944, in Lutrebois, and between January 10 and 13, 1945, in Petit Thier. The precise number of prisoners of war and civilians massacred attributable to Kampfgruppe Peiper is still not clear. According to the trial, between 538 and 749 POWs had been the victims of war crimes perpetrated by Peiper's men. The United States Senate subcommittee that inquired into the subsequent trial placed the number of dead at 362 prisoners of war and 111 civilians, largely Belgians.[134]

There were unfortunate cases of *tu quoque* which followed the Malmedy Massacre. Reports of the massacre led to retaliation against German prisoners of war during and after that battle. Few Waffen-SS soldiers came to be taken prisoner by units such as the 3rd Armored Division. An example of the reaction to the massacre is the written order from the Headquarters of the 328th Infantry, dated December 21, 1944: "No SS troops or paratroopers will be taken prisoner but will be shot on sight." Another example of a large-scale retaliation against German soldiers was the Chenogne massacre. At the Saar river the 90th Infantry Division executed Waffen-SS prisoners in a thoroughly systematic manner fashion in December 1944, prompting headquarters to issue explicit orders to capture Waffen-SS soldiers in order that they could be interrogated.

The trial was attached to what became collectively known as the Dachau Trials, which took place from May 16, 1946 to July 16, 1946. The defendants appeared before a military court of senior American

---

[134] Engels, Émile, ed. *Ardennes, 1944-1945, Guide du champ de bataille*. Bruxelles: Racine, 1994.

commissioned Officers. The court functioned according to rules founded previously by the international military tribunal at the Nuremberg Trials.

The counts of indictment related to the alleged massacre of more than three hundred American prisoners of war "in the vicinity of Malmedy, Honsfeld, Büllingen, Ligneuville, Stoumont, La Gleize, Cheneux, Petit Thier, Trois Ponts, Stavelot, Wanne and Lutrebois," between 16 December 1944 and 13 January 1945 during what was popularly known as the Battle of the Bulge. Additionally, the tribunal considered the massacre of about one hundred Belgian civilians in the vicinity of Stavelot.[135]

The defense was directed by Colonel Willis M. Everett Jr., a lawyer from Atlanta, assisted by other American and German lawyers. Everett had little or no experience in criminal law and was overwhelmed, if not intimidated, by having to defend 73 people on such short notice. The German lawyers, naturally, were totally unfamiliar with the American military judicial system. During the course of the trial the defense made the following argument:[136]

> As previously outlined, International Law laid down certain safeguards for treatment of prisoners of war, and any confession or statement extracted in violation thereof is not admissible in a court martial or any subsequent trial under a code set up by Military Government. If a confession from a prisoner of war is born in a surrounding of hope of release or benefit or fear of punishment or injury, inspired by one in authority, it is void in its inception and not admissible in any tribunal of justice. . . . Could anyone, by artifice, conjure up the theory that the Military Government Rules and Ordinances are superior to the solemn agreements of International Law as stated in the Geneva Convention of 1929? Is this court willing to assume the responsibility of admitting these void confessions?....It is not believed that the Court will put itself in the anomalous position of accepting statements into evidence which were elicited from prisoners of war in contravention of the Geneva Convention and therefore a violation of the Rules of Land Warfare on the one hand and then turn squarely around and meet out punishment for other acts which they deem violations of the same laws. To

[135]MacDonald, Charles. *A Time For Trumpets: The Untold Story of the Battle of the Bulge*. Bantam Book, 1984

[136] https://www.scrapbookpages.com/DachauScrapbook/DachauTrials/MalmedyMassacre03.html

> do so would be highly inconsistent and would subject the Court and all American Military Tribunals to just criticism.

The prosecution was led by Colonel Burton L Ellis, a knowledgeable and experienced officer. The prosecution's evidence was based primarily on affidavits collected before the trial from the defendants and from witnesses. Nine defendants testified, each minimizing his own role while placing the blame on others. As happened in all such trials, lawyers representing one defendant were willing to sacrifice all other defendants in order to save their client.

Lt. Col. Rosenfeld ruled against a defense motion to drop the charges, based on the above argument, by proclaiming that the Malmedy Massacre accused had never been Prisoners of War because they became war criminals the moment they committed their alleged acts and were thus not entitled to the protection of the Geneva Convention of 1929. On March 10, 1945, an order signed by General Dwight D. Eisenhower had reduced the status of all German POWs to that of "disarmed enemy forces," which meant that they were no longer protected under the rules of the Geneva Convention after the war. Moreover, as the law member of the panel of judges, Lt. Col. Rosenfeld ruled that "to admit a confession of the accused, it need not be shown such confession was voluntarily made...." Contrary to the rules of the American justice system, the German war criminals were presumed guilty and the burden of proof was on them, not the prosecution.

On July 16, 1946 the tribunal delivered its verdict regarding the 73 members of the SS Kampfgruppe Peiper, holding all members to be responsible to some degree. The first 43, including Peiper, were sentenced to death by hanging; 22 were sentenced to life imprisonment, including SS general, Sepp Dietrich; two were sentenced to 20 years imprisonment; one was sentenced to 15 years; and 5 were sentenced to 10 years. Upon receiving the verdict Colonel Everett immediately wrote of the trial:

> It is not only because of the fate of the seventy-four accused, but primarily of the historical significance and fundamental importance of the Malmédy Trial this Petition for Review may be justified. Unfortunately, the history of international law reveals that many injustices have been committed and many bad precedents have been established. This trial will receive a share of criticism in the future because its decision will necessarily serve as a precedent for the military profession of all of the

nations of the world.[137]

Some twenty-five German Catholic bishops wrote in 1948, "Will not the tortures at the preliminary inquests at Schwabische Hall and Obersesel, and the mass executions at Landsberg, later on do more harm to victorious America than a lost battle?" There were mock trials held in dark rooms before a table lighted only by candles around a crucifix; and bogus priests promised absolution if the prisoners would agree to sign false statements. Judge Edward L. Van Roden, in a series of speeches made to the National Council for the Prevention of War, and other similar organizations, made repeated these charges of priest imitators. Lutheran Bishop Wurm of Stuttgart protested to the American authorities against what he called "terrible investigation methods which mock description." These methods, the Bishop claimed, had consisted of beatings and kickings; knocking out of teeth and the breaking of jaws; starvation and solitary confinement for months without exercise or visitors or correspondence; promises of release from pain and the threat of death if the victim would sign statements incriminating others; and threats of reprisals on the prisoner's wife, children and parents if he refused to sign dictated statements.

While the tribunal had pronounced 43 death sentences, none were carried out; nor were the 22 life sentences. The sentence of Joachim Peiper, SS-Standartenführer and commander of the 1st SS-Panzer Division during the Battle of the Bulge, sentenced to death on 16 July 1946 for his role in the Malmedy Massacre, was subsequently commuted to life imprisonment and later to time served and he was released from prison in December 1956.

After the verdict, former German officers disputed the way in which the court had functioned. The prosecutors had readily admitted that many statements had been obtained from the defendants by various ruses and tricks. These illegal procedures were not repudiated by the court despite repeated defense objections, and the affidavits were accepted when they incriminated the informant himself and his co-defendants. Six of the defendants, including Peiper, complained to the court that they had been subjected to torture, physical violence, or threats of violence which sought

[137]In Whiting, Charles. *Massacre at Malmedy.* Stein & Day, 1984.

to coerce them into providing extrajudicial confessions. Only three of the defendants who testified claimed that they had suffered mistreatment during the pre-trial interrogation. Among the many claims were beatings and whippings, deprivation of food and sleep, and threat of execution. Some defendants were reportedly shown blood-stained walls against which other German soldiers had been lined up and shot. The most notorious case involved a conscript named Arvid Freimuth, a boy of 18, who had hung himself in his cell after repeated beatings rather than sign the confession dictated to him. The court would not permit the prosecution to bring in as evidence the prepared statement which Freimuth was told to sign.

Following the trial, various U.S. Army operatives talked about extracting confessions from the German prisoners of war. Colonel A.H. Rosenfeld, who was Chief of the Dachau branch of the U.S. War Crimes Administration until he resigned in 1948, when asked at a press interview before leaving Germany whether there was any truth in the German allegations concerning mock trials, replied, "Yes, of course. We couldn't have made those birds talk otherwise. It was a trick and it worked like a charm." One of the members of the Army's own investigative commission, Judge Edward L. Van Roden of Pennsylvania, made several public statements affirming the common use of physical violence had been inflicted on the accused. One observation stands out: "All but two of the Germans in the 139 cases we investigated had been kicked in the testicles beyond repair. This was standard operating procedure with our American investigators." Lt. Colonel Ellis and Lt. Perl, told Judge Von Roden that force was necessary in view of the difficulty in obtaining evidence. Perl said: "We had to use persuasive methods." He further admitted that these methods included "some violence and mock trials," and that the prosecution's case in the Malmedy cases rested on the evidence thus obtained.

The U. S. Senate Armed Services Committee which concluded that improper pre-trial procedures by U. S. authorities had unfairly affected the trial process. This drew attention to judicial irregularities that had occurred during the interrogations that preceded the trial. Congressmen from heavily German-American areas of the Midwest disputed the way in which the court had functioned. The case was appealed to the Supreme Court, which made no decision. The case then came under the scrutiny of a sub-Committee of the Senate of the United States. Senator Joseph McCarthy (R-WI) was Irish-American but represented a heavily German-American constituency. McCarthy joined those who had stated that the Court had not tried the defendants fairly. The Senate concluded that in 12 cases, mock trials were used in an effort to elicit confessions and to soften the suspects up for further interrogation. The evidence given concerning these trials is extremely conflicting, even among the persons who alleged they were subject to a mock trial. However, there is no question that mock trials were used. Many of the suspects in the Malmedy case were kept in separate cells for extended periods of time. The Senate Committee, however, dismissed charges of inadequate food and water and clean clothing. It also committee dismissed the allegation that hoods used on prisoners were dirty and bloody. The prosecutors had allegedly made threats against the families of the accused.[138]

The High Command Cases

Command responsibility issues were raised in several post World War II cases, notably, known as the High Command case, and Hostages case. These cases were prosecuted under Control Council Law No. 10, the law governing the trials of war criminals in Germany other than those prosecuted in the large Nuremberg trial. The High Command and Hostages cases further developed this area of the law.

The High Command case was part of the Nuremberg Subsequent Proceedings, whose defendants included Wilhelm von Leeb, the second highest ranking German officer of the Second World War. Fourteen senior German officers were tried in the High Command case, for a variety of offenses, including murder and mistreatment of prisoners of war, refusal of quarter, and other inhumane acts and violations of the laws or customs of war. The tribunal was in session from 30 December 1947 until 28

[138]Malmédy Massacre Investigation–Report of the Subcommittee of Committee on Armed Services. United States Senate Eighty-first Congress, first session, pursuant to S. res. 42, Investigation of action of Army with Respect to Trial of Persons Responsible for the Massacre of American Soldiers, Battle of the Bulge, near Malmédy, Belgium, December 1944. 13 October 1949.

October 1948. Unlike the Commission which tried Japanese General Yamashita in the Far East, this tribunal was staffed with professional judges trained in the law.

The main events for which the defendants were tried occurred on the Eastern Front. There was no question as to the authenticity and origin of orders under which the German Army proceeded. The accused officers were charged with committing and ordering actions which were obviously and blatantly criminal. Orders included Commissar Order which called for the immediate execution of all captured Red Army political officers. The Barbarossa Jurisdiction Order covered collective reprisals against civilians and directed summary executions of suspected saboteurs and guerillas. That order also precluded punishment of German soldiers or their allies who committed acts against civilians, a clear violation of the 4th Hague Convention.

Field commanders bore a great responsibility for the protection of civilians. Slave hunting, and the transportation of civilians to become workers in foreign factories were strictly forbidden and failure to guard against the transportation of civilians constituted a war crime. The tribunal made it clear that commanders must protect civilians in occupied areas.[139]

> One of the functions of an occupational commander endowed with executive power was to maintain order and protect the civilian population against illegal acts. In the absence of any official directives limiting his executive powers as to these illegal acts within his area, he had the right and duty to take action for their suppression. . . . Command authority and executive power obligate the one who wields them to exercise them for the protection of prisoners of war and the civilians in his area and . . . orders issued which indicate a repudiation of such duty and inaction with knowledge that others within his area are violating this duty which he owes, constitute criminality.

The prosecution argued that a form of strict liability should apply to commanders. The tribunal rejected this theory and held that for a commander to be criminally responsible for the acts of subordinates, the commander must breach a rule of international law and such a breach must

[139]Web Genocide Documentation Centre, at the Wayback Machine, known as the 13 Generals' trial; euRathlon, UWE Bristol.

have occurred voluntarily and with the knowledge that the act was criminal under international law. Other command responsibility issues raised during the course of the trial included: (1) the liability of a commander for actions committed by subordinates pursuant to criminal orders passed down independent of his or her command; (2) the liability of commanders for criminal orders issued by members of their staffs; and (3) the duties and responsibilities of the military commander of an occupied territory whose authority is limited. Prosecutors in both cases had argued in favor of strict interpretation of the command responsibility principle. Their precedent, of course, was the Yamashita case, already decided by Commission in the Philippines. The tribunal did accept the maxim that one may delegate authority, but never responsibility. However, the tribunal at Nuremberg rejected the concept of strict interpretation in a lengthy statement.[140]

> The authority, both administrative and military, of a commander and his criminal responsibility are related, but by no mean coextensive. Modern war, such as the last war, entails a large measure of decentralization. A high commander cannot keep completely informed of the details of military operations of subordinates and most assuredly not of every administrative measure. He has the right to assume that details entrusted to responsible subordinates will be legally executed. . . . Criminality does not attach to every individual in this chain of command. . . . [I]t must be borne in mind that a military commander, whether it be of an occupied territory or otherwise, is subject both to the orders of his military superiors and the state itself as to his jurisdiction and functions. . . . [C]riminal responsibility is personal. The act or neglect must be voluntary and criminal. . . . That can occur only where the act is directly traceable to him or where his failure to personally supervise his subordinates constitutes criminal negligence on his part. In the latter case, it must be a personal neglect amounting to a wanton immoral disregard of the action of his subordinates amounting to acquiescence.

Field Marshal Wilhelm Ritter von Leeb (1876—1956) testified that he was wholly unaware of any atrocities being committed by troops

---

[140] Hébert, Valerie Geneviève. *Hitler's Generals on Trial: The Last War Crimes Tribunal at Nuremberg.* University Press of Kansas, 2010.

under his command and that he certainly opposed any orders that bordered on criminality. In any event, orders concerning POWs, civilians in occupied areas, and acts of sabotage came from above and he was simply following orders. The tribunal held that in order to find a commander culpable for the transmission of superior orders, prosecution must show that that the orders were patently criminal. Commanders who knowingly participated in, or in any way agreed to, execution of orders that were criminal by their very nature, could be held legally responsible. During his defense Leeb showed that he had lodged protests with his superiors on account of the Commissar Order; he also made his subordinates aware of his opposition to that order and tried various subterfuges to avoid executing the order. For its part, the Tribunal made it clear that it expected Leeb to go no farther, as, for example, blatantly disobeying the order. It also accepted Leeb's reasoning that, once he made his opposition know, he had every reasonable expectation that subordinate officers would comply with his wishes. However, Leeb apparently agreed with, and passed along, the Barbarossa Jurisdiction Order, and received regular reports of reprisals that troops under his command had executed. Thus, Leeb was exonerated on the one charge, but held responsible on the second.[141]

Another high ranking defendant, Field Marshal Georg Karl Friedrich Wilhelm von Küchler (1881--1868), testified that he did not know that troops under his command had executed Soviet commissars although he had passed along the Commissar Order. The tribunal apparently did not believe Küchler was telling the truth, but must have known that the order was being applied. The tribunal held that "It was his business to know." But Küchler's credibility approximated absolute zero since reports received in evidence showed that reports of the implementation of the Commissar Order had been regularly delivered to his headquarters. On 27 October 1948 he was sentenced to twenty years' imprisonment for war crimes and crimes against humanity committed in the Soviet Union. The sentence was reviewed in 1951 and reduced to 12 years. He was released 1953 on medical grounds. Küchler died in 1968.[142]

---

[141]https://en.wikipedia.org/wiki/Wilhelm_Ritter_von_Leeb

[142]https://everipedia.org/wiki/lang_en/Georg_von_K%25C3%25BCchler/

Similar results were to be seen in the cases of other defendants, such as General Karl von Roques, General Hans Reinhardt, General Otto Wöhler, and General Hans von Salmuth. All had allowed the Sicherheitsdienst, or SD, the intelligence wing of the Schutzstaffel, or SS, to enter POW camps, interrogate prisoners, and remove and execute Soviet political officers. The SS had removed civilians and brought them to Germany or elsewhere as slave laborers. The SS also executed many of those who were physically unable to work. Essentially, the tribunal held in all cases that it was the business of the officers to know and generally discounted pleas of ignorance of events. Because if the Nazi obsession with record keeping, the tribunal did not need to impute anything; it had at its disposal an enormous collection of signed documents.

Like the High Command Case, the Hostages Case dealt with multiple accused and was prosecuted by authorities of the United States under Control Council Law No. 10. The judges dismissed the contentions of the accused that reports and orders transmitted to them were not brought to their attention by members of their staffs and addressed the issue of notice to the commander, making several important observations.

An army commander will not ordinarily be permitted to deny knowledge of reports received at his headquarters, they being sent there for his special benefit. Neither will he ordinarily be permitted to deny knowledge of happenings within the area of his command while he is present therein. It would strain the credulity of the Tribunal to believe that a high ranking military commander would permit himself to get out of touch with current happenings in the area of his command during wartime. No doubt occurrences result occasionally because of unexpected contingencies, but they are unusual.

The Hostage Case, involving a dozen German officers, was heard between 8 July 1947 and 19 February 1948. While the primary focus of the Hostage Case was on the taking, torture, and execution of civilian hostages, there were aspects of command responsibility. The Hostage Case applied a standard of strict interpretation of command responsibility even greater than the Command Cases. Its broad reading of command responsibility included a nearly absolute "should have known" standard. Lead defendant Field Marshal Wilhelm Siegmund Walter List and his co-defendants were charged with crimes against civilians in the Balkans during German occupation. List claimed that he knew nothing of any atrocities committed during his tenure. Here again meticulous German record keeping proved the undoing of the defense. The tribunal noted that a "commander will not ordinarily be permitted to deny knowledge of reports received at his headquarters, they being sent there for his special benefit." This may be regarded as "obliged to know" as an addition to "should have known." It was thus a moot point whether any of the officers had actually issued orders to take and execute hostages; if they had not issued such orders they were or should have been aware of these orders and events.

The tribunal made an interesting distinction during the Hostage Case. A commander is responsible for events that require individual and independent decision-making only if and when subordinates require his concurrence. If the atrocity occurs as a result of a decision made by a subordinate the tribunal is free to assume that the commander knew nothing of it and is thus not culpable. However, atrocities that occur pursuant to a commander's orders, including those which may occur during his absence, are attributable to the commander and thus he may be held criminally responsible. Since a commander may, indeed has the duty to, request adequate reports of all activities that are within his provenance, prudence requires him to make certain he receives full reports. "If he fails to require and obtain complete information, the dereliction of duty rests upon him and he is in no position to plead his own dereliction as a defense." In general, the tribunal did not view defendants in the Hostage Case as credible witnesses and found that they "must have known" and were thus criminally responsible for the atrocities.[143]

A case before the Supreme Court of Norway provides an example of obedience to illegal orders given by an officer of occupying power. Hauptsturm Fuhrer Wilhelm Artur Konstantin Wagner (1909—1978) was charged before the Eidsivating Lagmannsrett, a lower court, with having committed war crimes and crimes against humanity, in that he, in violation of the laws of humanity, was concerned in the deportation and death of

[143] *Law Reports of Trials of War Criminals,* Vol. XII, 1949 of the United Nations War Crimes Commission.

321 Norwegian Jews. The Lagmannsrett found him guilty and sentenced him to death. He appealed to the Norwegian Supreme court on the ground, *inter alia*, that the punishment decided by the Lagmannsrett. was too severe, the majority of the judges having failed to consider that he had acted on superior orders and that in his capacity of a subordinate he could not have prevented the carrying out of the decision of the German and Quisling Governments. When discussing the severity of the punishment decided upon by the Lagmannsrett, the President of the Court agreed with the minority of that court that it had been established that the defendant held a very unimportant position in the Gestapo and that there was nothing to show that he had taken any initiative in the action. His part had been to pass on the orders from Berlin to the Chief of the State Police and to execute the orders of his superiors. He was sure that if the defendant had refused to obey orders, he would have had to pay for the refusal with his life.[144]

Conclusions

When we consider the Nuremberg Tribunal as well as the secondary trials, we arrive at the conclusion that commanders could not always be held to a strict liability standard with respect to offenses committed by their subordinates. The law, however, does impose on them a duty to stay informed of the acts of such subordinates. Based on these tribunal rulings decided at the end of World War II, the meaning of the international law of command responsibility could be summed up as follows: (1) As long as there was a presumption that orders were legal, and that commanders could pass orders from higher headquarters to lower-level commands with minimal scrutiny. (2) Commanders were presumed to be aware of the contents of all reports received at their headquarters. If such reports were inadequate or unclear, commanders had a duty to request that additional reports be prepared. (3) Commanders were required to be aware of all events, including any criminal activity, that occurred within their areas of responsibility. (4) In order to be held criminally responsible, commanders must have known that criminal acts were committed and they

[144] https://forum.axishistory.com/viewtopic.php?t=148760; also https://sv.wikipedia.org/wiki/Wilhelm_Wagner_(SS-Hauptsturmführer)

acquiesced to, participated in, criminally neglected to interfere, or ordered them to be committed. (5) Even if commanders delegated authority, they could not delegate their responsibility for the conduct of the troops. Responsibility for the conduct of troops remained with the commander. (6) When tribunals examined alleged criminal conduct of commanders, a variety of factors could be relevant in determining whether the commander was on notice, including the scale and geographic scope of the alleged criminal acts.

Tribunals rejected the defense of superior orders in all European war crimes cases. They did generally accept as factors mitigating punishment, if not guilt, a wide variety of factors. First and foremost was the defense of following superior orders. Had they not followed the criminal orders from on-high they would have, at best, been relieved, and, at worst, been executed. Another would have carried out such orders and the atrocities would still have occurred. All German defendants charged with war crimes on the Eastern Front immediately used the *tu quoque* defense since the Russian atrocities against civilians, including their own dissident minorities, everywhere were numerous and great. The tribunal listed other mitigating factors, including "the nature of the crime, the age and experience of the person to whom it applies, the motives for the criminal act, . . . and the provocation, if any, that contributed to its commission." Notable is the fact that the tribunal held defendants in the Hostage Case to a higher standard than did the High Command Case tribunal. In the former a commander could be found guilty of criminal neglect for failing to gather, and then read, information about events occurring under his command, relieving the prosecution of the necessity of showing that the defendant knew of crimes being perpetrated in the ranks below him.

As in all other trials, the defense of *tu quoque*[145] was disallowed. Certainly Russian executions of Polish anti-communist prisoners at Katyn Forest was a violation of international law as were there genocidal policies against their own ethnic minorities. Various American units were charged with the shooting of German and Italian prisoners of war. One American

---

[145] Yee, Sienho. "The Tu Quoque Argument as a Defence to International Crimes, Prosecution or Punishment." *Chinese Journal of International Law* (January 2004).

captain was acquitted on the grounds that he had been following the orders of General Patton, who had discouraged American troops from taking prisoners during the landing of the US Seventh Army in Sicily. American soldiers executed German prisoners within half a mile of the Dachau courtroom on April 29, 1945. American soldiers of the 45th Thunderbird Division of the US Seventh Army lined up surrendered Waffen-SS soldiers against a wall and machine-gunned them. This was followed by the killing of SS guards at the Dachau concentration camp after they came down from their guard tower and surrendered. American soldiers of the 222nd Regiment of the 42nd Rainbow Division executed soldiers of the German Home Guard after they had surrendered. The Home Guard consisted of young boys and old men who were forced into service in the last desperate days of the war to defend their cities and towns. After an investigation by the US Army resulted in the court martial of the soldiers involved in these killings, General George S. Patton tore up the papers and tossed them in the wastebasket. Stephen E. Ambrose, the author of *Citizen Soldiers*, related that General Maxwell Taylor instructed the men of the 101st Airborne Division to take no prisoners during the Normandy invasion. After the war, Germany attempted to adjudicate 369 murder cases, involving U. S. Army soldiers killing German POWs and wounded men, before a German court.[146]

---

[146] MacLean, French L. *The Fifth Field: The Story of the 96 American Soldiers Sentenced to Death and Executed in Europe and North Africa in World War II.* Atglen, PA: Schiffer Publishing, 2013.

4
World War II in Asia

The war crimes trials for Europe had preoccupied the Allies during much of the Second World War, but they had shown little interest in Japan. Finally on 31 August 1945 Washington inquired of General Douglas MacArthur what his plans were for the punishment of the Japanese. MacArthur had already appointed Colonel Alva Carpenter chief of the War Crimes Branch and made him Judge Advocate General for the Pacific theater. There was no legal or political objection to MacArthur's establishment of rules and procedures for his area. Secretary of War Henry Stimson and his staff had argued as early as 1944 that the Allies should use military commissions to try war crimes as outlined in the War Department's field manual. In March 1944 the Joint Chiefs of Staff had made it clear that they opposed any limitation of the powers of military commanders over war crimes prosecution. Thus, Colonel Carpenter's War Crimes Branch operated on the assumption that it could formulate constitutionally whatever rules and procedures it thought to be appropriate and would expect no outside objections. The Branch would not be restricted to using traditional American rules of evidence and procedure.[147]

The Japanese record of war crimes in World War II was extensive. Most of the following figures are official, having been presented at the Tokyo War Crimes Trial. From the invasion of China in 1937 to the end of World War II, the Japanese military regime murdered near 3,000,000 to over 10,000,000 people, most probably almost 6,000,000 Chinese, Indonesians, Koreans, Filipinos, and Indochinese, [148] among others,

---

[147]Lael, Richard L., *The Yamashita Precedent.* Wilmington, DE: Scholarly Resources, 1982, 59-64.

[148]Kratoska, Paul H. *Asian Labor in the Wartime Japanese Empire.* Aemonk, NY: Sharpe, 2005

including Western prisoners of war. This democide[149] was caused by a morally bankrupt political and military strategy. Military expediency and custom prevailed, based on a unique national culture. For example, Japanese held the view that those enemy soldiers who surrendered while still able to resist were criminals and this deserving of ill treatment. It also harbored the illusion that the Japanese were a race superior to all others and were led by a divine emperor, a descendant of the sun goddess.[150] Anything the Japanese chose to do was justified by this superior status.[151]

One of the major Japanese war crimes was the mistreatment of prisoners of war [POWs] along with the impressment of civilian laborers in occupied lands. The overall number of POWs and internees killed was about 138,000. The prisoner of war death rate averaged nearly 29 percent. As many as 60,000 POWs were impressed to assist in building the Burma-Siam Railroad more than 25% died or were murdered. By comparison about 4% of British and American POWs died in German camps.

Of 41,862 known Chinese laborers sent to Japan, 2872 died in China before leaving, 600 on ships bound to Japan, 200 during their journey to the place of employment, and 6872 in Japanese workplaces. At least, 600,000 to 1,610,000 forced Asian laborers died. Of 300,000 Javanese, Tamils, Burmese, and Chinese who became forced laborers sent to build the Burma-Thailand railroad in 1942 to 1943 more than 60,000 died or were killed. Some 5,400,000 Koreans were conscripted for labor beginning in 1939 with at least 67,000, and perhaps as many as 80,000, dead between 1937 and 1945. Japan conscripted over a 1,000,000 forced laborers from Manchuria with at least 100,000 dying in servitude.[152] As an example of Japanese brutality, some 250 Tamil men, women, and children, forced laborers in June 1943 in Nieke, became infected with cholera and were confined to a single barracks. The Japanese set fire to the wooden

---

[149] Democide is the murder of any person or people by a government, including genocide, politicide, and mass murder.

[150] Dower, John, *War Without Mercy: Race and Power in the Pacific War.* New York: Pantheon, 1985.

[151] Lord Russell of Liverpool, *The Knights of Bushido: A Short History of Japanese War Crimes*. Berkeley Books, 1961

[152] Landas, Marc, *The Fallen: A True Story of American POWs and Japanese Wartime Atrocities.* Wiley, 2004.

building, immolating all within it.

Murder of citizens of occupied nations ranked high among Japanese war crimes. In the Philippines, where after the war American military teams made an effort to investigate Japanese massacres, about 159,000, and possibly as many as 318,000, civilians were reported killed.[153] The number of civilians murdered in the 43 known massacres in China exceeds 1,000,000.[154] Of 130,000 Europeans interned in the Dutch East Indies, 30,000 died, among whom were 4500 women and 2300 children. At least 42,000, and possibly 80,000, Indonesians were massacred during the Japanese occupation. From the Indochinese -- Vietnamese, Laotians, and Cambodians -- population there is a high estimate of 575,000 dead. The Chinese living in Malaya suffered from the Japanese occupation with at least 37,000 of them being executed.[155] The overall Japanese democide in World War II, including Japanese democide in China included, provides a total of 3,056,000 to 10,595,000 with a likely mid-total of 5,964,000 people killed.[156]

The Allies created three classes of war criminals charged with ordering, supervising, and committing war crimes. The A class defendants were the principal decision and policy makers. From early 1946 to late 1948, some two hundred top Japanese civilian and military leaders were designated as Class A war criminal suspects; twenty-eight of them were tried at the Tokyo War Crimes Tribunal from early 1946 to late 1948. Of the fifty-five counts of crime listed in the indictment, the overwhelming majority fell under crimes against peace, fifteen counts under murder, and three under other conventional war crimes and crimes against humanity. Virtually all of these defendants bore some responsibility under the principle of leadership responsibility.

Classes B and C included those who ordered atrocities, allowed them to occur, or actually committed them. Between 1946 and 1951, the

---

[153] Escoda, Jose M., *Warsaw of Asia: The Rape of Manila*, revised ed. Quezon City, Philippines: Giraffe Books, 2001.

[154] Li, Peter, *Japanese War Crimes*. Transaction Publications, 2013.

[155] Kratoska, Paul, ed., *Southeast Asian Minorities in the Wartime Japanese Empire.* London: Routledge Curzon, 2002.

[156] Rummel, R.J., *Genocide and Mass Murder Since 1900*. Charlottesville, VA: School of Law, University of Virginia, 1997, chapter 3.

U.S. and other governments separately tried about 5,700 Japanese officers and enlisted men in some 2,240 separate trials throughout the Asia Pacific. Among them were over three hundred Koreans and Taiwanese employed by the Japanese. These so-called B and C class tribunals were concerned with those perpetrating or ordering conventional war crimes. Only a comparative handful of these crimes involved leadership responsibility as most crimes committed by this group concerned principally the individual.[157]

The International Military Tribunal of the Far East (IMTFE) sat at Tokyo and conducted extensive investigations resulting in the compilation of large volumes of evidence. The B and C tribunals were conducted individually by the Allied powers and met at such sites as the individual nations designated. B and C defendants were frequently tried in batches with the trials lasting only a few hours. Executions were frequent and prompt.[158] There were and indeed still are major problems with the legality of some aspects of the trials. The charge of crimes against the peace and waging a war of aggression were not justified under existing code or customary law.

It was General Douglas MacArthur who decided to exonerate Emperor Hirohito and all members of the imperial family from criminal prosecutions.[159] It may have been that when the Truman Administration chose to broadcast that it would allow Japan to keep its *mikado* that General MacArthur found that granting the family immunity was the only way to honor that pledge. According to them, MacArthur and Brigadier General Bonner Fellers worked to protect the Emperor and shift ultimate responsibility to Tōjō.[160] According to the written report of Mizota Shūichi, interpreter for Admiral Mitsumasa Yonai, General Fellers met the two men at his office on 6 March 1946 and told Yonai: "It would be most convenient if the Japanese side could prove to us that the Emperor is completely

[157]Boister, N. & R. Cryer. *The Tokyo International Military Tribunal: A Reappraisal*. Oxford University Press, 2008.
[158] Maga, Tim, *Judgment at Tokyo: The Japanese War Crimes Trials*. University of Kentucky Press, 2001.
[159]Brines, Russell, *MacArthur's Japan*. Lippincott, 1948, 66ff; D. C. James, *The Years of MacArthur*. Houghton Mifflin, 1985, 111ff.
[160]Thurman, M. J., *War Crimes: Japan's World War II Atrocities*. Turner, 2001.

blameless. I think the forthcoming trials offer the best opportunity to do that. Tōjō, in particular, should be made to bear all responsibility at this trial."[161] It is less clear why MacArthur ordered his staff chose to grant immunity to all members of the royal family.[162]

The number one war criminal thus became Hideki Tōjō (1884–1948). He had graduated from the Army Cadet School, the Imperial Japanese Army Academy, and the Army War College, and, by 1928, he had become the bureau chief of the Japanese Army, and was shortly thereafter promoted to colonel. He began to take an interest in militarist politics during his command of the 1st Infantry Regiment. Tōjō was promoted to Chief of Staff of the Kwangtung Army in 1937. As Chief of Staff, Tōjō was responsible for the military operations designed to increase Japanese penetration into the Inner Mongolia border regions with Manchukuo. In July 1937, he personally led the units of the First Independent Mixed Brigade in Operation Chahar,[163] his only real combat experience. After the Marco Polo Bridge Incident marking the start of the Second Sino-Japanese War, Tōjō ordered his forces to attack Hopei and other targets in northern China. Tōjō was a general of the Imperial Japanese Army (IJA) and the 40th Prime Minister of Japan, serving during most of World War II, from 17 October 1941 to 22 July 1944.[164]

The list of charges against Tōjō was long indeed. As Prime Minister, he was directly responsible for the attack on Pearl Harbor, which led to the war between Japan and the United States, although planning for it had begun before he entered office. He was a strong supporter of the Tripartite Pact between Japan, Nazi Germany and Fascist Italy. As the

---

[161]Bix, Herbert P., *Hirohito and the Making of Modern Japan*. HarperCollins, 2001, 583-85; John W. Dower, *Embracing Defeat: Japan in the Wake of World War II*. Norton, 2000, 324-26.

[162] Brackman, Arnold C., *The Other Nuremberg*. New York: Morrow, 1987

[163]This action occurred in August 1937, following the Battle of Beiping-Tianjin at the beginning of the Second Sino-Japanese War. This was the second attack by the Kwantung Army and the Inner Mongolian Army of Prince Teh Wang on Inner Mongolia after the failure of the Suiyuan Campaign (1936). The Chahar Expeditionary Force was under the direct command of General Hideki Tōjō, the chief of staff of the Kwantung Army.

[164]Butow, Robert C. *Tōjō and the Coming of the War*. Stanford University Press, 1961. Paul Manning, *Hirihito: The War Years*. Dodd Mead, 1986

Army Minister, he continued to vastly expand the grueling war with China. His responsibility for waging a war of conquest and aggression throughout Asia was great. As Education Minister, he continued militaristic and nationalist indoctrination in the national education system, and reaffirmed totalitarian policies in government. As Home Minister, he ordered various eugenics measures, including the sterilization of those judged "mentally unfit".

Tōjō's war crimes against prisoners of war (POWs) was unprecedented. It was Tōjō who had said that if a POW did not work he would not eat. He knew of the Bataan Death March and the impressment of POWs in the building of the Burma-Siam Railroad. He was acutely aware that ill men were being driven out to work under conditions that would kill them. The death rate for POWs under Tōjō was appalling. Overall, 27% of all prisoners died, with the American rate at 34% highest of all nationalities. Some 33% of Australian and 32% of British POWs died under Japanese control, but less than 20% of the Dutch POWs died. By contrast, in Germany on the Western front the POW death rate was less than 4%.[165]

Tōjō was tried by the International Military Tribunal for the Far East for war crimes and found guilty of: waging wars of aggression, and war or wars in violation of international law; waging unprovoked war against the Republic of China; waging aggressive war against the United States of America, Great Britain, the Netherlands, and France; and ordering, authorizing, and permitting inhumane treatment of Prisoners of War. General MacArthur wanted to drop the charges of crimes against peace because that would have paced Tōjō under the control of the War Department and removed him from MacArthur's jurisdiction. If Tōjō was tried only for war crimes MacArthur would have full control. Washington preferred to try Tōjō before an international tribunal as was done with the highest Nazi war criminals in the IMTE.[166]

Tōjō was sentenced to death for Japanese war crimes by the International Military Tribunal for the Far East, and was hanged on 23

---

[165]Daws, Gavan, *Prisoners of the Japanese*. Morrow, 1994, 360. See also *Japanese Prisoners of War*, eds. Philip Towle et al. London: Hambledon and London, 2000.

[166] Lael, *op. cit.*, 68.

December 1948.[167]

Before his execution Tōjō accepted responsibility for his actions during the war, giving the following statement:

> It is natural that I should bear entire responsibility for the war in general, and, needless to say, I am prepared to do so. Consequently, now that the war has been lost, it is presumably necessary that I be judged so that the circumstances of the time can be clarified and the future peace of the world be assured. Therefore, with respect to my trial, it is my intention to speak frankly, according to my recollection, even though when the vanquished stands before the victor, who has over him the power of life and death, he may be apt to toady and flatter. I mean to. . . say to the end that what is true is true and what is false is false. To shade one's words in flattery to the point of untruthfulness would falsify the trial and do incalculable harm to the nation, and great care must be taken to avoid this.[168]

Yamashita Case

Tomoyuki Yamashita (1885-1946) was an Imperial Japanese Army general during World War II. He was most famous for conquering the British colonies of Malaya and Singapore. Yamashita was born the son of a local physician in Osugi village, in what is now part of Ōtoyo village, Kōchi prefecture, Shikoku. He attended military preparatory schools in his youth. After graduating from the Imperial Japanese Army Academy in 1905, Yamashita joined the Army in 1906 and fought against the German Empire in Shantung, China in 1914. He attended the Army War College, graduating sixth in his class in 1916. He married Hisako Nagayama, the daughter of retired General Nagayama in 1916. Yamashita became an expert on Germany, serving as assistant military attaché at Bern, Switzerland and Berlin, Germany from 1919–1922. On his return to Japan in 1922, Yamashita served in the Imperial Headquarters and the Staff College. While posted to the Imperial Japanese Army General Staff, Yamashita unsuccessfully promoted a military reduction plan.

Despite his ability, Yamashita fell into disfavor as a result of his involvement with certain political factions within the Japanese military

[167]Piccigallo, Philip R., *The Japanese on Trial: Allied War Crimes Operations in the East, 1945-51*. University of Texas, 1979

[168] "Tojo" on Wikipedia, quoting the *Journal of Historical Review* [unspecified date].

and became a rival to Hideki Tōjō. In 1928, Yamashita was posted to Vienna, Austria, as the military attaché. In 1930, Colonel Yamashita was given command of the elite 3rd Imperial Infantry Regiment.

After the February 26 Incident of 1936, Yamashita fell into disfavor with Emperor Hirohito due to his appeal for leniency toward the rebel officers involved in the attempted coup. The February 26 incident was an attempted coup d'état in Japan, occurring from February 26 to 29, 1936. It was carried out by 1,483 troops of the Imperial Japanese Army. Several leading politicians were killed and the conspirators briefly occupied the center of Tokyo. were some young activist officers, mostly below the rank of major. They deplored the political corruption in politics and noted the extreme poverty in rural areas. They decided the solution would be to remove some of the elder statesmen in the government. The Emperor was enraged and demanded that they be crushed for killing his loyal supporters. Loyal troops surrounded the rebels and eventually persuaded them to surrender. Considering their complaints to have some merit Yamashita attempted to mediate between the Emperor and the rebels. For that he was sent abroad to serve in unimportant posts.

Yamashita also insisted that Japan should end the conflict with China and seek to maintain peaceful relations with the United States and Great Britain. Since he was already in disfavor, he was ignored and subsequently exiled to an unimportant post in the Kwantung Army. From 1938 to 1940, he was assigned to command the IJA 4th Division which saw some action in northern China against Chinese insurgents fighting the occupying Japanese armies. Still the Emperor recognized Yamashita's considerable talents so in December 1940, the cabinet sent Yamashita on a clandestine military mission to Germany and Italy, where he met with Adolf Hitler and Benito Mussolini.

On 6 November 1941, Yamashita was put in command of the Twenty-Fifth Army. On 8 December, he launched an invasion of Malaya, from bases in French Indochina. In the campaign, which concluded with the fall of Singapore on 15 February 1942, Yamashita's 30,000 front-line soldiers captured 130,000 British, Indian, and Australian troops, the largest surrender of British-led personnel in history. He became known as the "Tiger of Malaya." The first of the atrocities with which the Allies charged Yamashita followed. The campaign and the subsequent Japanese occupation of Singapore included war crimes committed against captive Allied personnel and civilians. The two most notable war crimes were the Alexandra Hospital and Sook Ching massacres.[169]

At about 13:00 hours on 14 February, Japanese soldiers advanced towards the Alexandra Barracks Hospital. A British lieutenant, acting under a white flag, approached the Japanese forces but was bayoneted and killed. After the Japanese troops entered the hospital, a number of patients, including those undergoing surgery at the time, were killed along with physicians, surgeons, nurses, and orderlies. Approximately 200 male staff members and patients remained alive, but were rounded up and bound. The following day this group was assembled, many of whom were walking wounded. These men were ordered to walk to an industrial area. Anyone who fell was bayoneted. The Japanese guards forced the men into a series of small, badly ventilated rooms and were imprisoned overnight without water. Some died during the night as a result of their treatment. The remainder were bayoneted the following morning. The Japanese did not consider those who were weak, wounded, or who had surrendered to be worthy of life. Many who had not been imprisoned in the tiny rooms in the industrial area were systematically taken away in small groups and killed with machetes and bayonets. This carnage continued for 24 hours, leaving 320 men and one woman dead. There were only five known survivors.

General Tomoyuki Yamashita was the Commanding General of the Fourteenth Army Group of the Japanese Imperial Army and the Military Governor on the Philippine Islands from October 1944 until full control of the Islands was assumed by United States forces in September 1945. In the waning days of World War II, numerous atrocities were committed by troops under General Yamashita's control against the civilian population of the Philippines. With General MacArthur advancing on Manila, Yamashita had decisions to make. He maintained that he had only tactical, but not disciplinary, control over Japanese naval forces in the Philippines.

During the Japanese occupation of the Philippines, including the

---

[169] Havers, R. P. W., *Reassessing the Japanese Prisoner of War Experience: The Changi POW Camp, Singapore, 1942–45*. London: Routledge Curzon, 2003.

time during which Yamashita was stationed on the islands, the Japanese Army committed atrocities against the Philippine people. Most notorious were those committed against the inhabitants of Batangas Province, which was under the direct control of Colonel Masatocki Fujishige. He claimed that he never reported his actions to his immediate superior General Shizuo Yokoyama or to General Yamashita. All civilian deaths with in his area of responsibility were committed under his own orders. Fujishige's chief of staff quoted Fujishige during the war crimes trials as saying that "all the civilians have now turned into guerrillas; therefore, kill all of them."[170] That Yamashita did not know of the orders and subsequent atrocities the tribunal refused to believe; but even if Yamashita did not know it was his duty to have known. As the tribunal wrote

> The Japanese Commanders testified that they did not make personal inspections or independent checks during the Philippine campaign to determine for themselves the established procedures by which their subordinates accomplish their missions. Taken at full face value, the testimony indicates that Japanese senior commanders operate in a vacuum, almost in another world, with respect to their troops, compared with standards American Generals take for granted.[171]

General MacArthur's intelligence was correct in concluding that Yamashita did not wish to defend Manila. Yamashita ordered a withdrawal, declaring it to be an open city, and forbade unnecessary destruction. Presumably humanitarian concerns preoccupied him. He was also greatly concerned with being surrounded and cut off. Yamashita knew all too well that he had no way of supplying food and other basics to his own troops let alone to some 800,000 people in Manila. He thus ordered General Shizuo Yokoyama to destroy harbor installations and all bridges over the Pasig River and withdraw, joining him in the hilly country.

Although the Yamashita's Japanese main army withdrew into the hills, about 15,000 to 20,000 sailors and marines under Vice-Admiral Sanji Iwabuchi ignored the orders. Iwabuchi ordered his troops to stand and fight in the urban setting and die at their posts. Although legally it makes

---

[170] Testimony of Major Zenichi Uehara, chief of staff, in Lael, *op. cit.,* 34

[171] Decision of the U. S. Military Commission at Manila, 7 December 1945, in *The Law of War: A Documentary History*, 2: 1597.

no difference, it has never been clear whether Iwabuchi chose to make a dramatic last stand in Manila or whether his army was simply encircled too late to make an escape into the hills. Yokoyama apparently decided that if the Navy was going to salvage its honor by making a stand in Manila he should do no less and thus ordered the three Army battalions, about 4000 infantry, still in the city to stand with Iwabuchi's men. This combined force retreated across the Pasig River, destroying bridges and setting fires which quickly spread to residential areas. They made their initial stand in Manila's business district where they burned buildings and massacred civilians. In the bitter fight about 70% of the city was destroyed and at least 100,000 civilians died. The Japanese knew they were trapped and fought accordingly.

They made their final stand in Intramuros, the old Spanish fortified settlement that was surrounded by a 25 foot high wall some two and one-half miles in circumference. MacArthur, who thought of himself as a gentleman warrior, would not allow airplanes to bomb although he did order his artillery to destroy the compound and all within it. Iwabuchi and Yokoyama died as did nearly all their men. But before they died the Japanese committed terrible atrocities. Rape was common as officers allowed men who were about to die a final sexual escapade. Women of all ages were kidnapped and removed to temporary brothels set up in hotels and clubs. Even Germans, nominally allies in the Tripartite Pact, were not spared. They massacred twelve German Christian Brothers and killed others at the German Club. They bayoneted and shot all patients, nurses and physicians at the Red Cross hospital. It is obvious that such an orgy of destruction was not the isolated acts of some deluded, perhaps desperate, soldiers, but resulted from orders by commanders. If the Japanese were to die then they would not leave any cause for the victors to celebrate.[172]

When the orgy was finally over there was no officer left to charge with war crimes. Technically, Iwabuchi was not under Yamashita's orders because he was a naval, not army, officer; however, Yokoyama was a subordinate commander in Yamashita's army. The battle's principal victims were civilians who suffered enormously. MacArthur chose to

---

[172] Hastings, Max, *Retribution: The Battle for Japan, 1944-45*. New York: Knopf, 2007, 235-36.

place Yamashita on trial for the wanton destruction of life and property in Manila.[173]

Pursuant to Japan's unconditional surrender to the United States at the end of the war, General Yamashita also surrendered to United States troops present in the Philippines and immediately became a prisoner of war. He was detained by the United States Army in the Commonwealth of the Philippines. Upon his arrest as a prisoner of war, General Yamashita was charged by the Army's Judge Advocate General's Department with violations of the law of war. Included in this charge were allegations that forces under his command engaged in a "deliberate plan Ö to massacre and exterminate a large part of the civilian population of Batangas Province Ö as a result of which more than 25,000 men, women, and children all unarmed noncombatant civilians, were brutally mistreated and killed." Troops under Yamashita's command also had massacred POWs at Palawan. Because General MacArthur charged Yamashita only with war crimes, the MacArthur's Judge Advocate General could proceed without consulting the War Department. The prosecution could proceed without being hampered by traditional requirements for the admissibility of evidence and rules of procedure.[174]

The prosecution alleged that Yamashita did "unlawfully disregard and fail to discharge his duty as commander to control … his command, [and was] permitting them to commit brutal atrocities. . . ." The bill of particulars included incidents of gross misconduct, including murder, against prisoners of war and civilians, as well as execution of death sentences without procedures required by the 1929 Geneva Prisoner of War Convention.

The Allies might have brought Yamashita to trial in Malaya for crimes there and in Singapore. The charges would have been for crimes committed against British subjects in 1942. This would have fulfilled the Moscow Declaration which held that secondary war criminals would be tried in the nations "in which their abominable deeds were done." But

---

[173] Allen, Thomas B. and Norman Polmar, *Code Name Downfall*. Simon & Schuster, 1995, 70-71.

[174] J. Gordon Feldhaus, "The Trial of Yamashita," *South Dakota Bar Journal*, 15: 181-93 [1946]; John Ganoe, "The Yamashita Case and the Constitution" *Oregon Law Review*, April 1946, 143-58.

American forces had captured Yamashita and the Philippines was American territory with sovereignty residing in Washington. General MacArthur placed the trial in Manila, scene of the horrible atrocities at the end of the war.

The War Crimes Branch was scrupulous in its guarantee of basic procedural rights. Yamashita was guaranteed translators and a copy of all pertinent papers in his own language. He had the right to legal counsel, both American and Japanese lawyers. He could cross examine any witnesses. He was entitled to a copy of the indictment and thus to known the specific charges laid against him. However, the Branch dropped the usual rule that stated that the defendant be advised of facts, witnesses, and documents in advance of their admission in the court.

The Judge Advocate General's Office appointed six lawyers to serve as defense counsel, and was tried before a United States military commission of five United States Army Officers. The trial to be a grand American showcase. It was held in the ballroom of the former residence of the U.S. High Commissioner. There were 64 initial charges to which an additional 59 were added. In general terms the prosecution claimed that

> between 9 October 1944 and 2 September 1945, at Manila and other places in the Philippine Islands, while commander of armed forces of Japan at war with the United States of America and its allies [Yamashita] unlawfully disregarded and failed to discharge his duty as commander to control the operations of the members of his command, permitting them to commit brutal atrocities and other high crimes against the people of the United States and of its allies and dependencies, particularly the Philippines, and he, General Tomoyuki Yamashita, thereby violated the law of war.[175]

General Yamashita pled not guilty to all charges. In his defense he claimed that he did not personally engage in the criminal acts committed by the Japanese troops; nor had he ordered these acts to be committed; nor had he had control over the troops who were technically under his command. There was little evidence that Yamashita knew about the atrocities at the time they were actually committed. In fact not only had Yamashita not ordered the execution of prisoners, there was some

---

[175]Transcript of the case of Yamashita, cited in Lael, *op. cit.,* 80.

evidence that he had done his best to remove POWs from harm's way. His counsel argued vigorously, and Yamashita testified, that he assumed command in the midst of battle, that he was never able to assert actual control over those troops who committed war crimes, and that his ability to control his troops was severely degraded by enemy attacks on his routes and means of communication.[176] His defense argued that in most cases the prosecution really had not charged Yamashita with either committing directly, or ordering to be committed, any war crimes. Colonel Harry Clarke, senior defense counsel, provided an insight into the defense strategy.[177]

> The charge alleges that the Accused failed in his duty to control his troops, permitting them to commit certain alleged crimes. The Bill of Particulars, however, sets forth no instance of neglect of duty by the Accused. Nor does it set forth any acts of commission or omission by the Accused as amounting to a "permitting" of the crimes in question.
>
> The Accused is not charged with having done something or having failed to do something, but solely with having been something. For the gravamen of the charge is that the Accused was commander of the Japanese forces and by virtue of that fact alone, is guilty of every crime committed by every soldier assigned to his command. . . . The Articles of War denounce and punish improper conduct by military personnel, but they do not hold a commanding officer for the crimes committed by his subordinates.[178]

The contrarian view was presented by Major Robert Kerr for the prosecution.

> The record itself strongly supports the contention or conclusion that Yamashita not only permitted but ordered the commission of these atrocities. However, our case does not depend upon any direct orders from he accused. It is sufficient that we show that the accused 'permitted' these atrocities. . . . Who permitted them? Obviously the man whose duty it was to prevent such an orgy of planned and obviously deliberate murder, rape, and arson –

---

[176]Reel, A. Frank, *The Case of General Yamashita,* New York: Octagon Books, 1971.
[177]Guy, George, "The Defense of Yamashita," *Wyoming Law Journal* 4: 153-80 [1950].
[178]Transcript of the Trial of General Yamashita, quoted in Lael, *op. cit.*, 82-83.

the commander of those troops![179]

The atrocities, Kerr argued, "were so notorious and so flagrant and so enormous, both as to the scope of their operation, and as to the inhumanity, the bestiality involved, that they must have been known to the Accused if he were making any effort whatever to meet the responsibility of his command or his position." Moreover, if Yamashita really did not know he should have known. If he did not know "of those acts, notorious, widespread, repeated, constant as they were," Kerr said, "it was simply because he took the affirmative action not to know."[180] It is also true that on two occasions witnesses linked Yamashita directly to atrocities. Neither witness was especially reliable and neither held up well under cross-examination. That said, it must be clearly understood that Yamashita's conviction depended wholly upon the supposition that he should have known of the commission of the manifold atrocities his men perpetrated and thus failed to discharge his duty as commander adequately.

The "should have known" allegation the prosecutors made was relatively new to war crimes trials. Many felt that it had no place in prosecution of a case against a military leader. In fact, betting among the many reporters who covered the trial was that Yamashita would be acquitted.[181]

But Yamashita was found guilty by the commission after it heard testimony from two hundred and eighty-six witnesses. The tribunal held Yamashita to a high standard of responsibility.

> Clearly, assignment to command military troops is accompanied by broad authority and heavy responsibility. This has been true in all armies throughout recorded history. It is absurd, however, to consider a commander a murderer or rapist because one of his soldiers commits a murder or rape. Nevertheless, where murder and rape and vicious, revengeful actions are widespread offenses and there is no effective attempt

---

[179]*War Crimes Commission: Law Reports of Trials of War Criminals*, 4: 84. See also Franklin Hart, "Yamashita, Nuremberg, and Vietnam" *Naval War College Review*, 25 (1972) 19.

[180]*Id.*, at 83.

[181]Gavan Daws, *Prisoners of the Japanese*. Morrow, 1994, 365. See also E. B. Kerr, *Surrender and Survival: The Experience of American POWs in the Pacific, 1941–1945*. New York: Morrow, 1985.

> by a commander to discover and control the criminal acts, such a commander may be held responsible, even criminally liable, for the lawless acts of his troops, depending upon their nature and the circumstance surrounding them.[182]

Upon his conviction, General Yamashita filed a writ of habeas corpus with the Supreme Court of the Commonwealth of the Philippines. In his writ, General Yamashita challenged the jurisdiction of the military commission, asserted that he did not commit a violation of the law of war, and claimed that he was denied a fair trial under the United States Articles of War, the Geneva Convention, and the United States Constitution. The Supreme Court of the Commonwealth of the Philippines denied his writ in total. The General then appealed to the United States Supreme Court. In the Supreme Court's decision, rendered in February 1946, the Court articulated a clear standard for military commanders with respect to the actions of their subordinates. In responding to General Yamashita's assertion that he did not personally participate in or order the commission of these offenses, the Court described the heart of the charge as being "an unlawful breach of duty by [General Yamashita] as an army commander to control the operations of members of his command by 'permitting them to commit' the extensive and widespread atrocities." The Court recognized that international law, through the law of war, "presupposes that [violations of the law of war] are to be avoided through the control of the operations of war by commanders who to some extent are responsible for their subordinates." The Court believed that absent such a duty upon commanders, nothing would prevent occupying forces from committing atrocities upon the civilian population. The Court held that Yamashita was, by virtue of his position as commander of the Japanese forces in the Philippines, under an "affirmative duty to take such measures as were within his power and appropriate in the circumstances to protect prisoners of war and the civilian population."[183] Chief Justice Stone wrote,

> The question then is whether the law of war imposes on an army commander a duty to take such appropriate measures as are within his power to control the troops under his command from

[182] Decision of the U. S. Military Commission at Manila, 7 December 1945, in *The Law of War: A Documentary History*, 2: 1596-97

[183] *In Re Yamashita,* 327 U.S. 1 (1946).

> the prevention of specified acts which are violations of the law of war and which are likely to attend the occupation of hostile territory by an uncontrolled soldiery, and whether he may be charged with personal responsibility for his failure to take such measures when violations result. . . . It is evident that the conduct of military operations by troops whose excesses are unrestrained by the orders or efforts of their commander would almost certainly result in violations which it is the purpose of the law of war to prevent. Its purpose to protect civilian populations and prisoners of war from brutality would largely be defeated if the commander of an invading army could with impunity neglect to take reasonable measures for their protection. Hence the law of war presupposes that its violation is to be avoided through the control of the operations of war by commanders who are to some extent responsible for their subordinates.[184]

Although some of the evidence admitted against Yamashita was highly questionable, direct testimony established his approval of execution of hundreds of suspected guerrillas without trial, and of thousands more without any kind of fair trial procedure. It also established that his headquarters were within walking distance of POW camps where numerous atrocities occurred. Certainly, he had actual knowledge of criminal misconduct by his subordinates. The tribunal concluded that, in fact, "the occurrences were so widespread he had to have, at the least, discovered and controlled them. Clearly, assignment to command military troops is accompanied by broad authority and heavy responsibility. The prosecution readily admitted that Yamashita was probably unaware of many of the atrocities charged to troops under his command, be that he was: certainly aware of a certain portion of them." The atrocities, the prosecution charged, occurred precisely because Yamashita had had neglected his command responsibilities. This has been true in all armies throughout recorded history. It is absurd, however, to consider a commander a murderer or rapist because one of his soldiers commits a murder or a rape. Nevertheless, where murder and rape and vicious, revengeful actions are widespread offenses, and there is no effective attempt by a commander to discover and control the criminal acts, such a

[184]Id. at 14-16

commander may be held responsible, even criminally liable, for the lawless acts of his troops, depending upon their nature and the circumstances surrounding them. It is for the purpose of maintaining discipline and control, among other reasons, that military commanders are given broad powers of administering military justice. The tactical situation, the character, training and capacity of staff officers and subordinate commanders as well as the traits of character and training of his troops are other important factors in such cases. The Commission concluded: (1) That a series of atrocities and other high crimes have been committed by members of the Japanese armed forces under Yamashita's command, that they were not sporadic in nature but in many cases were methodically supervised by Japanese officers and non-commissioned officers; (2) That during the period in question Yamashita failed to provide effective control of his troops as was required by the circumstances. Thus, rather than finding any sort of "strict liability" the commission held that the facts were so egregious General Yamashita had to have discovered and controlled them.[185] As the Commission wrote,

> From all the facts and circumstances of record, it is impossible to escape the conclusion that the accused knew, or had the means to know, of the widespread commission of atrocities by members and units of his command; his failure to inform himself through official means available to him of what was common knowledge throughout his command and throughout the civilian population can only be considered as a criminal dereliction of duty on his part.[186]

Yamashita appealed to the U.S. Supreme Court, but his writ was denied. Justices Murphy and Rutledge wrote an especially critical dissenting opinion:

> He was not charged with personally participating in the acts of atrocity or with ordering or condoning their commission. Not even knowledge of these crimes was attributed to him. It was simply alleged that he unlawfully disregarded and failed to

---

[185] Parks, William H.,"Command Responsibility for War Crimes" *Military Law Review*, 28 (1973); Wallach, Evan and Maxine Marcus "Command Responsibility" in Cherif Bassouni, ed. *International Criminal Law*. 3rd ed., 2008, 5-8.

[186] Review of the Staff Judge Advocate of the Record of Trial by the Military Commission of Tomoyuki Yamashita, 9 December 1945.

> discharge his duty as commander to control the operations of the members of his command, permitting them to commit the acts of atrocity. The recorded annals of warfare and the established principles of international law afford not the slightest precedent for such a charge.[187]

Yamashita was executed by hanging, an ignominious exit for a professional soldier, and he was immediately buried in an unmarked grave. Yamashita's culpability for these events remains a matter of controversy, as some argued that he had failed to prevent them.[188] However, Yamashita had the officer who instigated the hospital massacre and some soldiers caught looting executed for these acts, and he personally apologized to the surviving Alexandra Hospital patients. He was the highest ranking officer of any army tried specifically for leadership responsibility.[189]

There remains to this day an enormous difference of opinion as to the justice of the verdict in the Yamashita case. Defense attorney Frank Reel argued that the strict liability interpretation of leadership responsibility used in Yamashita's case was a new and unprecedented case of extralegal expansion of an established doctrine.[190] Telford Taylor, chief prosecutor at Nuremberg, agreed that strict interpretation of leadership responsibility had been the order of the day in post-World war II war crimes trials. One academic critic of the Commission's verdict wrote, "The judgment appeared to impose strict liability on military officers. Clearly Yamashita was not cognizant and could not have been aware of each and every crime committed under his command."[191] One recent commentary concluded that "General Yamashita was tried and hanged on a doctrine of

---

[187] *In re Yamashita*, 327 US 1 (1945) at 13.–14. See also Bassiouni, M. C., *Crimes against Humanity: Historical Evolution and Contemporary Application*. Cambridge: Cambridge University Press, 2011, 535.

[188] Yamashita's conviction met all necessary elements of command responsibility with respect to war crimes committed in the Philippines. U.N. War Crimes Commission, *Law Reports of the Trials of War Criminals* I, "Trial of General Tomoyuki Yamashia" (1948)

[189] Ryan, Allan A., *Yamashita's Ghost: War Crimes, MacArthur's Justice, and Command Accountability*. University Press of Kansas, 2012.

[190] Stryszak, *op. cit.*, 43.

[191] Lippman, Matthew, "Conundrum of Armed Conflict: Criminal Defenses to Violations of the Humanitarian Law of War," *Dickinson Journal of International Law* 1 (1996) 75.

leadership responsibility that has since been repudiated because of the injustice of convicting an individual of crimes he did not, and could not, know were being carried out by his subordinates."[192] The most serious charge against the Commission was that the generals were prejudiced.[193] First, General MacArthur, critics claimed, had chosen five officers who were certain to find the defendant guilty. They may have done so because they had seen the results firsthand and felt some retribution should be forthcoming; because they understood MacArthur's wishes without having to be told; because they simply loathed the Japanese for any of a variety of reasons; or perhaps because of some private prejudices. At this late date, indeed if ever, this point cannot be proven one way or another. The charge does little more than cast a nasty shadow over the lives and careers of five outstanding American officers without an iota of proof beyond the authors' own opinions.

There is no question that the Commission accepted the "must have known" argument. Recent commentator Michael Stryszak argued that one must look at the concept of imputed knowledge, defined by *Black's Law Dictionary*, as "knowledge attributed or charged to a person because the facts in question were open to his discovery and it was his duty to inform himself as to them." Thus, Yamashita's culpability was great since that knowledge lay well within the parameters of his responsibility as Japanese military supreme commander. Put another way, would the ordinary person, given the overwhelming and widespread incidents of terror, really believe that such events occurred without Yamashita being aware? It was not the responsibility of the Commission to determine which of many incidents Yamashita knew and which he did not know. The number of them precluded total ignorance. While in a strict sense some acts may have been more morally reprehensible than others, there was such an incredible number as to preclude total ignorance.[194]

Case of Masharu Homma

Masharu Homma (1887-1946) was born on Sado Island, in the Sea

---

[192] Simpson, Gerry J., "Conceptualizing Violence: Present and Future Developments in International Law" *Alabama Law Review* 60 (1997) 801.

[193] Stryszak, *op. cit.,* 43

[194] Id. at 44.

of Japan. He graduated from the Imperial Japanese Army Academy in 1907, and from the Army Staff College in 1915. Homma spent eight years as a military attaché in the United Kingdom, including combat service in France in 1918 with the British Expeditionary Force. From 1930-1932, Homma was again served as a military attaché to the United Kingdom, where his proficiency in the English language was useful. He was also assigned to be part of the Japanese delegation to the Geneva Disarmament Conference in 1932 and served with the Press Section of the Army Ministry from 1932-1933. He was given a field command again, as commander of the IJA 1st Infantry Regiment from 1933–1935, and was promoted to command the IJA 32nd Infantry Brigade from 1935-1936. In 1937, Homma served as aide-de-camp to Prince Chichibu, a brother of Emperor Shōwa. The two men made a diplomatic tour in Europe which ended in Germany. They met Adolf Hitler with whom the prince was impressed.[195] Homma then served as the commander of the Taiwan Army of the Imperial Armed Forces. Homma was appointed commander of the 27th Division, Japanese Imperial Army, in China from 1938 until 1940.[196]

Homma was commander of the 14th Imperial Japanese Army which invaded the Philippines. He ordered his troops to treat the Filipinos as friends, and to respect their customs and religion. This liberal approach earned him the enmity of his superior, General Count Hisaichi Terauchi, commander of the Southern Army, who sent negative reports about Homma to Tokyo. There was also disloyalty and subversion within Homma's command led by a small group of subordinates, notably Colonel Tsuji Masanobu. In Homma's name, they sent out secret orders which ran contrary to his explicit orders and policies.

In conquering the Philippines rather than waste his men in furious frontal assaults, he tried to outmaneuver the American forces. His superiors then claimed that he had been "contaminated" by Western ideas regarding the conservation of the lives of his men. Deterioration in the relationship between Homma and the general staff led to the removal of Homma from command shortly after the fall of Corregidor, and he was thereafter only nominally commander of the 14th Army.

---

[195] Yoshimori Futara *et al. The Crown Prince's European Tour*. 1925.

[196] Bix, *op. cit.*;, 162.

After the surrender of Japan, the American authorities arrested Homma. General MacArthur ordered his extradition to the Philippines in order that he could be tried by an American court martial. Homma was convicted of the actions of his men during the march rather than having a direct hand in the actions themselves, that is, leadership responsibility. It is far from clear whether Homma ordered, or even was aware of, the atrocities that occurred during the Bataan Death March. However, it is clear that he lacked the administrative expertise and ability to adequately delegate authority and control his men which led to the atrocities. After American-Filipino forces surrendered the Bataan Peninsula, Homma turned logistics of handling the estimated 25,000 prisoners to Major-General Yoshitake Kawane. Homma had publicly stated that the POWs would be treated fairly. Kawane formulated a plan to transport and march the prisoners to Camp O'Donnell, which Homma approved. However, the plan was severely flawed.

Homma was indicted on 48 counts of violating the international rules of war, but during this first meeting with his lawyers the general said he was pleading *not guilty* to all of them. As the commander of the 14th Imperial Army he was "morally responsible," but he said he neither knew about nor condoned—let alone ordered—any of the crimes for which he was now being charged. Of all the charges, he seemed to understand that those associated with the Bataan Death March would be the hardest to defend against. And yet Homma appeared to have only a vague notion of what this incident was supposed to have been. He said the very first time he'd heard the term was shortly before being taken into American custody, when several reporters asked him about his role in the atrocity.

In his defense at his trial, Homma also claimed that he was so preoccupied with the plans for the Corregidor assault that he had forgotten about the treatment of the prisoners, believing that his Kawane was properly handling the matter. He claimed that he did not learn of the atrocity until after the war. But there were other charges. Atrocities continued at Camp O'Donnell and at Cabanatuan after the arrival of the POWs. Homma also bore responsibility for bombing Manila after it had been declared an open city. Troops under his command refused to grant quarter to troops on Corregidor.[197]

Homma was convicted by the U.S. military tribunal for war crimes in the Philippines, including the Bataan Death March, and the atrocities at O'Donnell and Cabanatuan which followed. As the commander of the 14th Area Army, it was his duty to ensure that the prisoners were properly cared for. He was responsible for ensuring that the logistics were ready to take care of the prisoners. He failed in his leadership responsibility to ensure that his troops behaved in a legal and humane fashion. All of these were tasks incumbent upon him based upon his position. Having failed, he was thus legally responsible and accordingly could be held accountable. As a matter of international law, this was actually a new interpretation of leadership responsibility. The first person who had been convicted on its basis had been Lt. General Tomoyuki Yamashita.

Homma's chief defense counsel, John H. Skeen Jr., stated that it was a "highly irregular trial, conducted in an atmosphere that left no doubt as to what the ultimate outcome would be." Associate Justice Frank Murphy of the U.S. Supreme Court protested the verdict, stating: "Either we conduct such a trial as this in the noble spirit and atmosphere of our Constitution or we abandon all pretense to justice, let the ages slip away and descend to the level of revengeful blood purges."

Homma's wife appealed to General MacArthur to spare his life but he denied her pleas. However, MacArthur, as a small token to the woman, ordered Homma to be shot, rather than hanged as Yamashita was. He was not allowed to wear the uniform of his rank as general. Homma was executed by firing squad by the Filipino and American forces on 3 April 1946 outside Manila.[198]

Hirota v MacArthur

Baron Koki Hirota, was a major player in Japanese politics in the 1930s, and was the only civilian sentenced to death by the IMTFE. A one-time Prime Minister of Japan and Foreign Minister during the earliest stages of World War II in Asia, Hirota was convicted on three of nine

---

197 Hampton Sides "The Trial of General Homma," *American Heritage*, February/March 2007.

198 Philip R. Piccagallo, *The Japanese on Trial: Allied War Crimes Operations in the East, 1945-1951*. University of Texas Press, 1980.

counts—for his role as one of the leaders, organizers, instigators, or accomplices in the formulation or execution of a common plan or "conspiracy . . . [to wage] . . . wars of aggression, and wars in violation of international law;" for "waging a war of aggression against . . . . China;" and for deliberately and recklessly disregarding his duty to take adequate steps to prevent atrocities. Essentially, Hirota was convicted for his complicity in the Rape of Nanking. Hirota was either derelict in his duty by not insisting before the cabinet that immediate action be taken to stop the Nanking atrocities, or he failed in other actions available to him to get the same results.

Notwithstanding his complicity for the events at Nanking, Hirota's indictment was marginal, best described it as a borderline case. One of twenty-eight Class A defendants tried before the IMTFE, Hirota was one of the eleven who sought post-conviction relief in the courts of the United States. Hirota's was one of hundreds of similar applications for "original" habeas relief filed in the U.S. Supreme Court by Axis prisoners convicted of war crimes by American or Allied military tribunals. The Court denied every other original application without argument or an opinion, usually by a 4–4 vote with Justice Jackson recused.

There was no proof that Hirota, as foreign minister, had any legal authority to repress any war crimes, most importantly those that the Japanese perpetrated in Nanking. Reportedly, he had opposed the army's criminal activity and, in turn, was assured by the war minister and the army that no such incidents would ever occur again and that those who were responsible would be punished. The tribunal held that Hirota had a grave obligation to make his own independent investigation whether these assurances had been honored. If he found that the assurances were unkept he had a legal obligation to convince the whole cabinet to require that changes be made. Failing that he must resign from the cabinet.[199]

Hirota v. MacArthur[200] was a decision by the Supreme Court of the United States, which was concerned with the jurisdictional aspect of war crimes trials and their apparent immunity to judicial review by U.S.

---

[199]Minear, Richard R., *Victors' Justice: The Tokyo War Crimes Trials*. University of Michigan, 1971, 71-72.

[200]338 U.S. 197 (1948)

Supreme Court. The case held that "the courts of the United States have no power or authority to review, to affirm, set aside or annul the judgments and sentences imposed by the International Military Tribunal for the Far East." The motions for leave to file petitions for writs of habeas corpus were thus denied. The appeal to the U.S. Supreme Court was made following the imposition of death sentences against Koki Hirota and six other Japanese leaders tried for war crimes. The military tribunal set up in Japan by General Douglas Arthur MacArthur as the agent of the Allied Powers was not a tribunal of the United States, and the courts of the United States have no power or authority to review, affirm, set aside, or annul the judgments and sentences imposed by it on these petitioners, all of whom are citizens of Japan.

Justice William Douglas agreed, but expressed his concern in a concurring opinion about a total lack of judicial control over the international tribunal. His concern was that the high court had held that "no court of the United States to which the potential appellate jurisdiction of this Court extends has jurisdiction over this cause." He wrote, "Today, Japanese war lords appeal to the Court for application of American standards of justice. Tomorrow or next year, an American citizen may stand condemned in Germany or Japan by a military court or commission. If no United States court can inquire into the lawfulness of his detention, the military have acquired, contrary to our traditions, a new and alarming hold on us." Further, "It has never been deemed essential that the prisoner in every case be within the territorial limits of the district where he seeks relief by way of habeas corpus." By removing itself wholly from such cases the Supreme Court "would have to conclude that the United States Generals who have custody of petitioners are bigger than our government to hold that the respondent officials of the War Department have no control or command over them."[201]

The Supreme Court was satisfied that the tribunal sentencing these petitioners was not a tribunal of the United States. The United States and other allied countries conquered, and then occupied and controlled, Japan. The Allied Powers chose General Douglas to act as the Supreme Commander for them. The military tribunal sentencing these petitioners

---

[201] 338 U. S. 197 at 202ff (1948)

was set up by General MacArthur as the agent of the Allied Powers. It was well within the authority of the Allied High Command to create and constitute the war crimes tribunals.

Other War Crimes

The Rape of Nanking,[202] was a mass murder and war rape that occurred during the six-week period following the Japanese capture of the city of Nanking, the former capital of the Republic of China, on December 13, 1937 during the Second Sino-Japanese War. Hundreds of thousands of Chinese civilians and disarmed soldiers were murdered by soldiers of the Imperial Japanese Army. Widespread rape[203] and looting also occurred. The commanding officer, General Iwame Matsui, had issued orders before the city fell instructing his troops to observe restraint in dealing with the civilian population. The man most clearly responsible for this atrocity was the uncle of Japanese Emperor Hirohito, Prince Asaka, a member of the imperial family. He escaped prosecution because General MacArthur earlier had granted immunity to all members of the royal family. According to one Japanese journalist embedded with Imperial forces at the time, "The reason that the [10th Army] is advancing to Nanking quite rapidly is due to the tacit consent among the officers and men that they could loot and rape as they wish."[204] Thus, it was Matsui whom the tribunal put on trial. Matsui could not possibly have prevented the events that occurred with the tacit approval of a member of the royal family and was thus powerless. Nonetheless, the tribunal found Matsui responsible for the criminal acts of the Japanese troops in Nanking. He was found

---

[202] Iris Change, Rape of Nanking. London: Penguin, 1998; Daqing Yang, "Convergence or Divergence? Recent Historical Writings on the Rape of Nanking" 104 *American Historical Rev.* (June 1999) 842-65.

[203] For so-called comfort women, really Chinese women who were brutally raped, see Hicks, George, *Comfort Women: Japan's Brutal Regime of Enforced Prostitution in the Second World War.* New York: Norton, 1997; and David Andrew Schmidt, *Ianfu–The Comfort Women of the Japanese Imperial Army of the Pacific War: Broken Silence.* Lewiston, NY: Edwin Mellen Press, 2000; and Yuki Tanaka, *Japan's Comfort Women: Sexual Slavery and Prostitution During World War II and the U.S. Occupation.* London: Routledge, 2001

[204] *Japan Advertiser*, 7 December 1937. This newspaper was an American owned and edited English-language daily paper in Tokyo.

guilty because he must have known of these criminal acts.[205] Historians have estimated that 250,000 to 300,000 people were killed. The International Military Tribunal of the Far East estimated more than 200,000 casualties in the incident.[206] The Nanking Massacre is usually said to have occurred over a six-week period after the fall of Nanking, the crimes committed by the Japanese army were not limited to that period. Many atrocities were reported to have been committed as the Japanese army advanced from Shanghai to Nanking.

In 1937, the Osaka Mainichi Shimbun and its sister newspaper the *Tokyo Nichi Nichi Shimbun* covered a "friendly contest" between two Japanese officers, Toshiaki Mukai and Tsuyoshi Noda, both from Island troops, the Japanese 16th Division, in which the two men were described as vying with one another to be the first to kill 100 people with a sword before the capture of Nanking. From Jurong to Tangshan, cities in Jiangshu Province, China, Toshiaki Mukai had killed 89 people while Tsuyoshi Noda had killed 78 people. The contest continued because neither of them had killed 100 people. By the time they had arrived at Zijin Mountain, Tsuyoshi Noda had killed 105 people while Toshiaki Mukai killed 106 people. Both officers supposedly surpassed their goal during the heat of battle, making it impossible to determine which officer had actually won the contest. Therefore, according to the journalists Asami Kazuo and Suzuki Jiro, writing in the English language newspaper in Tokyo, they decided to begin another contest, with the aim being 150 kills. The *Nichi Nichi* headline of the story of December 13 read "'Incredible Record' [in the Contest to] Behead 100 People—Mukai 106 – 105 Noda—Both 2nd Lieutenants Go Into Extra Innings". After Japan surrendered, Toshiaki Mukai and Tsuyoshi Noda were arrested, tried by the Chinese in a war crimes tribunal, convicted, and executed by firing squad in Nanking charged with being civilized public enemies.[207]

---

[205] *Official Transcript of the International Japanese War Crimes Trials in the International Military Tribunal for the Far East*, 49: 815-16. Herein after *Japanese War Crimes Trials*.

[206] Yamamoto, Masahiro, *Nanking: Anatomy of an Atrocity.* Westport, CT: Praeger, 2000.

[207] Wakabayashi, Bob Tadashi, "The Nanking 100-Man Killing Contest Debate: War Guilt Amid Fabricated Illusions," *Journal of Japanese Studies* 26: 2, [Summer

Chemical and biological warfare had long since been outlawed. Japan used both in China. The one trial of a Japanese officer for use of chemical warfare involved Kajiura Ginjirō, Commander of the 231st Regiment, 39th Division. He was tried and sentenced to life in prison by a military tribunal in China in 1947 for using poisonous gas in combat. From December 25 to 31, 1949, the Soviet government tried twelve Japanese officers involved in biological warfare operations. The transcript of the trial included both photocopied documents and photographs that supported this charge.[208]

General Shunroka Hata, commanding forces over a prolonged period in China, was tried for numerous criminal acts perpetrated by troops under his command. The tribunal assumed that Hata must have known of the atrocities because of their huge scale. It was his duty, the tribunal reasoned, to know of such matters and then take all corrective measures necessary to correct them. When he failed to restrain his troops who were committing atrocities against Chinese civilians he could be held responsible as a war criminal.[209]

The case of General H. Kimura, commander of the Burma area, is one of the more unusual post-war prosecutions. Kimura had issued orders to his troops to treat POWs fairly and well and to generally restrain themselves. There was no question that he had given these two specific orders in a clear and unequivocal manner. His subordinates evidently ignored and circumvented the orders resulting in maltreatment of the prisoners and numerous criminal activities regarding the Burmese natives. The tribunal found him guilty of violating his leadership responsibility for failing to follow up and ascertain if his orders were being followed.[210] In both the Hata and Kimura cases the defendants were found to be culpable because they had failed to gather facts, read and study reports, and otherwise become aware of what was transpiring in their respective commands.

2000)]: 307–4

[208] *Materials on the Trial of Former Servicemen of the Japanese Army, Charged with Manufacturing and Employing Bacteriological Weapons.* Moscow: Foreign Languages Publishing House, 1950.

[209] *Japanese War Crimes Trials*, 49: 784.

[210] Burnett, *Command Responsibility*, 114.

Hisakazu Tanaka (1889-1947) was a general in the Imperial Japanese Army, and head of the Japanese occupation force in Hong Kong in World War II. His name is occasionally transliterated Tanaka Hisaichi. He was charged with leadership responsibility for the illicit execution of an American POW committed by a subordinate while he was absent from his post. The fact that he absented himself without providing adequate safeguards for such possibilities was sufficient for the trial judges to convict. Upon conviction an appeals court overturned the conviction because there was no evidence that he had "wrongful knowledge" of the crime and had no effective way of preventing it.[211]

Admiral Soemu Toyoda had served as Chief of the Naval General Staff from May until September 1945, having previously served as Commander of the Japanese Combined Fleet, May 1944 until May 1945. Tried, but no convicted, of war crimes, Toyoda should have become aware of atrocities committed under his command because of their great number. The tribunal wrote "that a reasonable man could have come to no other inclusion that that the accused must have known of the offenses, or of the existence of an understood and acknowledged routine for their commission." Under the principle of leadership responsibility if the accused "knew, or should by the exercise of ordinary diligence, have learned of the commission by his subordinates" of extralegal and criminal activities he could be himself held criminally responsible.[212]

General Shigeru Sawada was commander of the Japanese 13th Army in China. Troops under Sawada's command executed 8 Americans, refusing to accord them status as prisoners of war. Specifically, Okada Ryuhei and Lieutenant Wako Yusei, both under Sawada's orders at Kiangwan Military Prison, Shanghai, China. Eight United States airmen, after taking part in a bombing raid on a Japanese steel mill, an oil refinery and an aircraft factory on 18th April, 1942, were forced to earth and captured by the Japanese and eventually held in Tokyo for about fifty-two days, during which time they were imprisoned in solitary confinement. There was evidence that, both during their period in Tokyo and previously,

---

[211] United Nations War Crimes Commission: Law Reports of Trials of War Criminals, 5:66.

[212] *U.N. War Crimes Commission: Law Reports,* 4: 118-19, *U.S. v Toyoda.*

they were subjected to various forms of torture during interrogations. On 28 August 1942, after spending approximately 70 additional days at the Bridge House Jail, Shanghai, in small verminous and insanitary cells, all eight fliers were removed to the Kiangwan Military Prison, on the outskirts of Shanghai. At the time of their transfer, all the fliers were weak and underweight and one was very ill. On arriving, they were assembled in a room before several Japanese officers, who, they later learned, constituted their court-martial. The accused Wako and Okado were among the members of the' court. Sawada's order was that they try as criminals the eight American airmen. Four fliers were sentenced to death by a Japanese military tribunal on false and fraudulent charges that Sawada had the power to commute. Instead Sawada refused to remit and revoke such sentences, thereby causing the unlawful death of four of the fliers and the imprisonment of the others.[213]

War Crimes Not Prosecuted

For various reasons, few of them valid, many war crimes and Japanese war criminals went untried. For the most part the decisions to not prosecute were personally made by General MacArthur. After the war General MacArthur was determined to make Japan into a Western style democracy. The image of Japanese as barbarians who violated all the rules of warfare would work against this conversion. Many of the atrocities committed against American invading forces, and some atrocities committed against POWs were well known and thus could not be suppressed. But few Japanese were known to the public in the Allied democracies the way the German leaders were known. Few Americans or British could name any Japanese except the Mikado and Tōjō. Thus MacArthur suppressed knowledge of the use of germ, biological, chemical, and gas warfare in China. Since only Russian forces had visited and then occupied the infamous Unit 731 that gruesome experimentation could be suppressed also. MacArthur's staff was most successful in withholding information on any experimentation on Westerners at Unit 731.[214]

---

[213] *U.S. v Shigeru Sawada.* U.S. Military Commission, case number 25, trial of Lt.-Gen. Shigeru Sawada and 3 others, Shanghai, 15 April 1946.

[214] Allen and Polmar, *op. cit.*, 173-74.

Among the true war criminals who escaped all trial and punishment were the following. Sasakawa Ryō'ichi was initially accused of war crimes and confined in Sugamo Prison, but was never tried, and then released. He joined the *yazuka*, Japan's mafia, working against the political left. Kodama Yoshio was also held in Sugamo Prison, but was soon released and was involved in various nefarious schemes. Colonel Naitō Ryō'ichi, the man who negotiated immunity for Unit 731 personnel, created a partnership with another Unit 731 figure General Kitano Masaji and both became multi-millionaires selling blood commercially.[215]

One of the worst war criminals of all times was Lt.-Col. Masanobu Tsuji (1901-1961). If one named a scene of carnage and atrocity it was likely under Masanobu's command. He was a leading proponent of *gekokujo*.[216] Tsuji was born in the Ishikawa Prefecture and received his education at a military academy and then graduated from the Imperial War College. Tsuji served as a staff officer in the Kwantung Army from 1937 to 1939. His aggressive posture contributed to the Soviet-Japanese Border Wars, particularly the Changkufeng Incident [217] and the Nomonhan Incident.[218] During the World War II he served principally in Malaya, Burma, the Philippines, and Guadalcanal. He served as a staff officer under General Tomoyuki Yamashita. Known as a brilliant tactician he planned the defense at Guadalcanal, he personally led the last two assaults by the Japanese forces which attempted to expel the Americans from the island. Tsuji returned to Tokyo after these failures to urge the evacuation of the troops from Guadalcanal. He impressed the Emperor with his candid

---

215 Tanaka, Yuki, *Hidden Horrors: Japanese War Crimes in World II*. Boulder: Westview Press, 1996.

216 "leading from below" or "loyal insubordination."

217 Also known as The Battle of Lake Khasan (July 29, 1938 – August 11, 1938) and also known as the Changkufeng Incident in China and Japan, was an attempted military incursion of Japanese occupied Manchukuo into the territory claimed by the Soviet Union. This incursion was founded in the beliefs of the Japanese side that the Soviet Union misinterpreted the demarcation of the boundary based on the Treaty of Peking between Imperial Russia and Manchu Empire and subsequent supplementary agreements on demarcation, and furthermore, that the demarcation markers were tampered with.

218 In August 1939 the Soviet Union and Japan fought the largest tank battle the world had thus far seen. Under General Georgy Zhukov, the Soviets won a crushing victory at the what the Soviets called the Battle of Khalkhin-Gol.

assessment of the military situation.[219]

He was involved in war crimes throughout the Pacific war including the massacre of Chinese civilians in Singapore, the executions of numerous surrendered POWs during the Bataan Death March.[220] He was personally on Bataan, informing his troops that the emperor desired that all white POWs be killed. Numerous POWs later claimed that Tsuji had himself killed various prisoners on the Death March. There were other war crimes in China. It was Tsuji who was actually responsible for the murder of physicians, nurses, and patients at the Alexandria Hospital in Singapore. Tsuji personally killed many Chinese soldiers, POWs, and civilians, and order the massacre of hundreds more by troops he commanded. He boasted that he carried in his body bullets from five different enemy nations.[221] Masanobu Tsuji was regarded as the most notorious Japanese war criminal to escape trial after the war.[222]

A recent historian has written,

> Col Masanobu Tsuji [was] a fanatic repeatedly wounded in action and repeatedly transferred by generals exasperated by his insubordination. Tsuji once burned down a geisha house to highlight his disgust at the moral frailty of the officers inside it. His excesses were responsible for some of the worst Japanese blunders on Guadalcanal. He was directly responsible for brutalities to prisoners and civilians in every part of the Japanese empire in which he served. In northern Burma, he dined on the liver of a dead Allied pilot, castigating as cowards those who refused to share his meal: "The more we eat, the brighter will burn the fire of our hatred for the enemy."[223]

Following the capitulation of Japan in September 1945, Tsuji went into hiding in Thailand anticipating being charged with war crimes. When

---

[219]Kent G. Budge, "Tsuji Masanobu" in The Pacific War Online Encyclopedia. http://pwencycl.kgbudge.com/T/s/Tsuji_Masanobu.htm.

[220] Falk, Stanley, *Bataan: The March of Death.* New York: W. W. Norton, 1962; Donald Knox, *Death March: The Survivors of Bataan.* New York: Harcourt Brace Jovanovich, 1981. Other estimates of American deaths range from 650 to over 2,000; estimates of Filipino deaths range from 9,000 to 16,500.

[221] Masanobu Tsuji, *Japan's Greatest Victory, Britain's Worst Defeat*. Trans. by Margaret E. Lake. Da Capo Press, 1997.

[222] Daws, *op. cit.,* 374.

[223] Hastings, Max, *Retribution: The Battle for Japan, 1944-45*. Knopf, 2008, 53.

it was clear that this not to be, he returned to Japan and wrote of his years in hiding.[224] That recollection became a best seller in Japan. In fact, his memoirs made him so famous that he later was elected a member of the Diet. In April 1961, he traveled to Laos but was never heard from again. He was presumed to have been a casualty of the Laotian Civil War, and was declared dead on July 20, 1968.[225]

At Pingfang, Manchuria (Japanese Manchoukuo), the Epidemic Prevention and Water Supply Unit attached to the Kwantung Army was a covert biological and chemical warfare research and development unit of the Imperial Japanese Army that undertook lethal human experimentation during the Second World War, beginning as early as 1937.[226] This unit showed no remorse and carried out some of the most heinous experiments in human history on men, women, children, and infants.[227] It was responsible for some of the most notorious war crimes carried out by Japanese personnel. Between 3,000 and 12,000 men, women, and children provided by the *Kempeitai* were murdered during the human experimentation conducted by Unit 731. This does not include victims from other medical experimentation sites. Almost 70% of the victims who died in the Pingfang camp were Chinese, including both civilian and military. Another 30% of the victims were Russian. Some others were South East Asians and Pacific Islanders, at the time colonies of the Empire of Japan, and a small number of the prisoners of war from the Allies of World War II. There were also Japanese criminals used although in very small numbers.

In 1932, General Shirō Ishii, a medical officer of the Japanese Army and close friend of Army Minister Sadao Araki was placed in command of the Army Epidemic Prevention Research Laboratory. Ishii organized a secret research group, the *Tōgō Unit*, to conduct various

---

[224]*Senko Sanzenri* literally lurking.

[225]"Masanobu Tsuji" in Wikipedia.

[226] Williams, Peter and David Wallace, *Unit 731: Japan's Secret Biological Warfare in World War II* New York: Free Press, 1989. We followed this scholarly work throughout our discussion of Unit 731. See also Sheldon H. Harris, *Factories of Death: Japanese Biological Warfare, 1932–1945, and the American Coverup.* New York; Rev. ed., Routledge, 1994.

[227] "Japanese Use the Chinese as 'Guinea Pigs' to Test Germ Warfare," *Rocky Mountain Medical Journal* 39: 8 [August 1942]: 571–72.

chemical and biological weapons. Ishii had proposed the creation of a Japanese biological and chemical research unit in 1930, after a two-year study trip abroad, rationalizing it on the grounds that Western powers were developing their own programs. One of Ishii´s main supporters inside the army was Colonel Chikahiko Koizumi, who became Japan's Health Minister, serving from 1941 until 1945. Koizumi had witnessed and had been impressed by the successful German use of chlorine gas at the Second Battle of Ypres.

Unit Tōgō was housed in the Zhongma Fortress, a prison camp about100 kilometers south of Harbin. A jailbreak in autumn 1934 and later explosion in 1935 led Ishii to abandon the Zhongma Fortress. The Army authorized him to move to Pingfang, some 24 kilometers south of Harbin, and to set up a much larger facility.

1936, Hirohito authorized, by imperial decree, the expansion of this unit and its integration into the Kwantung Army as the Epidemic Prevention Department. It was divided at the same time into the *Ishii Unit* and *Wakamatsu Unit* with a base in Hsinking. From August 1940, all these units were known collectively as the "Epidemic Prevention and Water Purification Department of the Kwantung Army."[228]

Those who surrendered to the American Forces were fortunate. On 6 May 1947, General Douglas MacArthur, as Supreme Commander of the Allied Forces, wrote to his superiors in Washington that "additional data, possibly some statements from Ishii probably can be obtained by informing Japanese involved that information will be retained in intelligence channels and will not be employed as *War Crimes* evidence." The reason they were not tried was that the information and experience gained in the studies of the biological warfare was of a great value for the United States biological weapons development program.

A few of the unlucky Unit 731 officers and enlisted men were arrested by Soviet forces and tried at the Khabarovsk War Crime Trials. The Japanese were also put on trial by the Soviet Union and China. The Soviet Union conducted a tribunal of twenty Japanese servicemen in the

---

[228] Charlotte Adele, *A Guide to Japanese War Crimes: Mass Killings, Human Experimentation and Biological Warfare, Sexual Assault, and More.* Webster Digital, 2013.

city of Khabarovsk in late 1949 and found twelve of them guilty of waging bacterial warfare. Most of those defendants were executed. Some of those in Unit 731 had committed suicide as all Japanese personnel were issued cyanide capsules as the Russians approached. Apparently the Chinese Nationalist government tried and executed no one for the events at this facility despite the fact that most human subjects were Chinese. In the mid-1950s, Communist China tried several hundred Japanese officers and civilians, many of whom had been transferred from the Soviet Union. Most of these later defendants were given reduced sentences in return for admission of guilt, and none received the death penalty.[229]

In 1981, historian Tsuneishi Keiichi published the first scholarly assessment of Unit 731, making extensive use of the postwar Khabarovsk trial records and wartime publications in Japanese medical journals. Few understood the extent to which Unit 731 interfaced with the military medical establishment in Japan during the war. Tsuneishi argued that even without the postwar sources such as the Khabarovsk trial records, articles published by Lt. Gen. Ishii Shirō, the head of Unit 731, and others during the war provided sufficient evidence that the Japanese had experimented on live humans.[230]

All of the belligerents had chemical and bacteriological warfare programs. The horrid experience in World War I had convinced nations to eschew the use of such weapons in war. Nonetheless, all the nations possessed a full range of these prohibited arms. Many such agents were simple to manufacture and at least two – chlorine gas and its close derivative phosgene—needed no improvement since their use in the Great War. Mustard gas, also used in the Western Front was readily available. Mussolini had used gas against Ethiopian troops in his conquest of that African nation. The fear of massive Allied retaliation, perhaps with even more ghastly chemicals, was the primary restraint operating on the Japanese government. But perhaps Japan could still use both biological

---

[229] *Materials on the Trial of Former Servicemen of the Japanese Army, Charged with Manufacturing and Employing Bacteriological Weapons.* Moscow: Foreign Languages Publishing House,1950.

[230] Yang, Daqing, "Documentary Evidence and the Studies of Japanese War Crimes: An Interim Assessment" in *Researching Japanese War Crimes Trials*. Inter-agency Working Group, 2006, 38-40.

and chemical weapons against the Chinese without fear of retaliation.[231]

Japan had its chemical weapons manufactory in Okunoshima, Hiroshima Prefecture, since the early 1930s. Reportedly, Japan used chemical warfare in 1939 in Shanshi Province, China, against the Soviet Red Army. Nanking became the center of Japanese research and development in chemical and bacteriological warfare. In what was originally a Chinese hospital the Japanese bred disease-bearing fleas and lice. And there were sporadic reports of the use of germ warfare and also chemicals against the Chinese in the early 1940s, especially in Chekiang Province. Both American President Franklin Roosevelt and British Prime Minister Winston Churchill then publicly threatened Japan with massive retaliation in kind if such weapons were used against Allied soldiers.[232] It is unclear if those threats included continued use against the Chinese Army and civilian population.

The Shimoda Case

During the Tokyo War Crimes Trial, several lawyers who defended the various Japanese war criminals tried to convince the IMTFE to consider the legality of the American use of nuclear weapons. Their motions were ignored largely because the tribunal had already rejected any use of the *tu quoque* defense. Shoichi Okamoto, a Japanese defense attorney, refused to accept the exclusion of consideration of atomic weapons and continued his quest to adjudicate that matter. In February 1953, he published a booklet entitled *Questions and Answers on the Civil Lawsuit over the Atomic Bombings*. He called upon citizens of Hiroshima and Nagasaki to take legal action against the U. S. government using the American legal system. Okamoto's plan met with opposition even in Hiroshima and Nagasaki.[233] The mayor of Hiroshima opposed the plan

---

[231]Powell, John W., "Japan's Germ Warfare: The U.S. Cover-up of a War Crime," *Bulletin of Concerned Asian Scholars* 12: 4 [Oct-Dec 1980]: 2–17; "A Hidden Chapter in History," *Bulletin of the Atomic Scientist* 37: 8 [October 1981]: 45–53.

[232] Allen and Polmar, *op. cit.*, 189-91

[233]Tanaka, Yuki, "The Atomic Bombing, The Tokyo War Crimes Tribunal" *Asia-Pacific Journal* (2 November 2009). 44-3-09. http://japanfocus.org/-Richard-Falk/3245. Richard Falk, "Shimoda Case: A Legal Appraisal of the Atomic Attacks upon Hiroshima and Nagasaki," *American Journal of International Law*, 59: 4 [October 1965]. Tanaka was one of the court appointed legal scholars involved in

purely on the technical grounds that the American legal system was not amenable to such a legal action. Okamoto then gave up the notion of trying the case in an American court and decided to seek action in the Japanese legal system.[234]

In co-operation with various organizations in Hiroshima and Nagasaki, five people were selected as litigants. Ryuichi Shimoda, the leader of the group, came from Hiroshima and was 57 years old. He lost four daughters and one son in the atomic attack on Hiroshima, and he, his wife and surviving son suffered from persistent health problems. Another lawyer, Yasuhiro Matsui, joined the legal team. Proceedings at the District Court in Tokyo began in April 1955, and the proceedings lasted until the court finally ruled on December 8, 1963.[235] Okamoto died in April 1958 and did not hear the final ruling. The court wrote,

> The plaintiffs, Japanese nationals, were all residents either of Hiroshima or of Nagasaki when atomic bombs were dropped on these cities by bombers of the United States [Army] Air Force in August 1945. Most of the members of their families were killed and many, including some of the plaintiffs themselves, were seriously wounded as a result of these bombings. The plaintiffs jointly brought the present action against the defendant, the State, for damages on the following grounds: (a) that they suffered injury through the dropping of atomic bombs by members of the [Army] Air Force of the United States of America; (b) that the dropping of atomic bombs as an act of hostilities was illegal under the rules of positive international law (taking both treaty law and customary law into consideration) then in force, for which the plaintiffs had a claim for damages; (c) that the dropping of atomic bombs also constituted a wrongful act on the plane of municipal law, ascribable to the United States and its President, Mr. Harry S. Truman; (d) that Japan had waived, by virtue of the provisions of Article 19 (a) of the Treaty of Peace with Japan of 1951, the claims of the plaintiffs under international law and municipal law, with the result that the plaintiffs had lost their claims for

---

the *Shimoda* case.

[234] *Ryuichi Shimoda et al. v. The State* I. Evaluation of the act of bombing according to international law in Wikisource.

[235] *Shimoda et al. v. The State*, Tokyo District Court, 7 December 1963. The full text is on line at http://www.icrc.org/ihl-nat.nsf/276c23458e6a0d2441256486004ad099/aa559087dbcf1af5c1256a1c0029f14d!

> damages against the United States and its President; and (e) that this waiver of the plaintiffs' claims by the defendant, the State, gave rise to an obligation on the part of the defendant to pay damages to the plaintiffs.

The plaintiffs' cause of action was based, more specifically, on the provisions of Article I of the State Redress Law, which was applicable to the case of injury to a private person through an unlawful act of a government official; on the provisions of Article 29 of the Constitution, which provided for the obligation to pay just compensation in every case of expropriation of private property by the State for public use; and, finally, on unlawful infringement of the rights of the plaintiffs through the omission of the defendant to take appropriate measures for recovery of compensation. [The court held] that the action must fail on the merits. The aerial bombardment with atomic bombs of the cities of Hiroshima and Nagasaki was an illegal act of hostilities according to the rules of international law. It must be regarded as indiscriminate aerial bombardment of undefended cities, even if it were directed at military objectives only, inasmuch as it resulted in damage comparable to that caused by indiscriminate bombardment. Nevertheless, the claimant as an individual was not entitled to claim damages on the plane of international law, nor was he able, as a result of the doctrine of sovereign immunity, to pursue a claim on the plane of municipal law. In these circumstances, the plaintiffs had no rights to lose as a result of the waiver contained in Article 19 (a) of the Treaty of Peace with Japan.[236]

> The Japanese court could have, at any time it wished, chosen to dismiss the case on the simple and traditional legal ground of act of state. Imbued with absolute sovereign immunity in international affairs, the Japanese government could have chosen to terminate the case immediately. Instead it chose to allow the litigation to labor on for eight and a half years. The case will bear the interpretation that the Japanese government wished to establish to its satisfaction that the atomic bombings were clear violations of International law. It is not especially surprising, given Japan's post war attitude toward its role in World War II, that a Japanese court would find that the atomic bombing constituted a war crime. What is surprising is the

[236] *The Japanese Annual of International Law*, 8 [1964] 231.[I]

> attitude of an American court on this subject. The Superior Court of Orange County, California, noted the opinion of the Japanese court in a decision involving POWs being forced to work in a metals plant, The California court cited the Japanese tribunal in the *Shimoda* case noting that it had found that "the United States had in fact violated international law" in dropping the atomic bombs. The Orange County Court made no attempt to reject the conclusion that the United States had indeed violated international law by using the atomic bomb.[237]

To many Americans there was no difference in kind between conventional and nuclear bombs; it was merely that atomic bombs were more effective. Fire bombing killed many more people than did atomic bombs. As General Curtis LeMay wrote, "We scorched and boiled and baked to death more people in Tokyo on that night of 9-10 March [1945] than went up in vapor at Hiroshima and Nagasaki combined." On 9 March 1945 American B-29s destroyed 16 square miles of Tokyo, including 10,000 acres of buildings of all types. On 25 May 1945 464 B-29s returned to Tokyo, dropping 3258 tons of incendiary bombs which destroyed 19 square miles of the city. By August 1945 American B-29 Super Fortresses had destroyed significant parts of 65 Japanese cities. After the war Intelligence estimated that strategic bombing had destroyed about 37% of all Japanese automobiles, 34% of its machine tools, and 20% of all household goods and furniture. At least 310,000 Japanese had died in the bombings or in the firestorms that accompanied many of the air raids; another 412,000 were injured. Destruction of factories and other workplaces displaced over 13,000,000 workers. Architect of the napalm bombing was General Curtis LeMay who estimated as early as 30 May 1945 that a million Japanese had been killed. Some 9,200,000 Japanese, or an estimated 25% of the nation, were made homeless. About two and one-half million houses were burned and another 600,000 were demolished by Japanese authorities to create fire-breaks. Secretary of War Henry Stimson was unconcerned about the results, but rebuked LeMay for revealing the estimates. After all, Stimson said, he "did not want to have

[237] *Mitsubishi Materials v Dillman* [1999], case 814430 Orange County. The U.S. State Department and the Justice Department worked with the defendants, both in court and behind the scenes, to oppose the plaintiffs' moves, arguing that the 1951 San Francisco Peace Treaty waives their claims.

the U.S. get the reputation for outdoing Hitler in atrocities." In short, Stemson told LeMay to continue the good work but just not brag about it.

If one considers the dropping of the atomic bomb on Japan in 1945 to have been a war crime one would be hard pressed to ignore the effects of conventional bombing upon civilian population. While no conventional bomb creates radioactive fallout and with it radiation poisoning, certainly the burns inflicted by napalm and thermite fire bombs create their own wounds.

War Crimes: Legacy

After the conclusion of the Tokyo trials and its adjunct tribunals in individual nations, neither the Western nor the Japanese governments seemed interested in continuing investigating Japan's war crimes. This stands in stark contrast to continued prosecution of Nazi war criminals in the United States and Europe. Japan seemed more preoccupied with rebuilding the nation and mourning its losses than in looking upon its crimes. The release of some Japanese war criminals from Chinese incarceration led a few of these veterans to publish accounts of atrocities in China. The first edition sold out quickly, but enormous pressures from former military leaders prevented publication of a second edition and of additional memoirs. This was soon followed by the publication of *An Affirmation of the Greater East Asian War*, a book which marked the beginning of open challenges to the legality of the Tokyo War Crimes Trial.[238] This was the opening volley in the campaign to invalidate the indictment of Japan's war crimes.

Among other authors, Ian Buruma compared responses to war crimes in postwar Germany and Japan in The Wages of Guilt. . According to Buruma, Germany publicly accepted responsibility for the evils perpetrated by the Nazi regime and educated future generations by discussing its sordid Nazi history in school textbooks and classes. Germany apologized to humankind. Conversely, Japan rejected responsibility, downplayed the historical evidence of aggression and atrocity in its schools with sophistry and euphemism, and apologized to no

[238]Hayashi Fusao, *Daitōa sensō koteiron* [*An Affirmation of the Greater East Asia War*]. Tokyo: Banchō shobō, 1964. A sequel was published in 1965.

one. Worse yet, ultra-conservative Japanese commentators insisted the war was wholly justified. In 1979 small stolen portions of the ashes of the Class A war criminals were entombed at the Yasukuni Shrine near the emperor's palace where, the Japanese believed, the spirits of the glorious war dead gathered. In the inner sanctum of Yasukuni, behind the sacred sword and mirror of the Shinto cult, one can find the register of the spirits of Japan's honored dead including the "seven martyrs." Japan also continues to downplay atrocities and maintains that the Rape of Nanking was an anomaly. It also refuses to accept responsibility for its many other war crimes.[239]

Many of the scientists involved in the infamous Unit 731 went on to prominent careers in post-war politics, academia, business, and medicine. Many Unit 731 scientists held prestigious posts at leading Japanese universities. Post war survivors of Unit 731 formed their own veterans' society, *Seikonkai*, the Refined Spirit Association. That organization created its own cemetery with a memorial tower dedicated not to the victims but to the masters.

[239]Ian Buruma, *The Wages of Guilt: Memories of War in Germany and Japan.* New York: Farrar, Straus, Giroux, 1994.

5
Command Responsibility in the United States

War crimes have accompanied every major military action in the United States, beginning when the nation was still a British colony. Perhaps the worst example occurred when the British were fighting the Amerindians. Lord Jeffrey Amherst (1717-1797) is best known as the architect of Britain's successful campaign to conquer the territory of New France during the French and Indian War. Under his command British forces captured the cities of Louisbourg, Quebec City and Montreal, as well as several major fortresses. He was also the first British Governor General in the territories that eventually became Canada. Under his instructions British officers distributed blankets infected with small pox, bringing about an epidemic that decimated the tribes.[240] Amherst's smallpox-infected blankets were used as germ warfare against American Indians during the siege of Fort Pitt by Chief Pontiac's forces during the summer of 1763. Smallpox had broken out at Fort Pitt in 1763, and the Commander of Fort Pitt proposed giving blankets infected with smallpox to American Indians.[241] Amherst approved the plan in theory and expressed his willingness to adopt any "other method that can serve to Extirpate this Execrable Race."[242] Major 19th century historian Francis Parkman quoted Amherst writing, "Could it not be contrived to send the

[240] "Captain Simeon Ecuyer had bought time by sending smallpox-infected blankets and handkerchiefs to the Indians surrounding the fort -- an early example of biological warfare -- which started an epidemic among them. Amherst himself had encouraged this tactic in a letter to Ecuyer" Carl Waldman, *Atlas of the North American Indian*. Facts on File, 1985, 108.

[241] Appel, J. M., "Is all fair in biological warfare? The Controversy over Genetically Engineered Biological Weapons", *Journal of Medical Ethics,* 35 (2009) 7: 429–432. This is also found as a document in the third series of *Pennsylvania Archives.*

[242] Amherst to Bouquet, dated 16 July 1763. See also Francis Parkman, *Conspiracy of Pontiac*. Boston, Little Brown, 1886, 2: 39.

Small Pox among those disaffected tribes of Indians? We must on this occasion use every stratagem in our power to reduce them." As a later historian wrote, "Captain Simeon Ecuyer had bought time by sending smallpox-infected blankets and handkerchiefs to the Indians surrounding the fort -- an early example of biological warfare -- which started an epidemic among them. Amherst himself had encouraged this tactic in a letter to Ecuyer."[243] William Trent (1715-1787), commander of the local militia of Pittsburgh during Pontiac's siege of Fort Pitt wrote the most detailed contemporary account of the Amerindian siege. In Trent's entry for May 24, 1763, he wrote, ". . . we gave them two Blankets and an Handkerchief out of the Small Pox Hospital. I hope it will have the desired effect."[244]

In fighting the native Americans neither Bouquet nor Amherst considered that any moral restraints should inhibit their conduct of war. Amherst referred to the Amerindians as "that Vermine" and Bouquet agreed, writing that he thought that the native aborigine "have forfeited all claim to the rights of humanity."[245] Amherst also discussed the use of dogs to hunt the Indians. This had been used successfully in Central and South America by various conquistadors and was thus called the Spaniard's Method. Amherst approved this in principle, but said he cannot implement it only because there are not enough dogs.[246] Quite naturally there was no statutory law, authority, or court with the proper authority to try and punish such clear violations of human ethics.

Henry Hamilton (c.1734–1796) was an Irish-born soldier and official of the British Empire. American forces under George Rogers Clark captured Hamilton, widely known as the Hair Buyer, for his purchases of scalps. Hamilton served as the Lieutenant Governor at Fort Detroit. In 1778, Clark captured several British posts in the Illinois country. Hamilton, accompanied by many of the Amerindians who sold him scalps, set out from Detroit on 7 October 1778 to recapture Vincennes, some 600 miles

---

[243]Carl Waldman, *Atlas of the North American Indian*. New York: Facts on File, 1985, 108.

[244] 24 May 1763 entry in *Journal of Captain William Trent from Logstown to Pickawillany*. 1871.

[245] Bouquet to Amherst, 25 June 1763.

[246] 26 July 1763, Bouquet acknowledging Amherst's instructions.

away. His force entered Vincennes on 17 December 1778. In February 1779, Clark returned to Vincennes, and in a surprise march, recaptured the outpost, taking Hamilton prisoner. Because of his support of the Amerindian raids, the Virginians regarded Hamilton as a war criminal rather than as a prisoner of war. It would have been the preference of virtually all frontiersmen, and especially Virginians, to have tried Hamilton for war crimes, especially against non-combatants. Clark, who killed a number of the accompanying native aborigine, sent Hamilton to Williamsburg, where he was jailed on the explicit instructions of Governor Thomas Jefferson. Eventually, George Washington ordered Jefferson to grant Hamilton parole. Hamilton was exchanged and sailed to London.[247] This was, of course, a clear case of a commander knowing what troops under his command were doing, even though they were at best very loosely under his control, but encouraging clearly most uncivilized behavior by purchasing the scalps of those the savages murdered. It had to be abundantly obvious that some scalps had been taken from women and children.

During the Mexican War Colonel David D. Mitchell was part of an outfit was known as the Kearney Campaign. Colonel, later General, Stephen W. Kearny commanded some 1,700 regular army and volunteer soldiers who mustered at Fort Leavenworth, Kansas. Kearny designated the force the Army of the West and advanced on the Santa Fe Trail by the end of June 1846.[248] Mitchell received an order to seize civilian goods, a command that he might have easily passed along to a subordinate officer or non-commissioned officer. Mitchell claimed as his defense that he was merely following superior orders. The U.S. Supreme Court in 1851 heard the case, affirming the conviction of Mitchell in the trespass suit. The Court held that "it can never be maintained that a military officer can justify himself for doing an unlawful act, by producing the order of his

[247] Bernard W. Sheehan, "'The Famous Hair Buyer General': Henry Hamilton, George Rogers Clark, and the American Indian." *Indiana Magazine of History* 69 (March 1983): 1–28. See also Weston D. Burnett, "Command Responsibility" *Military Law Review* 107 (1985) 71: 76.

[248] Susan Magoffin, *Down the Santa Fe Trail and Into Mexico*. University of Nebraska Press, 1982.

superior. The order may palliate; but it cannot justify."[249] No action was taken against the officer who ordered Mitchell to seize the civilian property.

There was, of course, no court martial or other punishment for employing such a immoral way of conducting war. Neither was there any criminal penalty attached to the many questionable acts committed during the American War for Independence. Brother fought against brother, often giving no quarter, taking no prisoners, and killing prisoners.[250] Reportedly, there were other violations of what little customary international law of warfare existed at that time, including rape and other sexual assault, pillage, wanton destruction of civilian property, and rapine.

Early in our national history Massachusetts indicated its dedication to command responsibility by enacting the following:

> Every Officer commanding, in quarter, or on march, shall keep good order, and to the utmost of his power, redress all such abuses or disorder which may be committed by any Officer or Soldier under his command; if upon complaint made to him of Officers or Soldiers beating or otherwise ill-treating any persons, or committing any kind of riots to the disquieting of the inhabitants of this Continent, he, the said commander, who shall refuse or omit to see Justice done to the offender or offenders, and reparations made to the party or parties injured, as soon as the offender's wages shall enable him or them, upon due proof thereof, be punished, as ordered by General Court Martial, in such manner as if he himself had committed the crimes or disorders complained of.[251]

In 1775 the Continental Congress adopted the American Articles of War and its article 12 resembled the Massachusetts provision for command responsibility. In September 1776 the Continental Congress revised its articles of war but the ninth article retained the language and thoughts of the previous directive on command responsibility.[252]

---

[249] *Mitchell v Harmony*, 54 US 115 (1851).

[250] The phrase "Tarleton's quarter" was coined by the rebels to mean "no quarter," i.e. "take no prisoners." It came into use after the Battle of the Waxhaws, where it was claimed that the British Legion slaughtered members of a defeated rebel army as they were attempting to surrender. The *Pennsylvania Archives* contains examples of other British massacres of defenseless men..

[251] Provisional Congress of Massachusetts, April 1775, Articles of War, art. 11

[252] Parks, William, "Command Responsibility for War Crimes" *Military Law Review*

Conditions changed little through the War of 1812. The British destruction of Washington, D.C., motivated by wanton destruction of private property along the north shores of Lake Erie by American forces in May1814, the most notable being the Raid on Port Dover. Both actions constituted a violation of the contemporary rules of civilized warfare.[253] The majority of British opinion believed that the burnings were justified following the damage that United States forces had done with its incursions into Canada and neither side considered attaching a penalty to the conduct of its armed forces.

The Civil War

In an effort to control the behavior of armies in the field, in the early 1860s the U. S. government attempted to codify the rules governing warfare. The United States adopted the results, a document, known as the Lieber Code, in 1863 at the outset of the Civil War. The Lieber Code of April 24, 1863, also known as *Instructions for the Government of Armies of the United States in the Field*, General Order № 100[254] or in short form the Lieber Instructions, was an order signed by President Abraham Lincoln to the Union Forces of the United States during the American Civil War that dictated how soldiers should conduct themselves in wartime.

The code was named after the German-American Francis Lieber (1800-1872), usually known as Franz Lieber, who was a jurist, gymnast and political philosopher. He edited an *Encyclopedia Americana* in 13 volumes, published between 1829 and 1833. Lieber was born in Berlin, fought in the Napoleonic Wars as a member of the Prussian Army, attempted to gain entrance to the University of Berlin, but was denied because he opposed the monarchy. He fought in the Greek War of Independence in 1821, moved to Italy, then England, and finally to Boston in 1827. In London he had married Mathilda Oppenheimer. He became a

---

62 (1973) 1: 4. See also Stryszak, Michael, "Command Responsibility" *U.S.A.F. Academy Journal of Legal Studies* 11 (2022) 27: 29-30.

253 Donald R. Hickey, *The War of 1812, A Forgotten Conflict*. University of Illinois Press, 1989.

254 *The War of the Rebellion: A Compilation of the Official Records of the Union and Confederate Armies,* (Washington, D.C.: Government Printing Office, 1899), Series III, 3: 148-164.

professor of history and political economics at South Carolina College, where he gained a dislike of the institution of slavery. As early as 1851, he delivered an address in South Carolina warning the southern states against secession. From 1856 until 1865, he was professor of history and political science at Columbia University. During the Civil War he headed a publication unit which wrote on behalf of the union. After the Civil War he collected and preserved the records of the Confederate States. From 1870 until his death in New York City, aged 72, Francis Lieber served as a diplomatic negotiator between the United States and Mexico.[255]

This code was a landmark document in the history of written international law regarding permissible national conduct during war. The Lieber Code influenced the Hague Regulations of 1907, which was the first important international treaty law on its subject. The main sections were concerned with martial law, military jurisdiction, and the treatment of spies, deserters and prisoners of war. The Lieber Code included practices that would be considered illegal by today's standards. In the event of the violation of the laws of war by an enemy, the Code permitted reprisal by musketry against the enemy's recently captured POWs. It also permitted the summary execution, likewise by musketry, of spies, saboteurs, *levees en masse*, and guerrilla forces, if caught in the act of carrying out their missions. It expressly forbade giving *no quarter* to the enemy, except in such cases where the there was an express threat to the survival of the unit that held these prisoners. It forbade the use of poisons; it prohibited the use of torture to extract confessions; and it delineated the rights and duties of prisoners of war and of capturing forces.

The Lieber Code mandated humane, ethical treatment of populations in occupied areas. Article 16 states, "Military necessity does not admit of cruelty; that is, the infliction of suffering for the sake of suffering or for revenge."[256] The code based its moral assumption of the existence of a reciprocal relationship between the population and the army.

---

[255] "Francis Lieber" in Wikipedia. See also Brown, Bernard Edward. *American Conservatives: The Political Thought of Francis Lieber and John W. Burgess.* New York: AMS Press, 1967

[256] *The War of the Rebellion: A Compilation of the Official Records of the Union and Confederate Armies,* (Washington, D.C.: Government Printing Office, 1899), Series III, 3: 148-164.

So long as the population did not resist military authority, it was to be well treated. However, if the inhabitants were to violate this contract by taking up arms and supporting guerrilla movements, then the army might apply much sterner measures, among which were the imposition of fines, the confiscation of private property, the destruction of such property, the imprisonment of civilians who aided guerrillas, the relocation of populations, the taking of hostages, and the execution of guerrillas who failed to abide by the laws of war as set down in the code.

One of the Code's principal aims was not to limit the Civil War, but to render legitimate its expansion in order to achieve full emancipation of the slaves. It also advocated a more aggressive war effort but along morally acceptable lines. It is apparent that commanders such as William Tecumseh Sherman rarely if ever consulted the Code in making combat decisions, the Code played a significant role nonetheless in the war's last two years. Its provisions regarding black soldiers bolstered the Union's decision to cease prisoner exchanges so long as the South refused to exchange black prisoners on equal terms with white ones.[257]

Civil wars attract the very worst of military behavior. The Civil War in America, 1861-1865 was no exception. Rarely are crimes in such conflicts punished. One can name many war crimes during the American Civil War. Even by standards of the mid-19th century Sheridan's raid through the Shenandoah Valley and what became known as Sherman's March to the Sea were war crimes of the highest order. These military campaigns were not aimed at destruction of enemy armies or supplies. Rather, they were designed to punish the civilians and terminate their support for the war. These two actions would seem to be clear violations of the Lieber Code.

However, Sherman did take action against one instance of wanton destruction of property. On July 24, 1863, Sherman arrested Captain William Keeler who had ordered the burning of a cotton gin. Keeler was court-martialed for arson, violation of a general order, and neglect of duty.[258] Keeler was acquitted, and Sherman disapproved the verdict,

---

[257]Witt, John F. *Lincoln's Code: The Laws of War in American History*. New York: Free Press, 2012, especially chapters 9 and 11.

[258]Eicher, David J., *The Longest Night: A Military History of the Civil War*. New York:

noting in a letter to General Grant that it was a "…volunteer court-martial tainted with the technicalities of our old civil courts."[259]

The Fort Pillow massacre marks one of the bleakest, saddest events of American military history. The Battle of Fort Pillow, also known as the Fort Pillow Massacre, was fought on April 12, 1864, at Fort Pillow on the Mississippi River in Henning, Tennessee. Fort Pillow was 40 miles north of Memphis. It was built by Confederate Brigadier General Gideon Johnson Pillow in early 1862 and was captured and used by both sides during the war. With the fall of New Madrid, Missouri, to Union forces, Confederate troops evacuated Fort Pillow on June 4, in order to avoid being cut off from the rest of the Confederate Army. Union forces occupied Fort Pillow on June 6, and used it to protect the river approach to Memphis. The Union garrison at Fort Pillow consisted of about 600 men, divided evenly between black and white troops. The black soldiers belonged to the 6th U.S. Regiment Colored Heavy Artillery and a section of the 2nd U.S. Colored Light Artillery (previously known as the Memphis Battery Light Artillery), under the command of Major Lionel F. Booth. Many of the black troops were former slaves and clearly understood the consequences of a loss to the Confederates. The best they could possibly hope for would have been an immediate return to slavery. No one considered their being treated as a prisoner of war. Some Confederates had already threatened to kill any Union black troops they encountered. Confederate officials such as President Jefferson Davis had announced that the South would treat black Union soldiers as criminals, subject to execution or re-enslavement upon capture.

Forrest arrived at Fort Pillow on April 12. By this time, Confederates had already surrounded the fort. He deployed sharpshooters around the higher ground that overlooked the fort, bringing many of the occupants into their direct line of fire. Major Booth was killed by a sharpshooter's bullet. By 11:00, the Confederates had captured two rows of barracks about 150 yards from the southern end of the fort. Heavy Confederate fire continued until 15:30, when Forrest sent a note demanding surrender, noting "Should my demand be refused, I cannot be

Simon & Schuster, 2001, 657.

[259]Kennett, Lee. *Sherman, A Soldier's Life*, Harper Collins, 2001, 225.

responsible for the fate of your command." Major William Bradford, now in command, replied, requesting an hour for consideration. Forrest, who believed that reinforcing Union troops would soon arrive by river, replied that he would only allow 20 minutes, adding that he was prepared to assault the fort. Bradford refused to surrender so Forrest ordered his bugler to sound the charge. The Confederate assault was furious.[260]

Both Union and Confederate sources claimed that even though the Union troops surrendered, Forrest's men massacred them in cold blood. Surviving members of the garrison said that most of their men surrendered and threw down their arms, only to be shot or bayoneted by the attackers, who repeatedly shouted, "No quarter! No quarter!" *The Joint Committee On the Conduct of the War* immediately investigated the incident and concluded that the Confederates shot most of the garrison after it had surrendered. There have been two modern studies which concluded that this was indeed a shameful massacre. But the Union took no judicial action against Forrest although this was a clear case of command responsibility.[261]

Even the re-enslavement of U.S.C.T. soldiers would have been a violation of the Lieber Code, Articles 42 and 43. Presumably, any Confederate officer attempting to return former slaves (and all Negroes were assumed to have been slaves) would have been guilty of abuse of command

> 42. Slavery, complicating and confounding the ideas of property, (that is of a thing,) and of personality, (that is of humanity,) exists according to municipal or local law only. The law of nature and nations has never acknowledged it. The Digest of the Roman Law enacts the early dictum of the pagan jurist, that "so far as the law of nature is concerned, all men are equal." Fugitives escaping from a country in which they were slaves, villains, or serfs, into another country, have, for centuries past, been held free and acknowledged free by judicial decisions of European countries, even though the municipal law of the

[260]Castel, Albert. "The Fort Pillow Massacre: A Fresh Examination of the Evidence." *Civil War History* 4 (March 1958); Ward, Andrew. *River Run Red: The Fort Pillow Massacre in the American Civil War*. New York: Viking Adult, 2005

[261]David J. Eicher, *The Longest Night: A Military History of the Civil War*. New York: Simon & Schuster, 2001, 657.

country in which the slave had taken refuge acknowledged slavery within its own dominions.

43. Therefore, in a war between the United States and a belligerent which admits of slavery, if a person held in bondage by that belligerent be captured by or come as a fugitive under the protection of the military forces of the United States, such person is immediately entitled to the rights and privileges of a freeman To return such person into slavery would amount to enslaving a free person, and neither the United States nor any officer under their authority can enslave any human being. Moreover, a person so made free by the law of war is under the shield of the law of nations, and the former owner or State can have, by the law of postliminy, no belligerent lien or claim of service.

Following the end of the American Civil War the sole trial for war crimes involved Captain Henry Wirz, M.D., commandant of Camp Sumter near Andersonville, Georgia. Known simply as Andersonville, this prison of war camp became known as the hell hole of the South. Of the 49,485 prisoners who entered the camp, nearly 13,000 died from disease and malnutrition. Henry Wirz was born in Zurich, Switzerland in 1822. After graduating from the University of Zurich he obtained medical degrees from Paris and Berlin. Wirz emigrated to the United States in 1849 when many were fleeing the Swiss Sonderbund War as well as the failed revolutions of 1848 in the German states and elsewhere. Dr. Wirz established a medical practice in Kentucky. He married a Methodist widow named Wolfe, and, along with her two daughters, he moved to Louisiana. In 1855 his wife gave birth to their daughter, Cora. By 1861, Wirz had established a successful medical practice.

At the outbreak of the American Civil War he joined the Confederate Army. As a sergeant in the Louisiana Volunteers, Wirz was badly wounded at the battle at Fair Oaks in May, 1862 and lost the use of his right arm. After returning to his unit on June 12, 1862, Wirz was promoted to Captain for bravery on the field of battle. Unable to continue in active service or medical practice, Wirz became a clerk at Libby Prison in Richmond. His commanding officer, Brigadier General John Henry Winder, was impressed by Wirz and promoted him to the rank of major.

Wirz spoke fluent English, German and Dutch, and on the advice of General John Henry Winder, President Jefferson Davis decided to send him on a secret mission to England and France. Davis made Captain Wirz a Special Minister and sent him to Europe carrying secret dispatches to the Confederate Commissioners, Mister Mason in England and Mister Slidell in France. When Wirz returned to America he rejoined General John Henry Winder, who was now in charge of all Union Army prisoners east of the Mississippi. During the summer of 1863 an agreement under which Union and Confederate captives were exchanged, came to an end. There was now a rapid increase in the number of prisoners and the Confederacy decided to build Andersonville Prison in Georgia. In April, 1864 Winder appointed Wirz as commandant of this new prison camp.

By August, 1864, there were 32,000 Union Army prisoners in Andersonville. The Confederate authorities were unable to provide enough food for the prison and men began to die of starvation. The inmates did not follow basic sanitary procedures water became polluted. Disease was a constant problem.

When the Union Army arrived in Andersonville in May, 1865, photographs of the prisoners were taken. The following month these photographs appeared in Harper's Weekly. The photographs caused considerable anger. The public demanded that the people responsible be punished for these outrages as war crimes. The Johnson Administration eventually decided to charge General Robert E. Lee, Confederate Secretary of War James Seddon, and several other Confederate generals and politicians with "conspiring to injure the health and destroy the lives of United States soldiers held as prisoners by the Confederate States."

In August, 1865 President Andrew Johnson ordered that the charges against the Confederate generals and politicians should be dropped. However, he did give his approval for Dr. Wirz to be charged with "wanton cruelty." Wirz appeared before a military commission headed by Major General Lew Wallace on 21st August, 1865. During the trial defense counsel showed a letter from Wirz in which he complained to his superiors about the shortage of food being provided for the prisoners. However, former inmates at Andersonville testified that Wirz inspected the prison every day and often warned that if any man escaped he would "starve every damn Yankee for it." Wirz fell ill during the trial but Wallace forced him to attend so Wirz was brought into court on a stretcher.

One of the pleas of the accused was that he merely acted as a subordinate in carrying out the orders of the commander of the post. The Judge Advocate admitted that the accused acted under orders, but replied, "A superior officer cannot order a subordinate to do an illegal act, and if a subordinate obey such an order and disastrous consequences result, both the superior and the subordinate must answer for it. General Winder could no more command the prisoner to violate the laws of war than could the prisoner do so without orders."

Wirz was found guilty on 6th November and sentenced to death. He was taken to Washington to be executed in the same yard where those involved in the assassination of Abraham Lincoln had died. Alexander Gardner, the famous photographer, was invited to record the event. The execution took place on the 10th November. The gallows were surrounded by Union Army soldiers who throughout the procedure chanted "Wirz, remember, Andersonville." Accompanied by a Catholic priest, Wirz refused to make a last-minute confession, claiming he was not guilty of committing any crime.

Major Russell read the death warrant and then told Wirz he "deplored this duty." Wirz replied that: "I know what orders are, Major. And I am being hanged for obeying them." The drop failed to break his neck and it took him two minutes to die. During this time the soldiers continued to chant: "Wirz, remember, Andersonville." To the Union, of course, Wirz was guilty of maltreatment of POWs and the torture of prisoners.[262]

Philippine Insurrection

Philippine occupation was the first war in which American officers and troops were officially charged with what we would now call war crimes. In 44 military trials, all of which ended in convictions, including that of General Jacob Smith, sentences, almost invariably, were light. Atrocities were committed on both sides. United States attacks into

---

[262]Page, James Madison. *The True Story of Andersonville Prison: A Defense of Major Henry Wirz.* Digital Scanning, 1999. See also Rutherford, Mildred L. *Facts and Figures versus Myths and Misrepresentations: Henry Wirz and the Andersonville Prison.* 1921; reprint by Pranava, 2018.

the countryside often included scorched earth campaigns in which entire villages were burned and destroyed, the use of torture, including the *water cure*; and the concentration of civilians into protected zones. The number of Filipino casualties was at the time, and still is, debated and politicized. One estimate concluded that some 34,000 Filipino soldiers lost their lives and that as many as 200,000 civilians may have died directly or indirectly as a result of the war.[263]

On September 22, 1901, two drunken American soldiers tried to molest a girl. Her two brothers rescued her but also mauled the soldiers. In retaliation, the Company Commander, Captain Thomas W. Connell rounded up 143 male residents, forcing them to clean up the town in preparation for an official visit by his superior officers. Connell detained the locals overnight without food. Connell retained 78 of the detainees, while he released 65 others due to age and physical infirmity. Finally, Connell ordered the confiscation of all bolo knives, and the destruction of stored rice. The townspeople plotted to attack the U.S. Army garrison. Valeriano Abanador, the local chief of police, and five other locals, and two guerrilla officers were involved in the plot. The lone woman plotter was Casiana "Geronima" Nacionales. About 500 men, representing virtually all families of Balangiga, took part. On September 28, Abanador grabbed Pvt. Adolph Gamlin's rifle and signaled the beginning of the revolt. They killed several Americans and freed their compatriots in the village square. A number of the men of C Company were able to arm themselves, retake the municipal hall, and fight back. The surviving Americans, led by Sergeant Frank Betron, then escaped by using native canoes. Capt. Edwin V. Bookmiller commanding the 9th US Infantry at Basey, commandeered a civilian coastal steamer, the *SS Pittsburg*, and with his men steamed to Balangiga. The town was deserted. The dead of Company C lay where they fell, many bearing horrible wounds. Bookmiller and his men burned the town to the ground. Of the original 74 man contingent, 48 died and 26 survived, 22 of them severely wounded.

[263] In 1908 Manuel Arellano Remondo, in *General Geography of the Philippine Islands*, wrote: "The population decreased due to the wars, in the five-year period from 1895 to 1900, since, at the start of the first insurrection, the population was estimated at 9,000,000, and at present (1908), the inhabitants of the Archipelago do not exceed 8,000,000 in number."

Media reports stated that many of the bodies were mutilated.[264]

President Theodore Roosevelt immediately ordered General Adna Chaffee to adopt "in no unmistakable terms," the "most stern measures to pacify Samar." [265] Chaffee's orders were largely responsible for the atrocities that marked the later stages of the war. In November 1901, the Manila correspondent of the a major newspaper reported: "The present war is no bloodless, *opera bouffe* engagement; our men have been relentless, have killed to exterminate men, women, children, prisoners and captives, active insurgents and suspected people from lads of ten up, the idea prevailing that the Filipino as such was little better than a dog. . . ."[266]

Under Chaffee's superior orders, American troops forced Filipino villagers into concentration camps. These camps were overcrowded and infected by various diseases. Conditions in these *reconcentrados* are generally acknowledged to have been inhumane. Men were frequently rounded up for questioning, tortured, and summarily executed. [267] In Batangas Province, where General Franklin Bell was responsible for setting up a concentration camp, a correspondent described the operation as "relentless." General Bell ordered that by December 25, 1901, the entire population of both Batangas Province and Laguna Province had to gather into small areas within their respective towns. Anything left behind was to be burned. Anyone found outside the concentration camps was shot.

The U.S. Army's retaliation measures included actions that resulted in the courts-martial of two field commanders, Brigadier General Jacob Smith (1840-1918)[268] and Marine Major Littleton Waller (1856-1926). After the massacre at Balangiga, General Smith had issued his infamous Circular No. 6, which stated his plans for crushing all resistance on the island "I want no prisoners" and "I wish you to kill and burn; and the more you burn and kill, the better it will please me." Then

---

[264]Boot, Max, *The Savage Wars of Peace: Small Wars and the Rise of American Power*. Basic Books, 2003, 204.

[265]*New York Times*, 30 September 1901.

[266]*Philadelphia Ledger*, 18 November 1901.

[267]Dumindin, Arnaldo, "The Last Holdouts: General Vicente Lukban Falls, February 18, 1902," *Philippine–American War, 1899–1902*, self-published, 2010.

[268]On 29 December 1890, as a cavalryman, Smith was present at Wounded Knee, South Dakota, when a massacre left about 300 Sioux men, women and children, and 29 Army soldiers dead

he tasked his men to reduce Samar into a wilderness, to kill anyone 10 years old and above capable of bearing arms.[269] General Smith and Major Waller underwent separate courts-martial for their roles in the suppressive campaign of November 1901 through January 1902. As a result of evidence introduced at the trial of Major Waller trial, General Smith was brought before a court martial, convicted, and admonished.[270] Several newspapers addressed him as "The Butcher Of Samar."[271] President Theodore Roosevelt personally ordered his dismissal from the army.[272] Roosevelt wrote,

> But the very fact that warfare is of such character as to afford infinite provocation for the commission of acts of cruelty by junior officers and enlisted men, must make the officers in high and responsible positions peculiarly careful in their bearing and conduct so as to keep a moral check over any acts of an improper character by their subordinates.[273]

Littleton "Tony" Waller Tazewell Waller was a career officer in thc Marine Corps, who served in the Spanish American War, the Philippines, the Caribbean and Asia. He retired from the Marines holding the rank of Major General. Brigadier General Jacob H. Smith asked for Marine Corps assistance to help subdue the Philippine population on the island of Samar. Major Waller and his Marine Battalion received the assignment. Waller received the "Kill all over ten" order from General Smith, but Major Waller countermanded it, telling his men not to obey it. Waller largely ignored these illegal orders. Waller and his battalion of 315 Marines departed Cavite on 22 October 1901 and landed at Catbalogan, Samar, on 24 October. In the southern half of Samar, Waller ran patrols, amphibious operations, and led a detachment of marines which defeated Philippine insurgents in a battle at Sohoton cliffs on 5 November 1901. He was having some success in registering the inhabitants and pacifying the Philippine towns.

---

[269] *New York Journal*, 5 May 1902.

[270] http://www.answers.com/topic/jacob-hurd-smith; "Jacob H. Smith" in Wikipedia.

[271] Arnaldo Dumindin, "Philippine-American War, 1899-1902," self-published, n.d.

[272] Fitz, David L., "Before the "Howling Wilderness": The Military Career of Jacob Hurd Smith, 1862-1902" *Military Affairs*, 43: 4 (December, 1979).

[273] In "Court Martial of General Jacob H. Smith" reprinted in Leon Friedman, *The Law of War: A Documentary History*. Abbey, 1977, 799

General Smith ordered Waller to scout a possible telegraph route across the island from Lanang on the east coast to Basey on the west coast, straight across trackless jungle. Waller's March across Samar began from Lanang on 28 December 1901 with 60 Marines, including Sgt. John H. Quick, two Philippine scouts and 33 Philippine porters. In terrible physical conditions, most of the men were soon sick and running out of food. To stave off disaster, Major Waller divided his force on 3 January 1902. Leaving Marine Captain David D. Porter in charge of a group remaining in the jungle, Waller and 14 others went for help at Basey, arriving there on 6 January. On 7 January, Waller led a relief operation back to Porter, but for nine days could not find them.

Growing more desperate for food, Captain Porter left the sick and dying behind, under the command of Marine Lieutenant A.S. Williams, and set out with 7 Marines and 6 porters to Lanang. Having arrived at Lanang on 11 January, Cpt. Porter then sent out a relief column to pick up his own stragglers and rescue Lt. William's command. By 18 January, when Williams was rescued, 10 marines had died, one had gone insane and the porters had mutinied. Williams later testified that their mutinous behavior left the Marines in daily fear of their lives; the porters were hiding food and supplies from the Marines and keeping themselves nourished from the jungle while the Marines starved; then three porters attacked and wounded Williams with a bolo knife. The other 11 porters were placed under arrest when Williams' command reached Lanang. Waller reported the executions to Smith, as he had reported every other event. "It became necessary to expend eleven prisoners. Ten who were implicated in the attack on Lieutenant Williams and one who plotted against me." Smith passed Waller's report to General Adna Chaffee. For some reason, Chaffee decided to investigate these executions, despite General J. Franklin Bell and Colonel Jacob H. Smith having carried out similar executions on a much larger scale months before with no subsequent investigations.

After an investigation, Waller ordered the summary execution, without trial, of the eleven Filipino porters for treason, theft, disobedience and general mutiny. Ten were shot in groups of three (one had been gunned down in the water attempting to escape) The bodies were left in the square as an example, until one evening under cover of darkness, some townspeople carried them off for a Christian burial. Waller's Marine Battalion on Samar was relieved by U.S. Army units on 26 February 1902. He and his Battalion left Samar on 29 February, returning to Cavite on 2 March 1902.

Waller was tried for murder in ordering the execution of the eleven Filipino porters. A court martial began on March 17, 1902. The court-martial board consisted of 7 Army officers and 6 Marine Corps officers, led by U.S. Army General William H. Bisbee. Waller's attorney, Commander Adolph Marix, USN, first argued that the Army had no jurisdiction over him, as he was still under Marine Corps command. General Bisbee initially agreed that the court was without jurisdiction in the case, but then reversed himself and held Major Waller for trial. The court martial board voted 11-2 for acquittal of Major Waller. Later, the U.S. Army Judge Advocate General dismissed the entire case, agreeing that a Marine Corps officer was not subject to an Army court.[274] Public outcry in America over the brutal nature of the Samar campaign cost Waller his chance to command the US Marine Corps.

The United States Senate Investigating Committee on the Philippines was convened from January 31, 1902 after word of the Army's Samar pacification campaign reached Washington. Chaired by Senator Henry Cabot Lodge, the committee heard testimony concerning crimes that had allegedly been committed by U.S. troops and officers in the Philippines. The policies behind the U.S. occupation were also examined. For six months officers and political figures involved in the Philippine adventure, both pro and anti-imperialists, testified as to the brutal nature of American anti-insurgent operations. Although attempts were made to justify the amount of damage U.S. troops were doing, as well as the number of Filipino lives lost, the evidence provided by several individuals was damning. Committee proceedings adjourned on June 28, 1902. For two months after that the legal team presenting evidence for the committee compiled its report. This report was released on August 29, 1902.[275]

---

[274] "Littleton Waller". *Hall of Valor*. Military Times. http://www.militarytimes.com/citations-medals-awards/recipient.php?recipientid=3429; Miller, op. cit.; "Littleton Waller" Wikipedia.

[275] *Manila Times*, 4 November 1901.

The report was a damning indictment of U.S. policy in the Philippines and the almost criminal conduct of the war by War Secretary Elihu Root, who multiple times had expressed support for the extreme measures implemented by the U.S. Army. The report found that the destruction of Filipino life during the war has been so frightful that it cannot be explained as the result of ordinary civilized warfare; that at the outset of the war there was strong reason to believe that our troops were ordered by some officers to give no quarter, and that no investigation was had; that the War Department never made any earnest effort to investigate charges of offenses or to stop illegal practices; that the Secretary of War never made any attempt to check, or punish, illicit methods of making war; and that from a very early day torture has been employed systematically to obtain information.[276]

Army General Otis stated that Filipino insurgents tortured American prisoners in "fiendish fashion." According to Otis, many were buried alive or were placed up to their necks in ant hills. He said others had their genitals removed and stuffed into their mouths and were then executed by suffocation or bleeding to death. There were also reports that Spanish priests were horribly mutilated before their congregations, and natives who refused to support Emilio Aguinaldo were slaughtered by the thousands.[277]

In 1909 two Filipino insurrectionists were brought to trial for war crimes based on the principle of command responsibility. Lieutenant Natalio Valencia received the death penalty for ordering the execution of a non-combatant. An American supervised court found Pedro A. Cruz, known only as a "guerrilla leader," guilty of permitting the murder of two American POWs. Assuming Cruz really was in command of his ragged band, his trial was based on his responsibility for the execution of American prisoners under his control by men over whom he retained command.[278]

---

[276] "War Crimes in the Philippines" http://www.worldfuturefund.org.

[277] Miller, Stuart Creighton, *Benevolent Assimilation: The American Conquest of the Philippines, 1899–1903*, Yale University Press, 1982, 89-93..

[278] Parks, *op. cit.,* 8; Stryszak, *op. cit.,* 32.

My Lai Massacre

On 16 March 1968 in Viet Nam soldiers from the United States massacred as many as 500 unarmed civilians, including old men, women, children. For a brief time there was a successful cover-up of that massacre. The American military suspected Quang Ngai Province, of being a Viet Cong stronghold. Thus the U. S. targeted the province for the first major American combat operation of the war. Military officials had declared the province a free-fire zone and subjected it to frequent bombing missions and artillery attacks. By the end of 1967, most of the dwellings in the province had been destroyed and nearly 140,000 civilians left homeless. Not surprisingly, the native population had come to distrust Americans

One combat unit assigned to Quang Ngai was led by Lt. Col. Frank Barker, Jr. Its mission was to pressure the Viet Cong in one area of the province. One combat outfit was Charlie Company, whose commanding officer was Ernest Medina, a thirty-three-year-old Mexican-American from New Orleans. One of the platoon leaders was twenty-four-year-old William Calley. On March 14, a small squad from Charlie Company ran into a booby trap, killing a sergeant, blinding one soldier, and wounding several others. After the funeral service, Captain Medina gave his soldiers a pep talk and discussed the next mission. He told them that the Viet Cong's crack 48th Battalion was in the vicinity of My Lai 4, and that the hamlet would be the target of a large-scale assault. Their mission would be to engage the 48th Battalion and to destroy the village of My Lai. Medina said that 7 A.M., the women and children would have left the hamlet and that all they could expect to find would be the enemy. The soldiers were to explode brick homes, set fire to thatch homes, shoot livestock, poison wells, and generally annihilate the enemy. Aerial gunships would support the 75 men. Medina's orders may have been vague although some soldiers recalled that Medina had ordered them to kill every person in My Lai Four.

The assault plan called for Lt. Calley's first platoon and Lt. Stephen Brooks' second platoon to sweep into the village, while a third platoon, under Captain Medina would be held in reserve. What they encountered was a group of 700 civilians. Initially there were few killings, but by 8 A.M. Calley's platoon had gathered a larger number in the town square. Calley told Private Paul Meadlo to kill them all. Meadlo and Calley began firing into the group from a distance of ten to fifteen feet, leaving few survivors. Meadlo was later to become a star witness in the ensuing courts martial. What Captain Medina knew of these war crimes is not certain. Medina later testified that he did not enter the village until 10 A.M., well after the shooting had stopped, and that he did not personally witness a single civilian being killed. Other witnesses placed Medina in the village closer to 9 A.M., and closer to the scene of many of the murders as they were happening.

Army photographer Ronald Haeberle said he saw about thirty different GIs kill about 100 civilians. Army helicopter pilot Chief Warrant Officer Hugh Thompson arrived in the My Lai vicinity about 9 A.M. and noticed dead and dying civilians all over the village. Thompson attempted to halt the carnage and later reported the wanton killings to brigade headquarters.[279] Twenty months later army investigators would discover three mass graves containing the bodies of about 500 villagers.

Meanwhile, Ronald Ridenhour, a private from Phoenix, learned what had happened at My Lai 4. Ridenhour was serving in a reconnaissance unit in Duc Pho, where he first heard five eyewitness accounts of the My Lai massacre. He started his own investigation, beginning with confirmation that Charlie Company had in fact been in My Lai. Ridenhour was shocked by what he learned and he made certain that the incident came to the attention of the American people. After his discharge he wrote to many public officials. Only Congressman Morris Udall, showed interest and he pushed for a full investigation of Ridenhour's allegations.

By late April, Army Chief of Staff General William Westmoreland turned the case over to the Inspector General for investigation. Over the next few months, it interviewed dozens of witnesses and it soon became apparent that war crimes had been committed. In June, 1969, William Calley was flown back from Viet Nam to appear in a line-up for identification.

On September 5, the Army filed formal charges, included six

---

[279] Trent Angers, *The Forgotten Hero of My Lai: The Hugh Thompson Story*. Acadian House, 1999

specifications of premeditated murder, against Calley. William Calley hired as his attorney George Latimer, a Salt Lake City lawyer. Latimer had considerable military experience, having once served on the Military Court of Appeals. Latimer pronounced himself impressed with Calley, noting that if Calley was guilty of anything it was only carefully and enthusiastically following orders.

In November, 1969, the American public began to learn the details of what happened at My Lai 4. Both *Time* and *Newsweek* ran the story with full coverage. Mike Wallace did an interview with Paul Meadlo. Journalist Seymour Hersh published in depth accounts based on his own extensive interviews.[280] *Life* magazine published Haeberle's graphic photographs. This raised questions on whether Calley could possibly receive a fair trial. There were, however, those who supported Calley.[281]

The Nixon Administration decided on a holding a closed-door investigation headed by William Peers, three-star general. For four months the Peers Panel interviewed 398 witnesses, ranging from General Koster to the GIs of Charlie Company, amounting to over 20,000 pages of testimony. Most of the enlisted men who allegedly committed war crimes were no longer members of the military, and were thus immune from prosecution by court-martial.[282] The Army decided to prosecute twenty-five officers and enlisted men, including General Koster, Colonel Oran Henderson, Captain Medina. In the end, only Medina and Calley were tried. According to the Peers Report, General Samuel Koster, the most senior officer, who failed to report known civilian casualties and conducted a clearly inadequate investigation found that the charges against him were dropped. Under the theory of command responsibility Koster received only a letter of censure and a reduction in rank for his part.[283]

---

[280]Articles on My Lai Massacre, Including: Colin Powell, William Calley, Seymour Hersh, Hugh Thompson, Jr., Lawrence Colburn, Glenn Andreotta. Hephaestus Books, 2011; Seymour Hersh, *Chain of Command.* Allen Lane, 2004.

[281]Greenhaw, Wayne, *The Making of a Hero: The Story of Lieut. William Calley, Jr.* Louisville: Tochstone, 1971; John Sack, *Lieutenant Calley: His Own Story*. Tempo Books, 1971.

[282]*Toth vs Quarles*, 350 U.S. 11 [1955] held that military courts cannot try former members of the armed services "no matter how intimate the connection between the offense and the concerns of military discipline."

[283]"Peers Report". http://www.law.umkc.edu/faculty/projects/ftrials/mylai/medina.html

On 16 March, Colonel Oran Henderson received reports of action over My Lai so he joined the crew of a helicopter for a reconnaissance flight. That same afternoon Hugh Thompson and his gunner Larry Colburn reported the killing of civilians at My Lai. Yet another report of civilian executions arrived later that same afternoon. On 24 April Henderson reported that 18 civilians had accidentally been killed. On 25 April he instructed Colonel Barker to review his findings. Barker's investigation concurred with Henderson's.

The Peers Report found that Colonel Henderson had committed grievous errors which come under command responsibility. When briefed on the concept of the operation of Colonel Barker into the Son My area, he did not insure that the plan included provisions for handling, screening, and treatment of noncombatants and refugees. After observing the bodies of non-combatants in and around My Lai Four during the morning of 16 March, and despite his knowledge that C Company had not encountered resistance, he failed to take effective action to prevent further killing of noncombatants by C Company. He failed to take any action to ensure that medical treatment was provided to noncombatants in the Son My area on 16 March. After C Company had reported killing 84 VC in My Lai 4 by 0840 hours, he either participated in or condoned the making of fictitious reports to higher headquarters and false entries in official records to the effect that 69 VC had been killed by artillery at a location north of My Lai 4. Having observed on 16 March that many of the dwellings and other structures in My Lai 4 were being burned in violation of division policy and the provisions of pertinent directives, he failed to take any effective action to stop such destruction and report the facts to higher headquarters. Having observed the bodies of women and children in and around My Lai 4, and after receiving subsequent reports and information on the same day indicating that many additional noncombatants may have been killed by artillery or gunship, he failed to initiate an immediate investigation to determine the extent and the causes of the casualties. Colonel Henderson then made a series of false and misleading reports to his commanding officer to the effect that he had made a thorough investigation of the Thompson Report and he had interrogated all of the commanders and many of the soldiers and aviation personnel involved. He also lied when he said Warrant Officer Thompson was the only person he had found who had seen anything unusual on 16 March and that there was no substance to Thompson's allegations. He gave false testimony before the Inquiry in a manner calculated to mislead this Inquiry in many particulars. He thus had concealed the existence of war crimes.[284]

Brought up before a court martial and charged with lying in his initial report and thus covering up the massacre, he was acquitted of all charges on December 17, 1971. He died on 5 June 1988.[285] Of 13 officers and enlisted men who were originally charged with the killings in My Lai, eight cases were dismissed and there were four acquittals before the Medina verdict.

Captain Ernest L. Medina now faced charges of murdering 102 Vietnamese civilians, based on the prosecution's theory of command responsibility. Captain Medina did not order the mass killings at My Lai but he "calculatingly chose not to intervene" while his troops were killing unarmed civilians, the military prosecutor said in opening the Government's case against the officer. The prosecutor, Major William G. Eckhardt, made it clear that the Government's strategy in seeking Captain Medina's conviction on a charge of premeditated murder would rely heavily for precedence on the World War II trial of Gen. Tomayuki Yamashita. Major Eckhardt said the Government would prove that Captain Medina knew that noncombatants were being rounded up and killed and did nothing to halt the "carnage." By failing to intervene, Captain Medina intended to give "protection and encouragement to his men in the perpetration of murder," the prosecutor charged.[286]

Captain Medina, as the officer in charge of Charlie Company was required to be accountable for the actions of the men under his command. The prosecution, led by Major William Eckhardt, argued that Medina had known that a massacre was taking place and had done nothing to stop it, and therefore he should be found guilty of murder. Medina was originally charged also with dereliction of duty for participating in the cover-up, but

---

284 http://law2.umkc.edu/faculty/projects/ftrials/mylai/Henderson.html contains the Peers Report "The Omissions and Commissions of Col. Oran K. Henderson."

285 Douglas Linder, "Biography of Oran Henderson". Law.umkc.edu; *Baltimore Sun*, 5 June 1988.

286 Homer Bigart in *New York Times*, 17 August 1971.

the offense was dropped because the statute of limitations had expired. Medina was subjected to a lie-detector test which tended to show he responded truthfully when he said that he did not intentionally suggest to his men that they kill unarmed civilians. A like test undermined his contention that he first heard of the killing of unarmed civilians about 10 to 10:30 A.M. It appeared that in fact he knew civilians were being killed sometime between 8 A.M. and 9 A.M., at which point there would still have been time to prevent many civilian deaths. The prosecution was unable to get the damaging lie-detector evidence admitted as evidence. The prosecution bitterly denounced Medina in the its summation as an officer who had abrogated his responsibility, and who "like Pontius Pilate cannot wash the blood from his hands." The military judge, Col. Kenneth A. Howard reduced the charge of killing 100 civilians from premeditated murder to involuntary manslaughter. Colonel Howard also dismissed the charge that Captain Medina had murdered a child.[287]

A millionaire named Glenn W. Turner who thought Captain Medina to be innocent of the charges contributed heavily to his defense and hired a top-notch lawyer. Medina's defense attorney F. Lee Bailey, conducted a highly successful defense, forcing the prosecution to drop key witnesses and keeping damaging evidence, notably Ronald Haeberle's photographs, from the jury. After fifty-seven minutes of deliberation, the jury acquitted Medina on all charges. Months later, when a perjury prosecution was no longer possible, Medina admitted that he had suppressed evidence and lied to the brigade commander about the number of civilians killed.[288] Of 13 officers and enlisted men who were originally charged with the killings in My Lai, eight cases were dismissed and there were four acquittals before the Medina verdict.

The strongest government case was that against Lt. William Calley. The trial began on 12 November 1970 in Fort Benning, Georgia. The prosecutor was Captain Aubrey Daniel who appeared before the panel of six military officers. evidence he would ask them to "in the name of justice" convict the accused of all charges. Daniel built the prosecution's case methodically although not a single witness directly placed Calley at the

---

[287]Bigart in *New York Times*, 23 September 1971.

[288]*United States v. Captain Ernest L. Medina*. Law.umkc.edu.

scene of a shooting. Daniel succeeded in having Ronald Haeberle's photographs admitted. In the second week of the trial Daniel began to call his more incriminating witnesses, men who did place Calley at the scene. They also described him killing civilians and also ordering others to do so. Some men testified that they had refused to carry out such orders.

The prosecution's final witness was also its most anticipated person. The Army had promised Paul Meadlo immunity from prosecution in return for his testimony in the Calley case. However, when he was called earlier in the trial, Meadlo had refused to answer questions about the incident, claiming his fifth amendment right against self-incrimination. Daniel called Meadlo to the stand for a second time, and Judge Kennedy warned Meadlo that if he refused to answer questions, U. S. marshals would take him into custody. Meadlo told the jury that Calley had left him with a large group of mostly women and children saying, "You know what to do with them, Meadlo." Meadlo thought Calley meant he should guard the people, which he did. When Calley returned a few minutes later he demanded that they kill all. They forced many into a large drainage ditch and Calley fired from 250 to 300 bullets into the ditch.

The defense employed two main strategies. First, it suggested that the stress of combat impaired Calley's thinking to such a degree that he could not be found guilty of premeditated murder. Here, Latimer relied on New York psychiatrist Dr. Albert LaVerne to sustain this assertion. Second, the defense claimed that Calley was merely following orders. Captain Ernest Medina had ordered that civilians found in My Lai 4 be killed and he was the real villain in the tragedy. Calley told the jury he could not remember taking a single army class on the Geneva Convention, but that he did know he could be court-martialed for refusing to obey an order. He testified that Medina had said the night before that there would be no civilians in My Lai, only the enemy. He said that while he was in the village, Medina called and asked why he had not yet killed the civilians. Captain Ernest Medina was called as a witness and he directly disputed Calley's testimony. In summary, Defense Attorney Latimer argued that Medina was lying about not giving the order to kill civilians, that Medina knew perfectly well what was going on in the village, and now he and the Army were now trying to make Calley the scapegoat.

After thirteen days of deliberations, the longest in U. S. court-martial history, the jury returned its verdict: guilty of premeditated murder on all specifications. After hearing pleas on the issue of punishment, jury head Colonel Clifford Ford pronounced Calley's sentence: "To be confined at hard labor for the length of your natural life; to be dismissed from the service; to forfeit all pay and allowances."[289] The public overwhelmingly disapproved of the verdict in the Calley case so President Nixon ordered Calley removed from the stockade and placed under house arrest. He announced that he would personally review the decision although not much came of that. Lieutenant General Albert O. Connor, the commanding the Third Army ordered Lieutenant Calley's life sentence reduced to 20 years. That decision meant that Lieutenant Calley would be eligible for parole in six to seven years. On 9 November 1974, the Army announced that William Calley would be paroled.

The Bales Case

On the night of March 10-11, 2012, Staff Sergeant Robert Bales reportedly left his base in Kandahar Province, Afghanistan, fully armed and unchallenged by base security. Then he allegedly murdered 16 innocent civilians in a nearby village. At a pretrial hearing, Lieutenant Colonel Joseph Morse testified that Bales went from house to house, firing his weapon with apparent intent to kill. At one point 11 bodies, mostly women and children, were "put in a pile and put on fire." The shootings are the worst case of civilian slaughter blamed on an individual U.S. soldier since the Vietnam War. The prosecution is seeking the death penalty. Various witnesses testified that. Bales, who was then serving on his fourth combat tour, had been upset over an incident that occurred 2 days earlier in which an improvised explosive device [IED] exploded, causing one U.S. soldier to lose the lower part of a leg.[290]

The murder of the 16 Afghan civilians in March came soon after another incident in February 2012, when American troops on Bagram airbase burned copies of the Koran. Riots ensued, leaving three NATO

---

[289] Everett, Arthur et al. *Calley: The Full Compelling Story of a Case as Bitterly Controversial as the Vietnam War Itself.* Dell/Associated Press N.Y., 1971.

[290] "Sgt Robert Bales: The story of the soldier accused of murdering 16 Afghan villagers." *The Telegraph*, 17 March 2012.

soldiers dead. Almost two weeks later, the sixteen Afghan civilians were murdered in what appears to have been a retaliatory strike, also a war crime. The fact that the commander of US and NATO forces in Afghanistan warned troops against carrying out retaliatory attacks could only mean that General Allen was fully aware of the possibility of retaliatory strikes and greatly concerned about the possibility of retaliatory strikes being carried out. Did General Allan do everything in his power, by taking action to prevent retaliatory strikes from being carried out on the civilian population of Afghanistan?

On 23 March 2012 Bales was formally charged with seventeen counts of murder and six counts of assault and attempted murder. He is currently being held in detention at the Midwest Joint Regional Correctional Facility in Fort Leavenworth, Kansas. On 18 December 2012 the U.S. Army referred Bales' case to court martial and will seek the death penalty.[291]

Bales had no history of mental disorder, and had undergone an expansive mental health screening to become a sniper in 2008. In 2010 he suffered a concussion in a car accident, underwent traumatic brain injury treatment at Fort Lewis, and was deemed healthy. Investigators examining his medical history described his 10-year Army career as "unremarkable" and found no evidence of serious traumatic brain injury or post-traumatic stress. As reported in told *The New York Times*, "When it all comes out, it will be a combination of stress, alcohol and domestic issues - he just snapped."[292]

---

[291] *New York Times*, 19 December 2012.
[292] *New York Times*. 15 March 2012.

6
Command Responsibility in Municipal Courts

By the very nature of international law it is fully applicable to states and theoretically exists on a higher level and is superior to municipal law. It is thus wholly desirable that states would choose to apply international law to circumstances within their boundaries and make their citizens responsible under it. Before there were international courts international law, like any and all law, could be imposed only by municipal courts. Even with the existence of international courts, especially the ICC, states are free to hold their own trials invoking international law.

The Boer War

The Anglo-Boer Wars, known to the Afrikaans as *Vryheidsoorloë* "(freedom wars,)" were two conflicts fought between 1880-1881 and again between 1899-1902 and pitted the British Empire against the Dutch settlers of two independent Boer republics, Orange Free State and the Transvaal Republic. The First Anglo-Boer War (1880–1881), was a rebellion of Boers farmers against British rule in the Transvaal that briefly re-established their independence. The British had annexed Transvaal in 1877 and naturally the Boers were angered. In 1877, the native Pedi had attacked the Boers of Transvaal who claimed that the British had not adequately assisted them. The British used force to bring Transvaal by force into a union. The British defeat by Zulus in 1879 at the Battle of Isandlwana had encouraged Boers to armed resistance. This war was over relatively quickly and resulted in a British victory.[293]

The Second War (1899–1902), by contrast, was a lengthy war that involved large numbers of troops, especially from British possessions. The

[293]Scholtz, Leopold. *Why the Boers Lost the War*. Basingstoke: Palgrave-Macmillan, 2005.

British fought directly against the Transvaal and the Orange Free State, defeating their forces first in open warfare and then in a long and bitter guerrilla campaign. British losses were high due to both disease and combat. The Boer policy of scorched earth provoked British response. The British created civilian internment in concentration camps to prevent support for the guerrilla fighters. This ravaged the civilian populations, news of which led to a significant erosion of support for the war in Britain. It ended with the conversion of the Boer republics into British colonies. These colonies later formed part of the Union of South Africa.

Harry Morant, an Australian; Peter Handcock, another Australian' and Edward Witton, a native of Great Britain, were charged with killing a German missionary who was allegedly carrying messages among the Boers, killing Boer prisoners who were caught wearing British uniforms, and killing of Boer POWs. Defense was provided by an Australian solicitor who had never defended a criminal, let alone capital, case where as the prosecution brought several high- powered and experienced barristers. The defense relied on the argument that the lieutenants were just following superior orders. It claimed that Lord Horatio Herbert Kitchener (1850-1916) had decided that the Boer guerrilla warfare required no adhesion to the customary laws of land warfare and had ordered that Boer prisoners be shot. Prosecution refused to allow Kitchener's appearance, but placed one Colonel John Hamilton on the witness stand. Hamilton denied that such orders existed. The two Australians lieutenants were summarily executed and the British lieutenant was sentenced to penal servitude for life. Mitten quietly received a pardon several years later and then wrote his account of the trial. The post war trial has become famous because of the movie *Breaker Morant* [1980], directed by Bruce Beresford, and made by the South Australia Film Company. The film was based heavily on *Scapegoats of the Empire* by Edward Witton, the young British lieutenant who was spared the death penalty in the proceedings.[294] The film has revived interest in Harry "Breaker" Morant and has spawned a number of studies and biographies.[295]

---

[294]Witton, Edward, *Scapegoats of the Empire: The True Story of Breaker Morant's Bushveldt Carbineers*. Clock & Rose Press, 2003 reprint.

[295]Bleszynski, Nick. *Shoot Straight You Bastards: The Truth Behind the Killing of*

The execution of Boer prisoners caught wearing British khaki was certainly defensible. The prosecution had attempted to make a distinction between wearing British uniforms with the intention of deceiving and merely using that clothing because they lacked other clothing. As late as World War II, the Allies executed without trial German soldiers caught wearing uniforms of any of the Allies. The execution of the missionary and prisoners of war were acts that violated the conduct of land warfare even in that time. The British government could have been charged with mistreatment of POWs for placing them in harm's way, as in putting them in carts in front of railroad engines to prevent mining of rails. The concentration camps were marginally legal, but were certainly run in cruel and inhuman fashion.[296]

Human Rights Trials in Argentina

The "Dirty War" in Argentina began when President Juan Peron died in 1974 and was succeeded by his second wife, Isabel Peron. Fighting between the Montoneros, an armed group coming out of the left wing of the Peronist movement, and security forces gave a pretext for Mrs. Peron to decree special repressive powers. The military took this as an opportunity to seize power, deposing Mrs. Peron in 1974 and setting up its own dictatorship under the name of "National Reorganization Process." The military, aided by the extreme rightist Argentine Anticommunist Army (AAA) moved to crush not only the Montoneros and other armed groups but all opposition to the Argentine ruling class and political right. Under the military dictatorship headed by General Jorge Videla, as many as 30,000 labor, peasant, student, and human rights activists were hunted down and killed or "disappeared," with many others imprisoned or driven into exile. The Videla regime cooperated in this with a number of other forces. Allied in "Operation Condor" with like-minded dictatorships in neighboring countries, it connived in the murder of many figures of the Latin American left. French experts helped the Argentine military develop

---

Breaker Morant. Green Earth Books, 1997; Kit Denton, *The Breaker*. St. Martins, 1997; F. M. Cutlack, *Breaker Morant: A Horseman Who Made History*. Smith, 1980.

[296]Wilcox, Craig, *Australia's Boer War: The War in South Africa 1899-1902*. Oxford University Press 2002.

the use of torture in interrogations. In 1986 and 1987 President Carlos Menem persuaded the legislature to issue sweeping amnesties, later reversed by legislative action.[297]

Several important human rights cases have emanated from Argentina regarding the military dictatorship of 1976-1983. Trials reopened in 2003 after Congress annulled the 1986 "Full Stop" law, which had stopped prosecution of such cases, and the 1987 "Due Obedience" law, which granted immunity in such cases to all members of the military except for those in positions of command. In 2005, the Supreme Court upheld the unconstitutionality of the amnesty laws, originally decided by a judge in 2001 in a case brought by CELS and Abuelas de Plaza de Mayo. Starting in 2005, federal judges struck down pardons that then-President Carlos Menem issued between 1989 and 1990 to former officials convicted of or facing trial for human rights violations. As of October 2011, according to the Center for Legal and Social Studies (CELS), 379 cases involving killings, "disappearances," and torture (in which CELS participated) were under judicial investigation or being tried in court. Of 1,774 alleged perpetrators, 749 were facing charges for these crimes, and 210 had been convicted.

In March 2011 the First Federal Oral Court sentenced an army general to life imprisonment and three agents to prison terms between 20 and 25 years for the murder, torture, and illegal arrest of detainees. Their prisoners had been held in the 1970s in a secret detention center known as Automotores Orletti located in Buenos Aires. It was the first conviction in Argentina of participants in Plan Condor, a scheme by which the military rulers of the region coordinated the abduction, interrogation, and "disappearance" of political opponents. Torture and ill-treatment were common problems.[298]

The Navy Mechanics School (ESMA) cases began in 2007, when a single defendant, former coast guard officer Héctor Febres, was tried. Febres committed suicide in his cell just four days before the verdict was to be handed down. Then in 2011, 16 of 18 defendants in another ESMA trial were convicted. According to government figures, 14,000 people

---

[297] *Washington Post*, 29 November 2012.

[298] http://www.hrw.org/world-report-2012/argentina

were forcibly disappeared during the dictatorship, although some human rights organizations have placed the number as high as 30,000.

The biggest trial for human rights crimes committed by Argentina's 1976-1983 dictatorship began in late 2012 in Buenos Aires. Some 68 people were accused of crimes involving nearly 800 victims of the Navy Mechanics School (ESMA). For the first time, six pilots who flew the so-called "death flights" will be tried. These flights dumped political prisoners from planes, drugged but alive, into the ocean. The planes often flew out over the turbid Rio de la Plata or over the Atlantic Ocean. Once over the water, prisoners were stripped naked and pushed one by one out of the cargo door of the plane, according to Adolfo Scilingo, a pilot who confessed in 1990 and is serving a sentence of 1,084 years in a Spanish prison. In total, eight pilots are accused of involvement in "death flights."[299]

The state charged the defendants with the kidnapping, torture, and participation in the disappearance of hundreds of victims. Some 5000 prisoners had been held in ESMA, the regime's biggest clandestine prison center. Of the defendants fifty-six belonged to the navy, and five belonged to the coast guard. There were also former members of the army, the police and the penitentiary service. Two civilians, lawyer Gonzalo Torres de Tolosa and former finance secretary Juan Alemann, were indicted. Five of the defendants are fugitives from justice. The national program for the search for wanted suspects offers a 100,000 peso award for information leading to their arrest.

The defendants include former navy captains Alfredo Astíz and Jorge Acosta, who were already convicted of other ESMA crimes. Acosta was also found guilty this year of involvement in stealing babies who were either born to political prisoners in detention or kidnapped along with their parents, who were later killed or "disappeared." The children were mainly raised by military or police families. In 1998, the government discovered that he had a secret Swiss bank account which may have been used to keep goods stolen from the "*desaparecidos*." He is also sought by Italy for crimes committed during the dictatorship against Italian citizens. He was sentenced to life imprisonment by one Argentine court on October 26,

---

[299] *Christian Science Monitor*, 7 December 2012

2011. He was sentenced to 30 years imprisonment by another Argentine court on July 5, 2012 for the systematic theft of babies from political prisoners.[300]

The case is the largest since the human rights trials got underway in Argentina again. The legislature had declared that the amnesty laws and pardons that had shielded human rights violators were unconstitutional. "This will be the biggest trial so far, because of the number of victims, defendants, and witnesses," said Carolina Varsky, a lawyer with the Centre for Legal and Social Studies (CELS), a human rights group taking part in the case. Varsky, the director of litigation in CELS, explained that the case had come to trial in bits and pieces, which she said "hid the true magnitude of the genocide committed" in ESMA.

One of the survivors who have most often testified is Mario Villani, a 73-year-old physicist who lived in Miami, Florida, at the time of the trial. Villani was kidnapped in 1977, and held in five different detention and torture centers, for a total of three years and eight months. ESMA was the last. Villani was tortured and forced to carry out different tasks during his detention. He gave his testimony to the National Commission on the Disappearance of Persons, and testified in the trials held after the dictatorship came to an end, in the 1980s, which were cut short by the amnesty laws and pardons of the members of the military junta. Since then he had provided his testimony in trials in Argentina, France, Italy, Spain, Germany and Israel. The testimony Villani and other survivors have given has helped keep the demand for justice alive for over three decades, bring the accused to trial, and identify some of the former torturers who were living their lives under new identities. Like other political prisoners, Villani not only suffered torture himself, but also witnessed horrendous crimes, like the murder by torture of a Jewish school teacher who belonged to the Communist Party, and whose name he never learned. "He made him strip, he tied him to the table with the bottom half of his body hanging off. He shoved a stick up his anus and gave him electric shocks," he testified in the trial against federal police official Héctor Simón, alias "Turco Julián" or "Julián the Turk." Simón, who was convicted in several cases,

---

[300]*Christian Science Monitor*, 7 December 2012

was known for his fierce antisemitism.[301]

The ESMA trial last is expected to last at least two years. Three hearings a week will be held, and every seven days the testimony of survivors and relatives of victims will be shown via DVDs.

Pinochet in Chile

Augusto José Ramón Pinochet Ugarte, more commonly known as Augusto Pinochet (1915-2006) was an army general and dictator of Chile from 1973 until transferring power to a democratically elected president in 1990. He was the commander-in-chief of the Chilean army from 1973 to 1998 and president of the government junta of Chile from 1973 to 1981. He assumed power in a coup d'état on 11 September 1973 that overthrew the government of communist Salvador Allende.

From the beginning, the government implemented harsh measures against its political opponents. According to human rights reports and investigations somewhere between 1,200 and 3,200 people were killed, up to 80,000 were imprisoned, and perhaps 30,000 were tortured by his regime including women and children. The Rettig Report found that at least 2,279 persons were conclusively murdered by the Chilean government for political reasons during Pinochet's regime, and the Valech Report found that at least 30,000 persons were tortured by the government for political reasons. Some of the most infamous cases of human rights violation occurred during the early period. In October 1973, at least 70 people were killed throughout the country by what became known as the Caravan of Death. Charles Horman, a leftist U.S. journalist, disappeared. And so did Víctor Olea Alegría, a leading member of the Socialist Party in 1973. General Carlos Prats, army commander under Allende, who had resigned rather than support the moves against Allende's government, was assassinated in Buenos Aires, Argentina, in 1974. A year later, the murder of 119 opponents abroad was disguised as an internal conflict, the regime setting up a propaganda campaign to accredit this allegation. Other victims included Juan José Torres, the former President of Bolivia, assassinated in Buenos Aires on 2 June 1976; Carmelo Soria, a U.N. diplomat assassinated in July 1976. Orlando Letelier, a former Chilean ambassador to the United

---

301 *New York Times*, 28 November 2012.

States and minister in Allende's cabinet, was assassinated in Washington, D.C. by a car bomb on 21 September 1976. Michael Townley, an American, had organized the murder on behalf of the Pinochet government. In 2011, commission identified an additional 9,800 victims of political repression during the Pinochet regime. This led to the total number of victims being revised to approximately 40,018, including 3,065 killed.[302]

In the 1988 plebiscite 56% of the voters cast their ballots against continuing his presidency. After peacefully stepping down in 1990, Pinochet continued to serve as Commander-in-Chief of the Chilean Army until 10 March 1998, when he retired and assumed a role as senator-for-life.[303]

A Spanish court indicted Pinochet on 10 October 1998 for human rights violations committed in his native Chile. Pinochet was arrested on the same date in London where he had gone for medical treatment. it was the first time that several European judges applied the principle of universal jurisdiction, declaring themselves competent to judge crimes committed by former heads of state, despite local amnesty laws. He was wanted in connection with numerous human rights allegations, but following a legal battle the Thatcher government released him and he returned to Chile in March 2000.

Although the state had granted Pinochet immunity for all acts committed during his regime, subsequent court decisions removed certain incidents from that blanket grant. Pinochet was first indicted by judge Juan Guzmán Tapia, and charged with a number of crimes.[304]

Pinochet's bank of attorneys was headed by Pablo Rodríguez Grez, a former leader of the rightist Fatherland and Liberty front. They argued that Pinochet was entitled to immunity from prosecution first as a former head of state, then under the 1978 amnesty law passed by the military junta. They furthermore claimed that his alleged poor health made him unfit to stand trial. Although supposedly gravely ill, the court deemed him fit to stand trial for Operation Colombo, during which 119 political opponents

---

[302] "Truth Commission: Chile 90" U.S. Institute of Peace. http://www.usip.org.

[303] Muñoz, Heraldo, *The Dictator's Shadow: Life under Augusto Pinochet*. Basic Books, 2008.

[304] Roht-Arriaza, Naomi, *The Pinochet Effect: Transnational Justice in the Age of Human Rights*. University of Pennsylvania, 2005.

had disappeared in Argentina. The Chilean justice also lifted his immunity on the Villa Grimaldi case, a detention and torture center in the outskirts of Santiago. Pinochet died on 10 December 2006, just after having been again put under house arrest on 28 November 2006 in the Caravan of Death case. At the time of his death, Pinochet had been implicated in over 300 criminal charges for numerous human rights violations, including the Caravan of Death case, as well as tax evasion and passport forgery.[305]

In 2003 the Supreme Court of Mexico agreed to honor the request from Spain to extradite Ricardo Cavallo, a former Argentine naval officer then living in exile in Mexico. The charges were all based on human rights abuses committed on Cavallo's watch and by those under his command. Miguel Angel Cavallo, who used the pseudonym Serpico, served as an officer of the military junta that ruled Argentina from 1976 to 1983, and was alleged to have committed crimes against civilians during the junta's "Dirty War." Mexico extradited him to answer charges of genocide and terrorism, but not on charges of torture, for which a lower court had ruled the statute of limitations to have expired. As Cavallo languished in Spain, awaiting trial, Argentina in 2003 repealed the two laws that had previously given immunity to individuals alleged to have committed crimes during the Dirty War. As a result, the National Court of Spain in December 2006 declared that since he could be tried in Argentine courts, which had priority, the Spanish courts lacked jurisdiction. He was briefly released from jail when an extradition request from Argentina failed to arrive within the required 40 days, but was rearrested a day later after a request was faxed. The Spanish Supreme Court reversed this decision in July 2007, ruling that Cavallo should still stand trial in Madrid, because the case against him in Spanish courts was more advanced than that in Argentina.[306] However, the Spanish government, upon reconsideration, granted Argentina's extradition request in February 2008, and extradited Cavallo to Argentina

---

[305] http://www.pinochet-a-biography.org.; Christopher Minster "The Life of Augusto Pinochet," http://latinamericanhistory . about . com/od/20thcenturylatinamerica/p/ pinochetbio.htm

[306] Smulovitz, Catalina, "The Discovery of Law: Political Consequences in the Argentine Case" in Dezalay, Yves and Bryant G. Garth, eds. *Global Prescriptions: The Production, Exportation, and Importation of a New Legal Orthodoxy*. University of Michigan, 2012, 249-75.

the next month.. Altogether 18 former military officers of the Naval Mechanics Training School (ESMA) were charged with failing to control those below them in the chain of command resulting in the commission of crimes against humanity -- illegal detention, torture, and murder— during the 1976-83 dictatorship.[307]

Spain tried Adolfo Francisco Scilingo, a former Argentine naval officer, for leadership responsibility for himself committing crimes against humanity, including extra-judicial execution, and not controlling those under his command. Specifically, Scilingo and those under his control were charged with genocide, 30 counts of murder, 93 of causing injury, 255 of terrorism and 286 of torture. Some 30 victims, who were thrown from planes to their deaths. The Spanish court convicted him on April 19, 2005, and sentenced him to 640 years imprisonment in Spain. The sentence was reduced to 30 years, the legally applied limit. One author in 2005 charged that use of a charge genocide to initiate proceedings, was a breach of the legal principle *Nullum crimen, nulla poena sine praevia lege poenali* which forms part of Spain's constitution, because at the time the offence was committed the Spanish provision on crimes against humanity was not yet in force.[308]

Guatemala: Jose Montt

A former U.S.-backed dictator who presided over one of the bloodiest periods of Guatemala's civil war will stand trial on charges he ordered the murder, torture and displacement of thousands of Mayan Indians, a judge ruled Monday. Human rights advocates have said that the prosecution of Jose Efrain Rios Montt would be an important symbolic victory for the victims of one of the most horrific of the conflicts that

[307] *Argentina Independent*, 31 October 2011. See also Kathryn Sikkink and Carrie Booth Walling, "The Impact of Human Rights Trials in Latin America." *Journal of Peace Research*, 44 (July 2007) 4: 427-45.

[308] *Nullum crimen, nulla poena sine praevia lege poenali* (Latin, *lit.* "No crime, no punishment without a previous penal law") is a basic maxim in continental European legal thinking. It was written by Paul Johann Anselm Ritter von Feuerbach as part of the Bavarian Criminal Code in 1813. The maxim itself is sometimes rendered: *nullum delictum, nulla poena sine praevia lege poenali nullum crimen, nulla poena sine praevia lege poenali nullum crimen, nulla poena sine lege praevia*

devastated Central America during the last decades of the Cold War. Rios Montt was *de facto* President of Guatemala, dictator, army general, and once president of Congress. Ríos Montt came to public office through a *coup d'etat* on March 23, 1982. In turn, he was overthrown by his Defense Minister, Óscar Humberto Mejía Victores, in another *coup d'etat* on August 8, 1983. Rios Montt served as a Guatemalan congressman for 15 years until he lost a re-election race in late 2012.

Ríos Montt was best known outside Guatemala for heading a campaign that was largely responsible for having defeated the guerrillas through the *guns and beans* campaign. The idea was simple: "If you are with us, we'll feed you, if not, we'll kill you." In 1996 Guatemala's 36-year civil war finally ended with the signing of a peace treaty. The civil war had pitted communist rebels against the Guatemalan state, including the army. Large numbers of civilians, both indigenous Mayas and *mestizo* Ladinos were caught in the crossfire. Human rights watch groups estimated that at least 200,000 people were killed during the conflict, making it one of Latin America's most violent wars in modern history.

Two truth commissions, the REMHI report, sponsored by the Roman Catholic Church, and the CEH report, conducted by the United Nations, documented widespread human rights abuses committed by the military that Ríos Montt's commanded. Both reports noted widespread massacres, rape, torture, and acts of genocide, especially against the indigenous population. Supporters claim that he had to rule with an iron hand because the country was becoming unstable due to the civil war. Several human rights organizations had called for his arrest on charges of war crimes and failures of leadership responsibility.

Despite a series of international inquiries finding him responsible for war crimes, no action was taken. In 1999, Guatemalan Nobel Peace Prize laureate Rigoberta Menchú announced charges for torture, genocide, illegal detention and state-sponsored terrorism against Ríos Montt and four other retired Guatemalan generals, two of them ex-presidents. Three other civilians who had been important governmental officials between 1978 and 1982 were also indicted. The Center for Justice and Accountability and Asociación Pro Derechos Humanos de España are co-counsel in the trial.

In September 2005 Spain's Constitutional Court ruled that Spanish courts can try those accused of crimes against humanity under the universality principle even if the victims were not of Spanish origin. In June 2006, Spanish judge Santiago Pedraz traveled to Guatemala to interrogate Ríos Montt and the others named in the case. However, defense attorneys for the proposed defendants filed at least 15 appeals that effectively prevented Pedraz from carrying out the inquiries.

Rios Montt was the first former president to be charged with genocide by a Latin American court. "It's the beginning of a new phase of this struggle," said Paul Seils, vice president of the New York-based International Center for Transitional Justice, which has worked extensively on war-crimes cases in Guatemala. He said the decision was "a good step forward" but he expected the prosecution of Rios Mont to encounter stiff resistance from forces in Guatemala opposed to the punishment of government-allied forces for their actions during the civil war.

Others hailed the judge's ruling as a less-qualified victory for justice in Guatemala. "The fact that a judge has ordered the trial of a former head of state is a remarkable development in a country where impunity for past atrocities has long been the norm," said Human Rights Watch. Guatemala's leaders have been criticized for years for their inability or unwillingness to prosecute government forces and allied paramilitaries accused of marching into Mayan villages, carrying out rapes and torture, and slaughtering women, children and unarmed men in a campaign of total desolation aimed at eliminating their support for the left-wing guerrilla movement.

Human Rights in Paraguay

Between 1904 and 1954, Paraguay had no less than thirty-one presidents, most of whom were removed from office violently. After World War II, politics became particularly unstable, with several political parties fighting for power in the late 1940s, which precipitated the Paraguayan civil war of 1947. A series of unstable governments ensued until the establishment, in 1954, of the stable regime of dictator Alfredo Stroessner, who remained in office for more than three decades. Stroessner modernized Paraguay in some ways, but at a terrible price in human suffering and misery. Stroessner and the Colorado party ruled the country from 1954 to 1989. As a dictator, Stroessner had a poor human right and environmental. Torture and death for political opponents were routine. He chose men to enforce his one-party rule who, in turn, gave orders for arbitrary arrests, torture, assaults, and murder to those below them. Even after Stroessner's overthrow, the Colorado continued to dominate national politics until 2008.

Some significant progress was made in bringing to justice some high-profile perpetrators of human rights abuses during Stroessner's military dictatorship. By the end of 2009, some 13,700 applications for reparations had been made to the Ombudsman after modifications to legislation on compensation were made in 2008. In October, the Defense Minister authorized the unsealing of files dating from the military regime, giving human rights activists investigating human rights violations during this period access to this information for the first time.

In May 2009, Sabino Augusto Montanaro, Interior Minister between 1968 and 1989, was arrested after voluntarily returning to Paraguay from exile in Honduras. He faced trial for a series of human rights violations including crimes allegedly committed as part of Operation Condor, a joint plan by Southern Cone military governments in the 1970s and 1980s to eliminate opponents. In August, a judge ordered the extradition of Norberto Bianco, an army physician at the Campo de Mayo military hospital, to Argentina to face trial for his alleged role in the illegal detention of more than 30 women and the subsequent kidnapping of their children in 1977 and 1978. He was awaiting extradition at the end of the year. In June, former diplomat Francisco Ortiz Téllez was arrested in connection with the enforced disappearance of Agustín Goiburú, a leading opponent of the Stroessner government, in 1977. Francisco Ortiz Téllez was under house arrest at the end of the year awaiting the outcome of his appeal.[309]

In May 2010, the body of 30-year-old *campesino* leader Enrique Brítez Irala was found hanging from a tree in the La Fortuna Agroganadera in the Jejuí colony, Choré district, San Pedro department. He had been involved in a dispute with a local landowner. Campesino groups reported that Enriquez Brítez Irala, who went missing three days before his body

[309] http://www.amnesty.org/en/region/paraguay/report for several years.

was found, had been tortured and claimed suggestions he had committed suicide were false. Investigations were under way at the end of the year.

As with most south and central American nations, Paraguay has shown little interest in protecting the land, property, persons, and lives of native aborigine. Various governmental and military officials had led their charges against the Yakye Axa, commanding various outrages, including rape, torture, rapine, and assault. The Inter-American Commission on Human Rights alleged that the Government of Paraguay ignored the ancestral property rights of the Yakye Axa Indigenous Community and endangered the Community's access to food and water, health care, and survival. These are serious violations of Articles 4 (right to life), 8 (right to fair trial), 21 (right to property) and 25 (judicial protection) of the American Convention on Human Rights.

Noting that States have an obligation to take into account the economic and social characteristics, special vulnerability, and customary laws, values and customs of indigenous peoples in order to effectively protect them, the Court found that Paraguay's delay in recognizing the Community's leadership, legal status and claims to land violated their rights to judicial protection, to a fair trial, to property, and ultimately to a decent life. The Court also found that the Community had a right to be granted legal status in order to take advantage of their full rights as a people, and that Paraguay's ongoing refusal to recognize that status was a violation of this right. As such, the Court ordered that Paraguay provide the Yakye Axa with reparations including compensation, food and water, sanitation, access to health care, and title to their traditional territory.[310]

El Salvador: Religious Murders

Not every prosecution of human rights violations and misuse of command powers makes its way to the criminal courts of the various states or the International Criminal Court. We will now look at two civil prosecutions which should have been heard before criminal tribunals but for whatever reasons were not. The United states opens its courts under the Alien Tort Claims Act (ATCA) for torts only in violation of

[310] *Yakye Axa Indigenous Community v. Paraguay*, Inter-American Court of Human Rights, 17 June 2005, citing the American Convention on Human Rights.

international law. With the expansion of code law through various treaties finding of appropriate law is not difficult.

Between 1980 and 1991, El Salvador was engaged in a civil war during which thousands of civilians were killed, tortured, or otherwise injured. Among those that were routinely victimized were priests and nuns, lay church workers. Others commonly arrested and injured were union leaders, land reform workers and students. Often these people were victims of spurious allegations that they assisted leftist guerrilla insurgents. The Salvadoran military was commonly the arresting party. During this period, the Salvadoran military was organized along hierarchical lines. At the very top of this organization was the Minister of Defense. Below the that office were the heads of the various armed forces along with the heads of the security forces, basically the National Guard. From 1979 to 1983, Jose Guillermo García was Minister of Defense and Carlos Eugenio Vides Casanova was Director-General of the National Guard.

In 1980, four American women were working with refugees in El Salvador. Ita Ford and Maura Clarke were nuns of the Maryknoll order, while Dorothy Kazell was a nun belonging to the Ursuline order and Jean Donovan was a Catholic lay worker. In this time frame, many Catholic nuns and priests received death threats along with threats of expulsion from El Salvador.

On the evening of December 2, 1980, Sister Kazel and Ms. Donovan went to the airport near San Salvador, to meet Sister Ford and Sister Clarke who were returning from Nicaragua. A Salvadoran official on duty at the airport saw Sister Kazel and Ms. Donovan arrive and called his superior officer, Sergeant Luis Antonio Colindres Alemán, who was in charge of the National Guard detachment at the airport. Earlier that day, Sergeant Colindres had ordered four National Guardsmen to wear civilian clothing and accompany him to the airport. Sergeant Colindres told the men that they had a special mission involving the capture of four persons arriving from Nicaragua. When the four women departed from the airport, their vehicle was followed by the National Guardsmen in a military jeep. When the Guardsmen pulled over the church-women's vehicle, Sergeant Colindres, who was in charge of the mission, began interrogating the women. Colindres then told the Guardsmen that they were to take the churchwomen to an isolated place. One Guardsman reported that he saw Sergeant Colindres make a telephone call and heard him say *muy bien* as if he was receiving orders. Colindres then told the guardsman that he had received an order to kill the women. Colindres' men followed the orders, first sexually assaulting and then killing the women. On 3 December 1980, people from a nearby village found the bodies.

After many complaints, some international in origin, the Salvadoran government launched several investigations, none of which were effective. In reality the inquiries actually covered up the fact that the order to kill the churchwomen came from higher levels in the Salvadoran military. The government finally arrested, tried, and convicted the four National Guardsmen. Despite considerable evidence that the Guardsmen had merely been following specific and direct orders to kill the American women, the government made no further investigation. Sometime around 1989, García and Vides Casanova, both of whom now hold the rank of General, emigrated to Florida. [311]

On May 13, 1999, the families of the women filed a federal civil lawsuit in Florida under the Torture Victim Protection Act [TVPA]. This federal statute gives torture victims or their families who are United States citizens the opportunity to confront the persons who committed crimes against them. This law holds strictly liable those officials who had the authority and responsibility to ensure that such acts did not take place. The TVPA provides that (A) an individual who, under actual or apparent authority, or under color of law, of any foreign nation, subjects an individual to torture shall, in a civil action, be liable for damages to that individual; or (B) subjects an individual to extrajudicial killing shall, in a civil action, be liable for damages to the individual's legal representative, or to any person who may be a claimant in an action for wrongful death. The theory was that Generals García and Vides Casanova had leadership responsibility for the soldiers under their control, like the National Guardsmen who committed the murders and the higher ranking officers that ordered the murders.

No one accused the defendants of actually committing the rapes. Nor did anyone suggest that they had pulled the triggers. In fact, Ford v.

---

[311] Amanda Smith, "Justice for the Generals" U.S. Law Background, PBS.org.

Garcia was not even a criminal trial. Instead, General Jose Guillermo Garcia and General Carlos Eugenio Vides Casanova faced the relatives of four slain churchwomen in a civil suit. The plaintiffs contended only that the two men bore leadership responsibility for the brutal rape and torture of the four women. Significantly, this action, brought in a federal court in southern Florida under the TVPA, was the first time a U.S. jury evaluated a foreign defendant's liability under this three-pronged leadership responsibility doctrine. Additionally, this was the first time a person accused under the TVPA of subjecting an individual to torture or extrajudicial killing had testified in his own defense in front of a lay jury. Unfortunately, the novelty of the experience resulted in an erroneous jury instruction. Thus, the court added an unprecedented fourth prong to the leadership responsibility doctrine. The additional element of proximate cause ran counter to the Senate's original intent, U.S. case law, international precedent, and common sense. Yet, despite the befuddled jury's pleas for clarification, the judge refused to give clear and concise directions and instructions.[312]

However, on 3 November 2000, the jury found for the defendants not guilty. The families of the churchwomen immediately appealed to the United States Court of Appeals for the Eleventh Circuit on the grounds that the trial court judge erred in issuing instructions to the jury on what they had to find in order to hold the generals responsible under the doctrine of leadership responsibility. The trial judge had instructed the jurors that, before they could hold the generals responsible, they had to find that the plaintiffs had proven that the generals had effective control over those who actually killed the churchwomen. Lawyers for the church women argued that the plaintiffs had demonstrated that the generals, by law, had authority over troops under their command. Thus, the burden should be on the generals to show that they did not have effective control over subordinate troops. Their appeal was denied, and in 2003, the United States Supreme Court refused to hear further proceedings.[313]

---

[312] Arthurs, Sean, "Comment and case Note: A Foolish Inconsistency: How Refusing to Review Ford v Garcia's Invited Error Demonstrates the 11th Circuit's Prioritization of Procedure over Justice" 72 *U. Cincinnati Law Review* [2004] 1707.

[313] John W. Brooker, "*Ford v Garcia*: A Puzzling Fusion of the Command Responsibility

El Salvador: Human Rights

On December 12, 1980, members of the Salvadoran National Guard abducted, detained, and tortured Juan Romagoza Arce, M. D., a physician who provided medical care at a church clinic. Dr. Juan Romagoza, was working in an impromptu health clinic in a church when a detachment of the army and security forces arrived in military vehicles. Because Dr. Romazoga had medical equipment and what appeared to be military boots, he was captured and taken to a local army base. Dr. Romagoza was then transferred by helicopter to the National Guard headquarters in San Salvador where he was tortured for three weeks. As part of his torture, he was hung by his fingertips with wire and shot through his left arm to signify that he was a leftist. That injury made it impossible for him to continue to practice surgery. He was also beaten, raped, starved, electro-shocked, burned with cigarettes, and kept in appalling conditions. Eventually released into his uncle's custody, Dr. Romagoza saw General Vides Casanova, one of the defendants in the case, talking to his other uncle and recognized the general's voice as belonging to the person who had interrogated him in the torture room. Dr. Romagoza was eventually released and was granted political asylum in the United States on April 21, 1987. Dr. Romagoza became a naturalized citizen of the United States in 1995.

On December 26, 1979, members of the Salvadoran National Guard abducted, detained, and tortured Neris Gonzalez, a lay worker and catechist with the Catholic Church in El Salvador. Ms. González was a catechist who taught literacy and simple mathematics to the peasants in the province of San Vicente. Members of the National Guard arrested her one day in the market and took her to a local headquarters. There, she was tortured for three weeks, raped repeatedly, and was forced to watch others be tortured, mutilated, and killed. At the time, she was eight months pregnant. The guardsmen damaged her belly repeatedly. Because of this trauma, Ms. González has no memory of how she escaped captivity. She was taken in the back of a truck full of dead bodies to a local dump. At some point, her baby was born, and local villagers heard the sound of her

---

Doctrine with the Torture Victim Protection Act," 28 *N.C. Journal of International Law* [2003] 701.

baby crying and rescued her. Her baby died two months later of injuries she suffered in prison.

On June 13, 1983, members of the Salvadoran National Guard abducted Dr. Carlos Mauricio, professor at the University of El Salvador. Professor Carlos Mauricio was teaching agronomy at the university when he was lured out of his classroom and taken to the National Police headquarters in San Salvador. Professor Mauricio was detained in a secret cell and tortured for approximately nine days, which included being beaten repeatedly with fists, feet, and metal bars; being hung for hours with his arms behind his back; and being forced to witness the torture of others. As a result of these beatings, two of his ribs were broken, and his vision was permanently damaged in one eye. Professor Mauricio was finally released due to the intervention of his then father-in-law, who was in the military. Professor Mauricio believes he was earmarked for capture because he had traveled out of the country for schooling and had worked with peasants to help them increase their agricultural yields.

General Carlos Eugenio Vides Casanova was the Director-General of the Salvadoran National Guard from 1979-1983 and then became Minister of Defense. General Jose Guillermo García was Minister of Defense from 1979-1983. Both men lived in retirement in Florida.

In May 1999, these three Salvadorans filed a civil lawsuit in U.S. District Court in Florida seeking damages for torture, and other grave human rights violations against and García and Vides Casanova. The plaintiffs claimed that these two men had leadership responsibility over the Salvadoran Military and Security Forces. These organizations had engaged in unlawful acts constituting torture; crimes against humanity; cruel, inhuman and degrading treatment; and arbitrary detention. The legal basis for the suit rests on two federal statutes: the Alien Tort Claims Act [ACTA] and the Torture Victim Protection Act [TVPA]. Under both of these statutes, a military commander may be held responsible for abuses by subordinate forces if the commander knew or should have known about and failed to take all reasonable measures to prevent, investigate or punish the abuses.[314]

---

[314]Van Schaack, *Beth, "Romagoza v. García*: Proving Command Responsibility under the Alien Tort Claims Act and the Torture Victim Protection Act." Center for

The attorneys for the plaintiffs attempted to prove three main elements: (1) that the direct perpetrators of the unlawful acts were subordinates of the defendant commanders; (2) that the defendant commanders knew (actual knowledge) or should have known (constructive knowledge) that his troops were committing, had committed, or were about to commit abuses; and (3) that the defendant commander failed to take steps to prevent or punish criminal conduct by subordinates. The plaintiffs, with the exception of Dr. Romagoza who identified General Vides Casanova in the torture chamber, did not argue that the generals personally participated in, or even knew about, their detention and torture. Instead, they argued that because the defendants were well aware that troops under their supervision were committing abuses, but nonetheless failed to supervise them properly or punish perpetrators, the commanders should be held liable for the abuses the plaintiffs suffered.

The defendants in the *Romagoza* case were the same as in the *Ford v. García*. The *Romagoza* case differs from the church women's case in important ways. First, in the *Romagoza* case, the victims themselves will be able to present testimony about what was done to them and by whom. Additionally, in the *Romagoza* case, the plaintiffs were tortured inside headquarters and posts of the National Guard and National Police, making it more difficult for the generals to assert that the abuses were carried out by rogue soldiers out of their control.[315]

The lawsuit was filed by the Center for Justice and Accountability on behalf of the survivors of torture during the Salvadoran Civil War. The appellants won, Garcia lost, and the Center won a judgment of over $54 million. Judgment was entered against the co-defendants, and upheld on appeal. Of course chances of actually collecting any significant portion of the judgment approximate absolute zero.[316]

A jury in Memphis, Tennessee, found Colonel Nicolas Carranza, formerly Vice Minister of Defense of El Salvador and now a U.S. citizen living in Memphis, responsible for overseeing the torture and killing in

---

Human Rights and Humanitarian Law in conjunction with the Washington College of Law at American University.

[315] Smith, Amanda, "Trial History: Romagoza et al. v. García et al. U.S. Law Background, PBS.org."

[316] "The Case Against the Generals" *Washington Post,* 17 August 2003

that country 25 years ago. Victims of armed forces under Carranza's superior control successfully sued for damages. To find Carranza guilty the jury applied the principle of "leadership responsibility," which holds a superior legally responsible for human rights abuses by subordinates if the official knew or should have known about them and failed to prevent them or punish those who committed them.[317]

Other Latin American Cases

Various human rights violations and other criminal activities against civilians have been the standard fare in most Latin and Central American nations at one time or another. Removal of authoritarian regimes by one means or another have generally been followed by amnesty laws which usually are short-lived. While in effect many amnesty laws exempt major criminal activities such as genocide, torture, and crimes against humanity.[318] As we write this, in Latin America, three nations – Grenada, Guyana, and Paraguay – do not have amnesties. Amnesties are operational in 16 of 19 transitional countries of Latin America. Fifteen of those 16 nations have held trials of those accused of ordering crimes against the civilian population and their subordinates who actually carried out those superior orders.[319] El Salvador actually has had no less than six amnesty laws, dated 1979, 1980, 1983, 1987, 1992, and 1993. Fourteen countries held human rights trials, with conditions reportedly improving in 11[320] and worsening in three – Mexico, Venezuela, and Haiti.[321]

In his *The Third Wave*, Samuel P. Huntington wrote that unless trials of former dictators and their henchmen occur soon after the transition to democracy there will be no retribution, no trials of criminals, and no

---

317 Preston, Julia, "Ex-Salvadoran Colonel is Ordered to Pay for Crimes against Humanity," *New York Times Pilar Domingo and Rachel Sieder, Rule of Law in Latin America: The International Promotion of Judicial Reform. University of London, 2001.*, November 19, 2005

318 Domingo, Pilar and Rachel Sieder, *Rule of Law in Latin America: The International Promotion of Judicial Reform*. University of London, 2001.

319 See Leslie Green, "War Crimes, Crimes Against Humanity, and Command Responsibility" *Naval War College Review*, 50 (1997) 1.

320 Human rights reportedly improved in Argentina, Bolivia, Chile, Ecuador, El Salvador, Guatemala, Honduras, Nicaragua, Panama, Paraguay, and Peru

321 Kathryn Sikkink and Carrie Booth Walling, "The Impact of Human Rights Trials in Latin America." *Journal of Peace Research*, 44 (July 2007) 4: 427-45.

justice. The authoritarian groups, Huntington thought, would eventually gain respectability and viability.[322] A recent article has shown that this is not always the case.[323] Two former officials of Uruguay, President Juan Maria Boysenberry, and Foreign Minister Juan Carlos Blanco, were charged with crimes against humanity, and for failing to control those under them, in 2006. Juan María Bordaberry Arocena (1928–2011) served as President from 1972 until 1976. In 1973, Bordaberry dissolved the General Assembly and was widely regarded as ruling by decree as a military-sponsored dictator. In 1976, Bordaberry proposed to abolish the parties and set up a corporatist state according to a pattern similar to fascist Italy and with little precedent in Uruguayan history. It was not until 17 November 2006 that he was arrested and charged with responsibility for four deaths, including two of members of the General Assembly during the period of civilian-military rule in the 1970s.[324]

In Brazil a jury found Lindonjonson Silva Rocha and Alberto Lopes do Nascimento, guilty of carrying out the killings of two Amazon activists in northern Brazil in 2011. Rocha was sentenced to 42 years and eight months and Nascimento was to be incarcerated for 45 years. However, Jose Rodrigues Moreira who was accused based on under whose command, and at whose orders the killings took place, was acquitted him due to insufficient evidence. Jose Claudio Ribeiro da Silva and his wife, Maria, were gunned down near a reserve in the jungle state of Para, where they were teaching farmers how to use land in a sustainable manner. Prosecutors had accused Moreira of ordering the killings because the Silvas had worked to prevent the eviction of three families occupying his land in the Nova Ipixuna reserve. Para is among Brazil's most violent and lawless states, notorious for land-related violence, contract killings, slave-like labor conditions and wanton environmental destruction. "The verdict was to a certain point a positive one because those who shot the guns were convicted," a government spokesman said, "but the verdict unfortunately

---

[322] Huntington, Samuel P. *The Third Wave: Democratization in the Late 20th Century*. U. Oklahoma Press, 1991, 228.

[323] Sikkink and Walling, *op. cit.*

[324] Alexei Barrionuevo and Charles Newbery "Juan Bordaberry, Who Led Uruguay in Dark Era, Dies at 83." *The New York Times*, July 17, 2011.

again showed that those who order people killed enjoy impunity."[325]

A mass incarceration program in place since the 1990s had resulted in a 350 per cent increase in the number of prisoners in Brazilian jails in the last 20 years. In September 2011, the United Nations Subcommittee for Prevention of Torture (SPT) concluded that torture and ill-treatment are widespread and systematic in detention centers all over the country and identified a generalized failure in bringing state agents to justice. During the dark years under authoritarian rule, the victims were political dissidents, students and intellectuals. Kicks and punches to the head and body, blows with truncheons and metal bars and electro-shocks were part of the standard routine in detention centers across Brazil. Both military and civil police forces made frequent use of torture on people arrested for political as well as ordinary crimes. In 2006 the first trials against reputed superiors and their subordinates for using torture took place. In May 2012, Brazil installed the Brazilian National Truth Commission to investigate human rights abuses committed in the past. The Commission's brief is to examine the period from 1946 to 1988, but the focus of the investigations will be on the military regime (1964–1985) when the use of torture against anyone who opposed the regime, even by peaceful means, was state policy. However, the Brazilian amnesty law did effectively shield many of the previous dictatorship's worst criminals because in September 2010, Brazil had the opportunity to do the same when the Federal Supreme Court tried a case brought by the Brazilian Bar Association (OAB) alleging the unconstitutionality of the Amnesty Law but, to the disappointment of families and human rights organizations, five out of the seven judges voted to uphold it.[326]

Israel

The Israeli occupation of Palestinian territory (the West Bank including East Jerusalem and the Gaza Strip) is in its fifth decade and the undercurrent of violence and inherent abuses of fundamental human rights and disregard for international law inherent in any long-standing military occupation is presented by both sides. Both Israeli and Palestinian civilians

---

[325] *The Independent*, 26 May 2013.

[326] "Torture Never Again," International Bar Association, 2 January 2013.

continue to bear the brunt of the violence in the region. Human rights violations by Israeli forces in the Occupied Palestinian Territories (OPT) have included, but are not limited to, home demolitions and the forced eviction of Palestinian families; punitive arrests, unfair trials, ill-treatment and torture of detainees and the use of excessive or lethal force to subdue nonviolent demonstrations as well as the use of restrictive legal means. In contravention of international law, Israel continues to build parts of the wall/fence in the OPT, expand settlements and use draconian restrictions on the movement of Palestinians with some 600 roadblocks and checkpoints. Amnesty International is also concerned about discriminatory policies affecting access to water for Palestinians.[327]

An instance, often mentioned in regard to treatment of Palestinians in the Occupied Territory, is the finding, in the Report of the Kahan Commission of Inquiry into the massacre at the refugee camps in Beirut in 1982, on the personal responsibility of then-Minister of Defense of Israel, Ariel Sharon.[328] The Kahan Commission formally known as the Commission of Inquiry into the Events at the Refugee Camps in Beirut, was established by the Israeli government on 28 September 1982, to investigate the Sabra and Shatila Massacre (16–18 September 1982). The Kahan Commission was chaired by the President of the Supreme Court, Yitzhak Kahan. Its other two members were Supreme Court Judge Aharon Barak, and Major-General (res.) Yona Efrat. The Commission was to make recommendations on Israeli involvement in the massacre. It concluded that direct responsibility rested with the Gemayel Phalangists led by Fadi Frem, and that no Israelis were deemed directly responsible, although Israel was held to be indirectly responsible. This case raises many issues, some of which are clearly outside the scope of this study.[329] It is nonetheless worth

---

[327] "Israel/ Occupied Palestinian Territories" http://www.Amnestyusa.org; see also "EU Slams Israel's Human Rights Record" *Israel News,* 29 July 2012.

[328] *Final Report of the Commission of Inquiry into the Events at the Refugee Camps in Beirut*, 7 February 1983; in *International Legal Materials* 22 (1983) 473-520.

[329] Linda A. Malone, The Kahan Report, Ariel Sharon and the Sabra-Shatilla Massacres in Lebanon: Responsibility Under International Law for Massacres of Civilian Populations", *Utah Law Review* (1985) 373-433; See also Weston B. Burnett, "Command Responsibility and A Case Study of the Criminal Responsibility of Israeli Military Commanders for the Pogrom at Shatila and Sabra," *Military Law Review* 107 (1985) 71-189.

noting that the Commission found that Sharon disregarded the danger of acts of vengeance and bloodshed by the Phalangists against the population of the refugee camps when he decided to have the Phalangists enter the camps, and failed to order appropriate measures to prevent or reduce the danger of massacre as a condition for that entry. These blunders constituted "the non-fulfillment of a duty with which the Defense Minister was charged," without clearly relying on the doctrine of superior responsibility. Ariel Sharon, as minister of defense, was found to bear personal responsibility "for ignoring the danger of bloodshed and revenge" and "not taking appropriate measures to prevent bloodshed." Sharon's negligence in protecting the civilian population of Beirut, which had come under Israeli control, amounted to a non-fulfillment of a duty with which the Defense Minister was charged, and it was recommended that Sharon be dismissed as Defense Minister. Sharon refused to resign, and Prime Minister Menachem Begin refused to fire him.[330]

In January 1988, a month into the Intifada uprising against Israeli occupation of the West Bank and Gaza Strip, Colonel Yehuda Meir ordered the troops under his command to round up twenty Palestinian men from Hawara and Beita, two Arab villages in the West Bank, bind them in handcuffs and blindfolds, and break their bones. The unit commander reporting to Meir passed on the order to his troops, but told them that it was not necessary for them to comply. Some soldiers refrained from doing so, but others carried out the order with such zeal that they broke their truncheons. The defense minister at the time, Yitzhak Rabin, had publicly spoken of the need to "break the bones of Intifada rioters." Although Meir was not present during the incident, he was the superior commanding officer in the area.

The International Committee of the Red Cross (ICRC) demanded that Israel inquire into the matter and at the same time launched its own investigation. The army chief of staff summoned Meir and offered him the choice: to appear before a disciplinary military court for a severe reprimand and discharge from the army, or to face a court martial. Meir accepted the first option. He was to go to work for the state security service

---

[330] *Report of the Commission of Inquiry into the Events at the Refugee Camps in Beirut, International Legal Materials* 22 (1983) 473-518.

and then he could begin retirement on his colonel's pension.

Word of the infamous back room deal became known and much of the Israeli public was outraged. The Association for Civil Rights in Israel approached the Israeli High Court of Justice, demanding that Meir be court-martialed. The High Court ruled unanimously that Meir should be tried in a special military tribunal for torture, intentionally causing bodily harm, grievous assault, all of which were grave breaches of international law. The Torture Victim Protection Act [TVPA] was especially applicable. The court also charged him with conduct unbecoming an officer. "These actions outrage every civilized person, and no lack of clarity can cover it up" Justice Moshe Bejski said. "Certainly, if the order is given by a senior officer, that officer must be aware that the morality of the Israeli Defense Forces forbids such behavior." The court martial was held before a special military tribunal in Tel Aviv in April 1991. He was found guilty, demoted to private's rank, and deprived of his colonel's pension.

Meir's case points to two traditional issues of international humanitarian law First, can obedience to superior orders be a defense against allegations of war crimes? The claim of superior orders cannot serve as a defense against an allegation of serious breaches of such law. The illegality of the orders was obvious, blatant, and undeniable in the Meir case.

The second issue is how far up the chain of leadership responsibility may leadership responsibility extend for ordering a war crime. Statutory international law holds that "the fact that a breach of the Conventions or of this Protocol was committed by a subordinate does not absolve his superiors from penal disciplinary responsibility as the case may be if they knew, or had information which would have enabled them to conclude in the circumstances at the time that he was committing or was going to commit such a breach and if they did not take all feasible measures within their power to prevent or repress the breach."[331] leadership responsibility extends as high as any officer in the chain of command who knows or has reason to know that his subordinates are committing war crimes and failed to act to stop them. Although Israel has

---

[331]Article 86 of Additional Protocol I to the 1949 Geneva Conventions.

not ratified Additional Protocol I, it is clear from Israeli Supreme Court practice that its domestic law embraces these internationally recognized standards for superior orders and leadership responsibility.

Under the doctrine of leadership responsibility, a military commander is liable for crimes about which he "knew or should have known" about under circumstances at the time, and only for those crimes committed by forces under his "effective command and control." He is liable if he "failed to take all necessary and reasonable measures" to prevent and repress such crimes that subordinates "were committing or about to commit" or for failing to report such crimes to proper authorities.[332] Meir argued in his own defense that he was acting in accord with his understanding of orders given by his superiors. The tribunal rejected that argument. The judges concluded that political and high-ranking military officials had not given orders to break bones. Consequently, the State prosecutor's office decided not pursue charges against Ehud Barak, the chief of staff at the time, Rabin, the minister of defense, or Maj. Gen. Yitzhak Mordechai, the commanding officer of the central zone. Officers and soldiers who carried out Meir's orders in the Hawara and Beita affair were tried in special military courts. Their arguments that they were merely "obeying orders" were rejected and they served time in prison.[333]

As recently as 2012 the Israeli Supreme Court has heard cases involving the targeted killing of Palestinians by the Israeli Defense Forces. One of the principal questions the Israeli high court had to ponder had precedence in the Nuremberg Trials: how does one separate civilians on the one hand and, on the hand, militia, guerrillas, and forces operating as *levees en masse*?[334] The court would obviously granted greater latitude to the military in the issuance of orders and leadership responsibility while dealing with recognized armed forces as opposed to those who are strictly civilians. Recognition of these categories is fundamental to the whole system because they are codified in conventional law.

---

[332] 1998 statute of the International Criminal Court

[333]Nomi Bar-Yaaco, "Command Responsibility," Crimes of War.Org.

[334] *Public Committee against Torture v. Israel* [2006] Israeli Supreme Court 597

Khmer Rouge Tribunal

The Extraordinary Chambers in the Courts of Cambodia (ECCC), commonly known as the Khmer Rouge Tribunal is a court established to try the most senior and most responsible members of the Khmer Rouge. Cambodia and the United Nations agreed to establish this tribunal. Although it is a national court, its members include both local and foreign judges. It is a hybrid court because the ECCC was created by the government of Cambodia in conjunction with the U.N., it remains independent of them. Its jurisdiction extends to serious violations of Cambodian penal law, international humanitarian law and custom, and violations of such international conventions as are recognized by Cambodia. This includes crimes against humanity, war crimes, and genocide. The chief purpose of the tribunal was to provide justice to the Cambodian people who were victims of the Khmer Rouge regime's policies between April 1975 and January 1979. In May 2006, Justice Minister Ang Vong Vathana announced that Cambodia's highest judicial body approved 30 Cambodian and United Nations judges to preside over the long-awaited genocide tribunal for surviving Khmer Rouge leaders.[335]

Kang Kek Iew was one of the leaders of the Khmer Rouge. He headed the a special branch of the Khmer Rouge in charge of internal security which also ran the prison camps. He ran the notorious Tuol Sleng (S-21) prison in Phnom Penh. Kang Kek Iew, or "Comrade Duch," was the first of the five brought before the tribunal. His hearings began on 17 September 2009 and concluded on 27 November 2010. On 26 July 2010 the tribunal found Kang guilty of crimes humanity, genocide and the breaches of the Geneva Convention and was sentenced to 35 years imprisonment.[336]

Nuon Chea was the principal adviser and assistant to dictator Pol Pot during the rule of the Khmer Rouge. Charges lodged against Nuon Chea included murder, extermination, enslavement, deportation, imprisonment,

---

[335] "The Extraordinary Trial of Khmer Rouge Leaders" New York Times, 16 January 2013;" 'Prosecutors Describe Khmer Rouge Leaders' 'Organized and Systematic' Atrocities, Ibid., 22 November 2011.

[336] http://www.asianews.it/news-en/Comrade-Duch,-from-Khmer-Rouge-to-Christian,-alone-to-ask-for-forgiveness-14897.html; "Kang Kek Iew" in Wikipedia.

torture, persecution on political, racial, and religious grounds, genocide, torture, willfully and causing great suffering or serious injury to body or health. In 1960 he was appointed Deputy Secretary to oversee the security of the party and the state. His charges included supervising Phnom Penh's S-21, the notorious torture facility. Human rights organizations estimated that Nuon Chea was responsible for the death of 1.7 million people during the rule of the Khmer Rouge. In 1998, Nuon Chea reached an agreement with the Cambodian government which allowed him to live near the border of Thailand. He was arrested and taken into custody in 2007. His case has been under investigation since 2007 and hearings began in 2011. Chea is the highest ranking official to be detained although he denies much of his role in the Khmer Rouge. In Fact, he has testified that he admired the Khmer Rouge because it saved Cambodia from Vietnamese aggression.[337]

Ieng Sary joined the Khmer Rouge in 1963. He had studied in France where he joined the Communist Party and upon his return to Cambodia, he joined communists there. When the Khmer Rouge took control in 1975, Ieng became the Deputy Minister for Foreign Affairs. When the regime fell, Ieng fled to Thailand. The People's Revolutionary Tribunal of Phnom Penh convicted him of genocide and sentenced to him death. Ieng remained a member of the Khmer Rouge government in exile until 1996. Ieng Sary was arrested on 12 November 2007 and charged with planning, instigating, ordering, aiding/abetting, or overseeing of the crimes of the Khmer Rouge between 1975 and 1979. Allegations against Ieng Sary include crimes against humanity, and genocide.[338]

Ieng Thirith was the wife of Ieng Sary and sister-in-law of Pol Pot was the first Cambodian to receive a degree in English. Upon her return to Cambodia, she joined CPK and was allegedly appointed Minister of Social Affairs in Democratic Kampuchea. She was a senior member of the Khmer Rouge. Thirith remained with the Khmer Rouge until her husband, Ieng Sary, was pardoned by the Cambodian government in 1998. Later she and Sary lived near Phnom Penh until both were arrested by Cambodian police

---

[337] *New York Times*, 23 November 2011.

[338] "Prosecutors Describe Khmer Rouge Leaders Organized Atrocities," *New York Times*, 22 November 2011; "Trial Begins for Khmer Rouge Leader," *Ibid.*, 17 February 2009; "Ieng Sary" ICC Justice Portal, http://www.haguejusticeportal.net/index.php?id=8570

and tribunal officials on 12 November 2007. The tribunal held her responsible for the planning, instigating, and aiding crimes against humanity. In September 2012 Ieng, 80, was declared mentally unfit for trial and released. The decision was based on her mental deterioration probably caused by advanced Alzheimer's disease.

Khieu Samphan was one of the Khmer Rouge's most powerful officials. Before joining the Khmer Rouge, Khieu Samphan was Secretary of State for Trade in the regime headed by Prince Sihanouk in 1962. Sihanouk's security forces sought Samphan who went into hiding in 1969 and emerged as a member of the Khmer Rouge in the early 1970s. He succeeded Pol Pot as leader of the Khmer Rouge in 1987. Khieu Samphan in 1998 and left the Khmer Rouge and pledged allegiance to the Cambodian government. He was arrested on 12 November 2007 for crimes against humanity and genocide.[339]

In June 2011 the court closed its investigation of Case 003 prematurely, inviting the accusation that the judges were ignoring the case. The Case 003 involves Meas Muth and Sou Met, two Khmer Rouge army commanders who reportedly supervised the arrests and transportation of prisoners to the infamous S-21 prison. There was international concern that the court was yielding to government pressures not to indict and try additional defendants. Similar allegations of political pressure have been alleged in case 004 involving former mid-level Khmer Rouge commanders Im Chaem, Ta Ann and Ta Tith. These men ran a forced labor camp which was to create a massive irrigation project. In reality they supervised genocide in the camp. Many critics argue that these closings stem from a reluctance by the Cambodian government to try Khmer Rouge officials who managed to switch alliances towards the end of the conflict.[340]

Ieng Sary, a co-founder of Khmer Rouge movement in the 1970s, died while on trial for atrocities. He was 87. He had been on trial with two other former Khmer Rouge leaders by a joint Cambodian-international

---

[339]http://www.eccc.gov.kh/en/indicted-person/khieu-samphan

[340] "After the First Trial - A Population-Based Survey on Knowledge and Perception of Justice and the Extraordinary Chambers in the Courts of Cambodia." Human Rights Centre, University of California Berkeley, School of Law, 26. .

tribunal. He had been in declining health and tribunal spokesman Lars Olsen confirmed he died. Ieng Sary founded the Khmer Rouge with its leader, Pol Pot, who was his brother-in-law. The communist regime, which ruled Cambodia from 1975 to 1979, claimed it was building a pure socialist society by evicting people from cities to work in labor camps in the countryside. Its radical policies led to the deaths of an estimated 1.7 million people from starvation, disease, overwork and execution. Ieng Sary was foreign minister in the regime and as its top diplomat became a much more recognizable figure internationally than his secretive colleagues. In 1996, years after the overthrown Khmer Rouge retreated to the jungle, he became the first member of its inner circle to defect, hastening the movement's final disintegration.[341]

[341]*The Guardian*, 14 March 2013.

7
Command Responsibility in the International Criminal Court

The father of International Law, Grotius, wrote that "a community or its rulers may be held responsible for the crime of a subject if they knew of it, and did not prevent it, when they could or should prevent it."[342] Punishment, presumably, would be meted out by some unspecified court. The Hague Convention of 1907 provided for assigning "responsibility and potential payment of compensation by the state for breeches committed by members of its armed forces." [343] In 1919 the Commission on the Responsibility of the Authors of War and on the Enforcement of Penalties, recommended that "all persons belonging to enemy countries . . . without distinction of rank . . . who have been guilty of offenses against the laws and customs of war, or the laws of humanity, are liable to criminal prosecution."[344] What was needed of course was a forum appropriate to handle crimes on the international scale.

The International Criminal Court, commonly known as the ICC, is a permanent tribunal to prosecute individuals for genocide, crimes against humanity, and war crimes. It will not be until 2017 at the earliest that the ICC can exercise jurisdiction over the crime of aggression. The Rome Statute of the International Criminal Court of 1 July 2002 created this tribunal. It can prosecute only crimes committed on or after that date. The official seat is in The Hague, Netherlands, but it may hold sessions and superintend prosecutions anywhere. As of December 2012, some 121 states are states parties to the Statute of the Court, including all of South America, most of Europe and about half the countries in Africa. An additional 32 countries, including Russia, have signed but not ratified the

---

[342]Grotius, *On the Law of War and Peace*, II: 21: 2.
[343] Hague Convention, article 3.
[344] 19 March 1919, *American Journal of International Law* 14 (1920) 95.

Rome Statute. An additional 41 United Nations member states have neither signed nor ratified or acceded to the Rome Statute; some of them, including China and India, are critical of the Court. On 21 January 2009, the Palestinian National Authority formally accepted the jurisdiction of the Court .On 3 April 2012, the ICC Prosecutor announced that he was unable to determine whether Palestine was a *state* under the Rome Statute. On 29 November 2012, the United Nations General Assembly voted in favor of recognizing Palestine as a non-member *observer state*. The prevailing law of treaties mandates that these states refrain from "acts which would defeat the object and purpose" of the treaty until such time as they declare that they no longer wish to be parties to the treaty. Three such states -- Israel, Sudan and the United States -- have informed the U.N. Secretary General that they no longer intend to become states parties and, as such, have no legal obligations arising from their former representatives' signature of the Statute.[345]

The Court can generally exercise jurisdiction only in three cases, *viz.* if the accused is a national of a state party, if the alleged crime took place on the territory of a state party, or if a situation is referred to the Court by the United Nations Security Council. As of this writing the Court has opened investigations into eight incidents in Africa: the Congo; Uganda; Central African Republic; Darfur, Sudan; Kenya; the Libyan Arab Jamahiriya; Ivory Coast; and Mali. Of these eight, four were referred to the Court by the states themselves-- Uganda, Congo, Central African Republic and Mali. The United Nations Security Council ordered inquiries into Darfur and Libya, and the final two -- Kenya and Ivory Coast--were begun *proprio motu* by the ICC Prosecutor. The ICC has indicted 30 people, proceedings against 24 of whom are ongoing. The ICC has issued arrest warrants for 21 individuals and summonses to nine others. Five individuals are in custody; one of them has been found guilty and sentenced, one has been acquitted and released, and three are being tried. Ten individuals remain at large as fugitives. Additionally, three individuals

---

[345] http://www.haguejusticeportal.net; "International Criminal Court" on Wikipedia; Bruce Broomhall, *International Justice and the International Criminal Court: Between Sovereignty and the Rule of Law*. Oxford University Press, 2003; Roy S Lee (ed.), *The International Criminal Court: The Making of the Rome Statute*. The Hague: Kluwer Law International, 1999.

have been arrested by national authorities, but have not been transferred to the Court. Proceedings against six individuals are completed following the death of two and the dismissal of charges against the other four.[346]

The creation of the office in June 2003, the Prosecutor (OTP) has received and analyzed information about alleged crimes in many conflicts around the world and subsequently initiated a few investigations. Situations can be referred to the Court by a State Party to the Rome Statute, the UN Security Council, and the Prosecutor through his/her proprio motu power. The Court may then exercise its jurisdiction over the matter if either the State in whose territory the crime was committed (Territorial Jurisdiction), or the State of the nationality of the accused, is a party to the Statute (Active Nationality Jurisdiction). Non-States Parties may accept the Court's jurisdiction on an ad hoc basis. When a matter is referred by the Security Council, the Court has jurisdiction regardless of whether the State concerned is a party to the ICC treaty.

The trial, prosecution, and verdict in all the cases we have presented below are predicated upon the applicability of the doctrine of leadership responsibility. Unless the person on trial knew, should have known, or had a responsibility to know, of the illegal acts committed by persons under their command, one would have to show that the persons themselves committed illegal acts. In nearly every case it was a matter of knowing, perhaps even ordering, the outrageous acts with which the defendant is charged.

The Congo Cases

The ICC opened its investigation in the situation of the Democratic Republic of Congo (DRC) in 2004. Seven arrest warrants have been issued for war crimes and crimes against humanity against Thomas Lubanga Dyilo, Germain Katanga, Matthieu Ngudjolo Chui, Bosco Ntaganda, Sylvestre Mudacumura and Callixte Mbarushimana. The situation in the DRC was previously assigned to Pre-Trial Chamber I, composed of Presiding Judge Sylvia Steiner, Judge Sanji Mmasenono Monageng, and Judge Cuno Tarfusser. The situation is currently assigned

---

346 Schabas, William A., *An Introduction to the International Criminal Court.* 2nd ed.; Cambridge University Press, 2004; Wikipedia.

to Pre-Trial Chamber II, composed of Judge Cuno Tarfusser, Judge Hans-Peter Kaul, and Judge Ekaterina Trendafilova. The government of the Congo formally referred the situation on 19 April 2004, requesting that the Prosecutor investigate potential crimes under the Court's jurisdiction were committed anywhere in the territory of the DRC since the entry into force of the Rome Statute, on 1 July 2002. On 23 June 2004, after a thorough analysis of the situation in the DRC, especially in the eastern region of Ituri, the Prosecutor announced his decision to open the first investigation of the ICC. The trial against Congolese warlords Germain Katanga and Matthieu Ngudjolo Chui which opened on 24 November 2009 is ICC's second trial. Katanga and Ngudjolo are accused of war crimes and crimes against humanity allegedly committed in the village of Bogoro in the Ituri district of eastern DRC from January to March 2003.

Thomas Lubanga Dyilo is a convicted war criminal from the Democratic Republic of the Congo (DRC) and the first person ever convicted by the ICC.[347] He founded and led the Union of Congolese Patriots (UPC) and was a major operative in the Ituri conflict which took place between 1999 and 2007. During the Second Congo War, Lubanga was a military commander and self-styled minister of defense in the pro-Uganda Congolese Rally for Democracy-Liberation Movement (RCD-ML). In July 2001, he founded another rebel group, the Union of Congolese Patriots (UPC). In early 2002, Lubanga was superseded in the control of the RCD-ML so consequently he split from the group. In September 2002, he appointed himself president of the UPC and created a military wing, the Patriotic Force for the Liberation of the Congo (FPLC). Under Lubanga's leadership, the largely ethnic Hema UPC became one of the main participants in the Ituri conflict which pitted the Hema and against the Lendu. The UPC seized control of Bunia, capital of the gold-rich Ituri region, in 2002, and demanded that the Congolese government recognize Ituri as an autonomous province. The government arrested Lubanga on 13 June 2002, but he was released ten weeks later it exchanged him for a kidnapped government minister.

Human Rights Watch and other humanitarian groups accused the

---

[347] "Congolese Warlord Lubanga Gets 14 Years" CNN Wire Staff, updated 10 July 2012; See also http://www.lubangatrial.org.

UPC under Lubanga's command, of "ethnic massacres, murder, torture, rape and mutilation, as well as the recruitment of child soldiers." Between November 2002 and June 2003, the UPC allegedly killed 800 civilians on the basis of their ethnicity in the gold mining region of Mongbwalu. Between 18 February and 3 March 2003, the UPC destroyed 26 villages in one area, killing at least 350 people and forced 60,000 to flee their homes. Human rights organizations claim that at one point Lubanga had recruited some 3,000 child soldiers between the ages of 8 and 15 years. He reportedly ordered every family in the area under his control to help the war effort by donating something: money, a cow, or a child to join his guerrillas. The Ugandan Army forced the UPC out of Bunin in March 2003. Lubanga later moved to Kinshasa and registered the UPC as a political party.[348]

In March 2004, the government of Congo authorized the ICC to investigate and prosecute "crimes within the jurisdiction of the Court allegedly committed anywhere in the territory of the DRC since 1 July 2002. The government arrested Lubanga on 19 March 2005 in connection and charged him with the killing of nine Bangladeshi citizens who were functioning as United Nations peacekeepers in Ituri on 25 February 2005. On 10 February 2006, a Pre-Trial Chamber of the ICC found that there were reasonable grounds to believe that Lubanga bore individual criminal responsibility for the war crime of "conscripting and enlisting children under the age of fifteen years and using them to participate actively in hostilities," and issued a sealed warrant for his arrest. Rebels under his command also committed human rights violations, including ethnic cleansing, murder, torture, rape, and mutilation. His trial for the war crime of "conscripting and enlisting children under the age of fifteen years and using them to participate actively in hostilities" began on 26 January 2009. The tribunal found Lubanga guilty on 14 March 2012. On 10 July 2012, Trial Chamber I of the ICC sentenced Lubanga to a total of 14 years imprisonment.[349]

---

[348] "ICC Issues First Conviction" Stop Rape in Conflict, 12267 July 2012

[349] Alexandra Hudson, "*Congo suspect to face war crimes charges*." Reuters, 18 March 2006; "Congo warlord jailed for 14 years in landmark case," Reuters, 10 July 2012; "Thomas Lubanga Dyilo" on Wikipedia.

On 18 October 2007, a warrant of arrest listing nine counts of war crimes and four counts of crimes against humanity in the Ituri district of eastern DRC was unsealed for Germain Katanga, alleged commander of the Force de résistance patriotique en Ituri (FRPI). Alleged acts include murder or willful killing, inhumane acts, sexual slavery, rape, cruel or inhuman treatment, using children to participate actively in hostilities, outrages upon personal dignity, intentional attack against the civilian population, pillaging and destruction of property. The arrest warrant had been issued on 2 July but made public on 18 October 2007. Katanga was surrendered by the Congo and transferred to the ICC on 17 October 2007. His Initial appearance of Germain Katanga took place on 22 October 2007 at the ICC premises in The Hague.

On 7 February 2008, an arrest listing similar war crimes and crimes against humanity was unsealed for Mathieu Ngudjolo Chui, a Congolese national and alleged former leader of the National integrationist Front (FNI) and a Colonel in the National Army of the government of the Democratic Republic of the Congo [Forces armées de la RDC/ Armed Forces of the DRC] (FARDC). The warrant had been issued on 6 July 2007 but made public on 7 February 2008. Ngudjolo Chui was surrendered by the DRC authorities and transferred to The Hague on 7 February 2008. He appeared for the first time before ICC Pre-Trial Chamber I on 11 February 2008.

On 10 March 2008 Pre-Trial Chamber I decided to join the Katanga and the Ngudjolo Chui cases as the two defendants were prosecuted for the same crimes. Initially scheduled on 28 February 2008 and then on 21 May 2008, the hearing was postponed twice by the Chamber to afford more preparation time to the parties involved. From 27 June to 18 July 2008, ICC Pre-Trial Chamber I held a confirmation of charges hearing in the case against Germain Katanga and Matthieu Ngudjolo Chui. Germain Katanga was represented by David Hooper and Matthieu Ngudjolo Chui by Jean Pierre Kilenda Kakengi Basila. Fifty-seven victims participated in the hearing through their legal representatives, Carine Bapita Buyagandu, Joseph Keta, Jean Louis Gilissen, Franck Mulenda and Hervé Diakiese. On 26 September 2008, ICC Pre-Trial Chamber I sent the case against Germain Katanga and

Matthieu Ngudjolo Chui to trial, by confirming all but three of the alleged charges. Pre-trial judges confirmed seven counts of war crimes and three counts of crimes against humanity. They found insufficient evidence to try Katanga and Ngudjolo for inhuman treatment, outrages upon personal dignity and inhumane acts. In a decision issued on March 27, 2009 the Trial Chamber II set the commencement of the trial in the case of *The Prosecutor v. Germain Katanga and Mathieu Ngudjolo Chui* for 24 September 2009.

On 31st August 2009, ICC Trial Chamber II decided to postpone the commencement of the trial to 24 November 2009. On 8 December 2010, the prosecution completed presenting its case, following which the legal representatives for victims presented two witnesses. The defense began presenting its case on 24 March 2011. On 15 August 2011, the defense of Mathieu Ngudjolo Chui began to present its evidence before TC II. Eight witnesses were called by the defense of Ngudjolo Chui, who also testified in his own defense from 8 November 2011. On 27 September 2011, Germain Katanga also testified before TC II in his own defense. Closing arguments in the case are expected in early 2012.On 15-23 May 2012 closing oral statements were given by the prosecutor, the defense teams and participating victims. The judges will now determine the verdict. Some 366 victims participated during the proceedings, several of whom are former child soldiers. On 21 November 2012, ICC judges decided to separate the two.

On 29 April 2008, Pre-Trial Chamber I unsealed an arrest warrant against Bosco Ntaganda, alleged former Deputy Chief of the General staff of the Forces Patriotiques pour la Libération du Congo (FPLC), and alleged current chief of Staff of the Congrès National pour la Défense du People (CNDP), an armed group, active in North Kivu, Congo. The arrest warrant lists three war crimes: 1) the enlistment of children under the age of fifteen; 2) the conscription of children under the age of fifteen; and 3) using children under the age of fifteen to participate actively in hostilities. This is the fourth arrest warrant unsealed within the context of the DRC situation. The suspect remains at large. On 13 July 2012, Pre-Trial Chamber II issued a second warrant of arrest for Bosco Ntaganda following the Office of the Prosecutor's 14 May 2012 request. The additional charges in the second arrest warrant include the crimes against humanity of murder, persecution based on ethnic grounds and rape/sexual slavery, as well as the war crimes of intentional attacks against civilians, murder, rape/sexual slavery and pillaging allegedly committed from September 2002 to September 2003 in Ituri, DRC.[350]

Northern Uganda

The Lord's Resistance Army (LRA) is a Christian-based rebel group that has been active in Uganda and neighboring countries since 1987 and is led by Joseph Kony, a former faith healer. Kony founded the group which derived its theology from Alice Auma's unsuccessful Holy Spirit Movement. Kony claims to communicate with, and receive instructions from, spirits and God. He also claims that his insurgency works for the betterment of his Acholi people.

On 29 July 2004, the ICC Prosecutor determined that there is a reasonable basis to open an investigation into the situation concerning Northern Uganda, following the referral of the situation by Uganda in December 2003. Unable to deal with Kony, the government of Uganda on 16 December 2003 referred the problem to the ICC. The decision to open an investigation was reportedly taken after thorough analysis of available information in order to ensure that requirements of the Rome Statute are satisfied. On 14 October 2005, arrest warrants for crimes against humanity and war crimes were publicly announced and unsealed and were issued on 8 July 2005 by Pre-Trial Chamber II for the five senior leaders of the Lord's Resistance Army (LRA), Joseph Kony, Vincent Otti, Okot Odhiambo, Dominic Ongwen, and Raska Lukwiya. Following its investigation the ICC issued an indictment which lists 33 crimes: 21 counts of war crimes and 12 counts of crimes against humanity. The indictment sought Joseph Kony and also Vincent Otti, Okot Odhiambo and Dominic Ongwen. Kony and Ongwen are apparently still leading the LRA, which has since committed additional crimes.

On 30 September 2005, media reports indicated that Dominic Ongwen had been killed. On 6 July 2006, ICC Pre-Trial Chamber II

[350] Coalition for the International Criminal Court, http://www.iccnow.org/?mod=casessituations

announced that it had received negative results of DNA tests conducted on what was reputed to be Ongwen's corpse. On 11 July 2007, the proceedings against Raska Lukwiya were terminated following his death. Lukwiya, had been killed in a battle with the Ugandan military. In December 2007, Kony had Vincent Otti executed. On 8 November 2007, the ICC Office of the Prosecutor informed the Pre-Trial Chamber that it is taking steps to assess his fate. On 6 October 2008, the OTP publicly called for renewed efforts to arrest top LRA commanders Joseph Kony, Okot Odhiambo and Dominic Ongwen "in the light of serious and converging information on attacks by the LRA against civilians in the DRC."[351]

On 6 October 2008, the OTP publicly called for renewed efforts to arrest top LRA commanders Joseph Kony, Okot Odhiambo and Dominic Ongwen "in the light of serious and converging information on attacks by the LRA against civilians in the DRC." On 21 October 2008, ICC Pre-Trial Chamber II requested the DRC to provide information on the measures taken for the execution of these arrest warrants. The same day, the UNSC issued a resolution reminding the international community of the ICC indictments against the LRA.

Meanwhile, the European parliament adopted a resolution on the indictment and prosecution of Joseph Kony at the ICC. In March 2008, the Government of Uganda submitted a response to the Court explaining that the "establishment of the special division of the High Court and the enactment of the relevant legislation shall take place after the signing of the final peace agreement with the Lord's Resistance Army/Movement. With respect to the impact of these developments on the execution of the arrest warrants, the Government of Uganda stated that the special division of the High Court is not meant to supplant the work of the International Criminal Court and accordingly those individuals who were indicted by the International Criminal Court will [sic] have to be brought before the special division of the High Court for trial."

On 18 June, 2008, Pre-Trial Chamber II requested further information from the Republic of Uganda, after the reported failure to sign

---

[351] McKinley, James C. Jr., "Uganda's Christian Rebels Revive War in North." *New York Times*, 1 April 1996; Jeffrey Gettleman, Jeffrey (2010-04-10). "Uganda Enlists Former Rebels to End a War." *New York Times*, 10 April 2010.

the final peace agreement by the respective parties. The Chamber requested information as to the steps undertaken by the Republic of Uganda with a regard to the service of arrest warrants. On 9 July, 2008, Uganda responded that the comprehensive peace agreement was indeed not signed; that the Republic of Uganda remained committed to executing the warrants of arrest; and that the government of Uganda continues to spare no effort in its attempt to secure the cooperation of the DRC in order to trace the LRA in the Garamba National Park, which is territory belonging to Congo. In 2009 Odhiambo reportedly defected from the LRA, but would only surrender if his captors guaranteed that he would not be tried for his crimes.[352]

Darfur, Sudan

The War in Darfur was a guerrilla conflict or civil war centered on the Darfur region of Sudan. It began in February 2003 when the Sudan Liberation Movement/Army (SLM/A) and Justice and Equality Movement (JEM) groups in Darfur took up arms, accusing the Sudanese government of oppressing non-Arab Sudanese in favor of Sudanese Arabs. The conflict is also known as the Darfur Genocide. The Arab government of Sudan has been practicing apartheid against the nation's black ethnic groups. Sudan also has practiced discrimination against Christians in what is now South Sudan where tens of thousands of black Africans in the country's southern region, most of them Christians or animists, have been abducted and sold into slavery by Arab militias backed by the Islamist regime in Khartoum.

One side of the conflict was composed mainly of the official Sudanese military and police, and the Janjaweed, a Sudanese militia group recruited mostly from the local Arabs and few Arab Bedouin of the northern Rizeigat. The majority of other Arab groups in Darfur remain uninvolved in the conflict. The other side was made up of rebel groups, notably the SLM/A and the JEM, recruited primarily from the Fur, Zaghawa, and Masalit ethnic groups. Although the Sudanese government publicly denies that it supports the Janjaweed, it has been providing financial assistance and weapons to the militia and has been organizing

[352]https://www.state.gov/j/drl/rls/hrrpt/2008/af/118995.htm

joint attacks targeting civilians. The better-armed Janjaweed quickly gained the upper hand. By the spring of 2004, several thousand people – mostly from the non-Arab population – had been killed and as many as a million more had been driven from their homes

The crisis took on an international dimension when in 2004 over 100,000 refugees sought refuge in neighboring Chad. Janjaweed militiamen pursued the fleeing black displaced persons. Troops from Chad governmental forces attempted to stop the Janjaweed along the border. The army of Chad killed some 70 Janjaweed militiamen while losing 10 soldiers in one gun battle in April. A United Nations observer team reported that non-Arab villages were singled out while Arab villages were left unscathed. Several thousand people, mostly from the non-Arab population, had been killed and as many as a million more had been driven from their homes, causing a major humanitarian crisis in the region. In September 2004, the World Health Organization estimated that there had been 50,000 deaths in Darfur since the beginning of the conflict, mostly due to starvation.

In February 2008 the Sudanese government soldiers and Arab militiamen launched a new offensive against Darfur rebels. This action trapped thousands of refugees along the Chadian border, the rebels and humanitarian workers said 20 February 2008.[353] As of 21 February 2008, the total dead in Darfur stood at 450,000 with an estimated 3,245,000 people displaced. In January 2010, one recent authoritative study estimates with 95% confidence, that the excess number of deaths is between 178,258 and 461,520 (the mean being 298,271), with 80% of these due to diseases. As of 2010 a total of 51 International peacekeepers have been killed in Darfur.[354]

Having previously authorized an investigation into war crimes in Darfur,[355] in March 2005 the Security Council formally referred the situation in Darfur to the prosecutor of the ICC, without mentioning any specific crimes. The ICC investigation into the situation in Darfur, Sudan,

---

[353] "ICC Considers New war Crimes Charges Against Sudan" 13 Dec. 2012, Allafrica.com.

[354] Centre for Research on the Epidemiology of Disasters, "Patterns of mortality rates in Darfur Conflict," *The Lancet* [Jan. 2010], Thelancet.com.

[355] UN Security Council Resolution 1564 of 2004.

continues. The ICC has reason to believe criminal acts have been committed during the War in Darfur. Sudan is not a state party to the Rome Statute. As of the end of 2012 seven suspects have been indicted by the court: Ahmed Haroun and Ali Kushayb, Omar al-Bashir, Bahar Abu Garda, Abdallah Banda and Saleh Jerbo, and Abdel Rahim Mohammed Hussein.

Ahmed Haroun was formerly Minister of the Interior for the government of Sudan; later he served as the Minister of State for Humanitarian Affairs. He is alleged to have commanded and coordinated the counterinsurgency in Darfur and provided arms to the Janjaweed. Ali Muhammad Ali Abd-Al-Rahman, or Ali Kushayb, was allegedly the leader of the Janjaweed. Hauron and Kushayb were charged with the total of 51 counts of war crimes and crimes against humanity against the Fur people. The first nine counts concern attacks in and around the Kodoom villages about 15 August 2003 and around 31 August 2003. Additional counts concern attacks in and around the town of Bindisi from or around 15 August 2003 to or around 31 August 2003. Other counts concern attacks in and around the town of Mukjar in or around August 2003, September 2003, October 2003, December 2003, and March 2004. Last, more counts concern attacks in and around the town of Arawala in or around December 2003. Haroun is charged with 20 counts of crimes against humanity and 22 counts of war crimes while Kushayb is charged with 22 counts of crimes against humanity and 28 counts of war crimes.[356]

Omar Hassan al- Bashir became president of Sudan on 16 October 1993. On 4 March 2009 the prosecutor of the ICC issued its first warrant for Bashir's arrest, followed by a second warrant on 12 July 2010. [357] The warrants allege that Bashir is criminally responsible for intentionally directing attacks against a civilian population; five counts of crimes against humanity, including murder, torture, and rape; and genocide.[358] The prosecutor alleged that Bahar Idriss Abu Garda Abu Garda is criminally responsible as a co-perpetrator or as an indirect co-perpetrator for three war crimes: murder; intentionally directing attacks against

[356] "Situation in Darfur, Sudan". International Criminal Court website; "ICC Investigation in Darfur" in Wikipedia.

[357]"Omar al-Bashir" Wikipedia.

[358]"Sudanese President Bashir Charged," *The Guardian*, 4 March 2009.

personnel, installations, material, units or vehicles involved in a peacekeeping mission; and pillaging. The tribunal rejected the prosecutor's request because of the lack of evidence. Warrants may be issued at a later date if evidence can be discovered. Abdallah Banda Abakaer Nourain was commander of Justice and Equality Movement, one of the components of the United Resistance Front. He was indicted by the ICC on 27 August, 2009 with the indictment being unsealed on 15 June, 2010. He was charged with pillaging and attacking peace keeping forces. Saleh Jerbo Jamus, former chief of staff of SLA-Unity which is currently integrated into Justice and Equality Movement, was indicted on 27 August 2009 and the indictment unsealed on 15 June 2010. The prosecutor charged Jamus with murder or attempted murder; pillaging; and attacks upon peace keeping forces. Abdel Raheem Muhammad Hussein is Sudan's Minister of National Defence and former Minister of the Interior and former Sudanese President's Special Representative in Darfur. The prosecutor charged him with rape, false imprisonment, pillaging, and torture.[359]

There are various estimates on the number of human casualties which range up to several hundred thousand dead, from either direct combat or starvation and disease inflicted by the conflict. There have also been mass displacements and coercive migrations, forcing millions into refugee camps or over the border and creating what is regarded by many as a genocide.

Aftermath of Voting in Kenya

The ICC has been conducting an on-going investigation in the Republic of Kenya regarding the 2007–2008 post-election violence in Kenya. These acts followed the presidential election that was held on 27 December 2007. Because of Kenya's role as a Western ally and regional business hub, external intervention was almost immediate. The severity of the crisis led French Foreign Affairs Minister Bernard Kouchner to appeal to the U. N. Security Council in January 2008 to react "in the name of the responsibility to protect" before Kenya plunged into a deadly ethnic conflict. On 31 December 2007, U. N. Secretary-General Ban Ki-

[359]ICC "Situations and Cases" Darfur.

moon issued a statement expressing concern for the ongoing violence, calling for the population to remain calm and for restraint to be shown by Kenyan security forces. On the same day, then UN High Commissioner for Human Rights Louise Arbour called on the Kenyan Government to abide by its international human rights obligations. There were approximately 112 people were killed in Nakuru between 24 and 27 January 2008 and by 31 January at least 50 people had been killed in Naivasha.[360]

The case which concerns the Orange Democratic Movement's supporters' actions against the supporters of the government, William Ruto, Henry Kosgey, and Joshua Sang were charged with four counts of crimes against humanity. They were all accused of committing the crimes as indirect co-perpetrators at locations including Turbo town, the greater Eldoret area, Kapsabet town, and Nandi Hills town. Their charges were murder, deportation and forced transport of populations; torture, persecution, and commission of inhumane acts. The prosecutor alleges than in Nakuru there occurred forty-five cases of sexual violence including rapes and penile amputation. One of the factors that triggered that violence was the inflammatory language of politicians, has remained a serious threat to peace and stability.[361] The Electoral Commission of Kenya officially declared that the incumbent President Mwai Kibaki to have been re-elected. Supporters of the opposition candidate Raila Odinga accused the government of electoral fraud and rejected the results. A series of protests and demonstrations followed, and fighting, mainly along tribal lines, led to many deaths, injuries, and other violence. The government of Kenya and its National Assembly both attempted to stop the ICC process. On 26 October 2011 the tribunal confirmed all charges against William Ruto and Joshua Arap Sang; confirmed all of the charges with the exception of sexual violence against Uhuru Kenyatta and Francis Muthaura; and declined to confirm the charges against Mohammed Hussein Ali and Henry Kosgey.[362]

---

[360] Mba Chidi Nmaju, "Violence in Kenya: Any Role for the ICC in the Quest for Accountability?" 3 *African Journal of Legal Studies* [2009] 78-95.

[361] "Taming Hate Speech in Kenya" Humanitarian News and Analysis, 24 August 2012. irinews.org.

[362] "ICC investigation into Kenya" Wikipedia; *New York Times*, 19 March 2012.

On 15 December 2010, Chief Prosecutor Luis Moreno Ocampo named six suspects, and made an application to Pre-Trial Chamber II for summonses to be issued for their arrest. Moreno Ocampo named the following: Major General Mohammed Hussein Ali, the chief executive of the Postal Corporation of Kenya, who at the time of the post-election violence had been the Commissioner of the Kenya Police. Uhuru Muigai Kenyatta – the Deputy Prime Minister and Minister for Finance who is also chairman of the KANU political party which is part of President Kibaki's Party of National Unity. Henry Kiprono Kosgey – the Minister for Industrialization and member of the National Assembly for the Tinderet Constituency who is also chairman of the Orange Democratic Movement. Francis Kirimi Muthaura – the Head of Public Service, Cabinet Secretary and chairman of the National Security Advisory Committee. William Samoei Ruto – the Minister for Higher Education, Science and Technology and ODM member of the National Assembly for the Eldoret North Constituency. Joshua Arap Sang, the head of operations at the Kalenjin language radio station KASS FM, who at the time of the post-election violence was a radio announcer. The six men became colloquially known as the Ocampo Six. The charges against the group included rape, forced depopulation and dislocation of population, commission of inhumane acts, and murder. By 2013 human rights watch groups estimated that 1,300 Kenyans were killed and more than half a million displaced in the wake of a presidential election.

On 22 December 2010, a week after the ICC Prosecutor announced the list of persons indicted, the Kenyan National Assembly passed a motion to withdraw Kenya as a party to the Rome Statute. As originally written and introduced to the Kenyan National Assembly, the motion was ruled it was unconstitutional. An amended version introduced the following day passed. Minister for Energy Kiraitu Murungi denounced the court, claiming that the ICC was a colonialist, imperialist institution. The Rome statute seemed to contradict parts of Kenya's International Crimes Act as well as its constitution. In February 2011, Kenya appealed to the United Nations Security Council, asking it to defer the trials at The Hague. The African Union endorsed the position of the Kenyan government.

Civil War in Libya

The situation in Libya is the International Criminal Court's sixth investigation. Libya is not an ICC member so the Security Council referred Muammar Gaddafi's violent crackdown on pro-democracy protesters during last year's Arab Spring uprising to the ICC in February 2011. That referral mandates Libyan cooperation with the court. On 4 March 2011, the ICC Presidency assigned the situation in Libya to Pre-Trial Chamber I. The Chamber is currently composed of Judge Christine Van den Wyngaert (Belgium), Judge Hans-Peter Kaul (Germany), and Judge Silvia Fernandez Gurmendi (Argentina). Chief ICC Prosecutor Fatou Bensouda said that the ICC's pre-trial chamber would decide "in due course" on which figures associated with the ouster of Libyan leader Gaddafi should be charged and with what specific crimes.

Bensouda's office is continuing to gather information on a Libyan case focusing on allegations of rape and sexual violence targeting men and women, allegations against other members of Gaddafi's government, as well as charges of crimes committed by rebel forces. She pleaded with the Libyan government to withhold amnesty until the ICC's work was completed. She pointed to a recently approved Libyan law that raises the possibility of amnesty for "acts made necessary by the 17 February revolution," apparently creating the possibility of not prosecuting crimes committed by anti-Gaddafi fighters. Bensouda said she understood that the Libyan government has committed itself to a strategy of addressing all crimes committed in the country.

The ICC issued three arrests warrants in this investigation naming Muammar Gaddafi, Saif Al-Islam Gaddafi and Abdullah Al-Senussi. On 27 June 2011, ICC Pre-Trial Chamber I (PTC I) issued warrants of arrest for Libyan leader Muammar Mohammed Abu Minyar Gaddafi, his son Saif Al-Islam Gaddafi, Libyan government spokesman, and Abdullah Al-Senussi, Director of Military Intelligence, for alleged crimes against humanity (murder and persecution) committed in Libya from 15 February until at least 28 February 2011. The ICC Prosecutor applied for arrest warrants against Muammar Al-Gaddafi, Saif Al-Islam Gaddafi and Abdullah Al-Senussi on 16 May 2011. On 22 November 2011, Pre-Trial Chamber I decided to terminate the case against Muammar Mohammed

Abu Minyar Gaddafi following his death.[363]

PTC I judges decided that there were reasonable grounds to believe that the three suspects committed crimes against humanity and that the warrants of arrest were necessary to ensure their appearance before the ICC, to prevent interference in the ongoing investigation and to prevent the commission of further crimes. Responsibility for the implementation of arrest warrants lies with the Libyan national authorities. Libya is obliged to cooperate fully with the ICC and the prosecutor, under the terms of United Nations Security Council (UNSC) Resolution 1970 (2011). However, cooperation from the Libyan Transitional National Council and other states may be needed to ensure the arrest of the three suspects.

Libyan authorities have refused to extradite Saif al-Islam Gaddafi to face charges in war crimes committed during the NATO-backed revolt that toppled his father in 2011. Libya wants to try Saif al-Islam in its own courts. In the case of Qaddafi, who had been his father's heir apparent, officials have said confidently in recent interviews that the ICC had consented to a trial in Tripoli under its supervision, but the ICC disputed that. Libya also wishes to try Gaddafi's former intelligence chief Abdullah al-Senussi, one of the most feared members of Gaddafi's inner circle, for war crimes. On 17 March 2012, Al-Senussi was arrested in Mauritania. France and Libya are also reported to be seeking his extradition to their custody. His capture triggered a tug of war between Libya, France and the ICC for his extradition.[364] The new Libyan government in Tripoli issued a call for countries to extradite to Libya any members of the Gaddafi regime wanted in connection with past crimes. For its part the Tripoli government believes that the ICC opposes a trial in Libya because it has no confidence in any part of the state's court system.[365]

Among the charges Bensouda's office is pursuing is the execution

---

[363] "ICC Investigation in Kenya" Wikipedia.; "Disputed 2007 Presidential Election" International Coalition for the Responsibility to Protect. Responsibilityto protect.org.

[364] France has also sought Senussi, who was convicted in absentia there of murdering 170 people, including 54 French citizens, in the bombing of a passenger jet in 1989. *New York Times*, 21 March 2012.

[365] "Libya Resists International Court's Claim on War Crimes Case," *New York Times*, 21 March 2012

without trial of Gaddafi supporters. She is working on the assumption that the rebels summarily executed scores of Gaddafi loyalists, and perhaps Gaddafi himself when rebels sacked the ruler's final stronghold. When a team of Human Rights Watch researchers arrived in Sirte in October 2012 following the battle they found the decomposing remains of at least 53 people at the nearby Mahari Hotel, some with their hands still bound behind their backs. Rebels assassinated most of these persons during Gaddafi's last days before he was himself killed. Anti-Gaddafi forces captured alive an estimated 150 persons after the battle. They transported some 70 of these survivors to Misrata and held them there in custody, but at least 53, and possibly as many as 66 people, were found dead the next day at the nearby Mahari Hotel. The execution of prisoners is a war crime and those who issued such orders can be tried in the ICC.[366] Members of Gaddafi's family filed a complaint against the North Atlantic Treaty Organization (NATO) with the International Criminal Court for its alleged role in Gaddafi's death. Also last October, the UN Office of the High Commissioner on Human Rights which called for a full investigation into his death.[367]

Election Violence in Ivory Coast

Félix Houphouët-Boigny became Ivory Coast's father of independence as he led the separation from France. In 1956 France enacted the Overseas Reform Act which transferred a number of powers from Paris to elected territorial governments in French West Africa. In 1958, Ivory Coast became an autonomous member of the French Community. Houphouët-Boigny's one-party rule was not amenable to political competition. In 1990, hundreds of civil servants went on strike, joined by students, all protesting institutional corruption. This forced the government reluctantly to allow multi-party democracy. Houphouët-Boigny became increasingly feeble and died in 1993.

Houphouët-Boigny's hand-picked successor was Henri Konan Bédié. In October 1995, Bédié overwhelmingly won re-election against a

[366] "Death of a Dictator: Bloody Vengeance in Sirte," Human Rights Watch, on jurist.org.

[367] "War Crimes Committed At Gaddafi Death Site" 18 October 2012, Allafrica.com

fragmented and disorganized opposition. He tightened his grip on political life, jailing several hundred opposition supporters. In late 1999, a group of dissatisfied officers staged a military coup, putting General Robert Guéï in power. Bédié fled into exile in France.

A presidential election was held in October 2000 in which Laurent Gbagbo vied with Guéï, but it was peaceful. The lead-up to the election was marked by military and civil unrest. In the early hours of 19 September 2002, while President Gbagbo was in Italy, there was a coup d'etate. The government claimed that former president Robert Guéï had led a coup attempt, and state TV showed pictures of his dead body in the street. Guéï's supporters claimed that he and fifteen others had been murdered at his home and his body had been moved to the streets to incriminate him. Rebel forces made their stronghold in the northern city of Bouake and threatened to move on Abidjan. France deployed troops.

In January 2003, Gbagbo and rebel leaders signed accords creating a "government of national unity". French troops patrolled the western border of the country. The unity government was. In March 2004, some 120 people were killed in an opposition rally. A peace accord between the government and the rebels, or New Forces, was signed on 4 March 2007, and subsequently Guillaume Soro, leader of the New Forces, became prime minister. The presidential elections that should have been held in 2005 were finally held in November 2010. The Electoral Commission reported a loss for Gbagbo in favor of his rival, former prime minister Alassane Ouattara. The presidential election led the Second Ivorian Civil War. Ouattara's forces seized control of most of the country, with Gbagbo entrenched in Abidjan, the country's largest city. International organizations reported numerous instances of human rights violations by both sides. In the city of Duékoué, hundreds of people were estimated to have been killed, predominantly by advancing pro-Ouattara militias. In nearby Blolequin, dozens of people were killed, reportedly by retreating Liberian mercenaries whom Gbagbo had been hired.[368]

---

[368]"Ivory Coast" Wikipedia; Robert J. Mundt, "Côte d'Ivoire: Continuity and Change in a Semi-Democracy," in John F. Clark and David Gardinier, eds. *Political Reform in Francophone Africa*, Boulder: Westview Press, 1997; Robert E. Handloff, ed. *Ivory Coast: A Country Study*, Library of Congress Country Studies, Government Printing Office, 1991.

On 29 March 2011 forces loyal to President Alassane Ouattara captured the western town of Duékoué as they swept through Côte d'Ivoire before ultimately arresting former President Laurent Gbagbo. After taking over the town, pro-Ouattara forces committed horrific abuses, killing several hundred people. Human Rights Watch in June 2012 reported that armed militants hostile to the government of Ivory Coast recruited Liberian children to carry out deadly cross-border raids on Ivorian villages in recent months said today. Liberian authorities have failed to investigate and prosecute dozens of Liberian and Ivorian nationals who crossed into Liberia after committing war crimes during Côte d'Ivoire's 2010-2011 post-election crisis, some of whom have been implicated in the recent attacks. on June 8, 2012, in which at least 17 people, including seven United Nations peacekeepers, were killed in southwestern Côte d'Ivoire. In June 2012, Human Rights Watch reported that dozens of former Ivorian and Liberian combatants loyal to the previous government of Ivory Coast were using Liberia as a base to launch raids into Côte d'Ivoire. They targeted civilians perceived as supporting President Alassane Ouattara. Since July 2011, attackers killed at least 50 people during these raids and displaced thousands more. United Nations and French forces took military action against Gbagbo who was taken into custody after a raid into his residence on 11 April 2011. It was initially reported that he was captured by French forces; however, Ouattara's envoy to the UN claimed it was their forces who captured him, and the French deny any involvement in his arrest.

On 14 December 2010, President of Côte d'Ivoire Alassane Ouattara sent a letter to the Office of the Prosecutor reaffirming the Côte d'Ivoire government's acceptance of the Court's jurisdiction. On 3 May 2011, President Ouattara reiterated his wish that the Court open an investigation. The ICC opened its investigation in the situation of the Republic of Côte d'Ivoire in 2011. Two arrest warrants have been issued for crimes against humanity for Laurent Gbagbo and Simone Gbagbo. Côte d'Ivoire signed the Rome Statute on 30 November 1998 but has not yet ratified it. However, in April 2003, Côte d'Ivoire accepted the jurisdiction of the ICC under the provisions of article 12 (3) of the Rome Statute. It is the first time that the prosecutor has opened an investigation on this basis. The investigation was assigned to Pre-Trial Chamber I, composed of Judge Hans-Peter Kaul, Judge Christine van den Wyngaert, and Judge Silvia Fernández de Gurmendi. It had previously been assigned to Pre-Trial Chamber III.

After conducting a preliminary examination of the situation in Côte d'Ivoire from 2003 onward, the prosecutor concluded that there was a reasonable basis to believe that crimes within the jurisdiction of the Court had been committed in Ivory Coast since 28 November 2010. On 23 June 2011, Prosecutor Luis Moreno-Ocampo requested authorization from ICC judges to open an investigation in Côte d'Ivoire in relation to war crimes and crimes against humanity allegedly committed following the disputed presidential election of 28 November 2010. It was the second time that the prosecutor used his *propriu motu*[369] powers to initiate an investigation without first having received a referral from a state or by the United Nations Security Council. It is the seventh situation under investigation by the Office of the Prosecutor. On 22 February 2012, ICC judges expanded authorization for the investigation in Ivory Coast to include crimes within the jurisdiction of the Court allegedly committed between 19 September 2002 and 28 November 2010, considering that the violent events in Ivory Coast in this period (including the events since 28 November 2010) are to be treated as a single situation, in which an ongoing crisis involving a prolonged political dispute and power-struggle culminated in the events in relation to which the Pre-Trial Chamber earlier authorized an investigation.

In July 2012 government officials in Côte d'Ivoire used the fact that the ICC has issued arrest warrants against people from only one side of the recent conflict to justify their own selective approach to justice. That approach ignores many thousands of victims and threatens the country's ability to return to the rule of law. Ivory Coast's military was responsible for widespread human rights abuses in August and early September 2012. The abuses included arbitrary arrests, illegal detentions, extortion, inhuman treatment, and, in some cases, torture. The former leader of the Young Patriots militia, Charles Blé Goudé, was arrested on 17 January

[369] A *motu proprio* (Latin "on his own impulse") is a document issued by the Pope or a monarch on his own initiative and personally signed by him.

2013, accused of serious crimes allegedly committed under his command during Côte d'Ivoire's 2010-2011 violent post-election crisis.

On 23 November 2011, judges of Pre-Trial Chamber III issued an arrest warrant, following a request made by the prosecutor for Laurent Koudou Gbagbo, former president of Ivory Coast. Following the arrest warrant, on 30 November 2011 Gbagbo was transferred to the ICC in The Hague. The suspect appeared before Pre-Trial Chamber III on 5 December 2011 at which time the Chamber informed him of the charges brought against him, as well as of his rights. On 12 June, at the request Gbagbo, Pre-Trial Chamber I postponed the commencement of a confirmation of charges hearing to 13 August 2012. Originally scheduled to start on 18 June, the postponement of the hearing is intended to give the defense more preparation time. However, on 3 August, the hearing was postponed for a second time until a medical evaluation of Gbagbo's fitness to take part in the case is carried out. On 24-25 September 2012, Pre-Trial Chamber I held a closed hearing to discuss the fitness of Gbagbo to take part in the pending confirmation of charges hearing and subsequently found him competent. Following a hearing on the status of the case on 11 December 2012, pre-trial judges decided that a key confirmation of charges hearing to decide whether the case against Mr. Gbagbo will move to trial will begin on 19 February 2013. On 13 July, PTC I refused Gbagbo's request for provisional release. On 26 October 2012, the Appeals Chamber rejected Gbagbo's appeal challenging a decision denying him interim release.[370]

Mali

The Republic of Mali is a landlocked country in West Africa that was once part of French West Sudan. There are eight regions in the nation. In the north its borders reach deep into the middle of the Sahara Desert, while in the south water is abundant in the Niger and Sénégal rivers. The country's economic structure centers on agriculture and fishing although it is also a major producer of gold and salt. Since independence it has struggled politically and economically. Approximately half its population lives below the international poverty line of $1.25 a day.

[370] ICC "Situations and Cases" Ivory Coast; Coalition for the International Criminal Court, http://www.iccnow.org

In January 2012 a Tuareg rebellion began in Northern Mali, led by the National Movement for the Liberation of Azawad. In March, military officer Amadou Sanogo seized power in a coup d'état, citing Touré's failures in quelling the rebellion, and leading to sanctions and an embargo by the Economic Community of West African States. The MNLA quickly took control of the north, declaring independence as Azawad. However, Islamist groups including Ansar Dine and Al-Qaeda in the Islamic Maghreb (AQIM), who had helped the MNLA defeat the government, turned on the Tuareg and took control of the North with the goal of implementing Sharia Law in Mali.[371] Since the March 2012 coup, Mali had been ruled in theory by a series of civilian leaders while the military has appeared to retain power in fact. In April 2012, under international pressure, the military junta agreed to a civilian government led by an interim president, Dioncounda Traoré, the former leader of the national assembly, and an interim prime minister, Cheick Modibo Diarra, an astrophysicist who once worked at NASA. In December 2012, in an apparent second coup, soldiers arrested Diarra, the prime minister, who then announced his resignation on television. Three days later, a new prime minister, Diango Cissoko, was sworn in and took office.

At the same time, the upheaval in the government and military left the Malian Army unable to defend Mali's northern desert region. That area has become an enclave and training ground for radical jihadi factions, including Al Qaeda in the Islamic Maghreb, who have imposed a brutal application of Shariah law that includes public whippings, beatings, amputations and stonings.

On 18 July 2012, the government of Mali formally asked the International Criminal Court to investigate atrocities attributed to groups of armed rebels, including Islamic extremists. Mali had ratified the ICC's founding document, the Rome Statute, in 2000. One of the atrocities occurred on July 29, when Islamists in control of a town in northern Mali stoned a couple to death after accusing them of having children outside of marriage. In early August, Islamists publicly amputated the hand of a man they accused of robbery.

On 12 October 2012 the Security Council passed resolution 2071

[371] "Mali clashes force 120 000 from homes," *New York Times*, 22 February 2012.

concerning Mali. It pledged assistance in re-establishing control over areas lost in the Taliban and in creating and maintaining democratic institutions in the nation. Its greatest concern was for restoration of human rights and personal security.

In late November 2012, U. N. Secretary General Ban Ki-moon, recommended that the Security Council endorse a plan suggested by the African Union and the Economic Community of West African States to deploy a security force as requested by the Mali government to reclaim the north from the extremists. The Security Council unanimously approved a resolution to send thousands of African troops into Mali to help oust Islamist extremists who have turned its northern half into a vast Qaeda enclave and training ground. But the resolution also made clear that such a military intervention will not happen until Mali's own dysfunctional army is adequately trained and a framework for political stability and elections is restored in the country, which has been in turmoil since a military coup in March.

The weak Malian army had retreated south while African nations and the U.N. debated how to find money and soldiers to recapture the territory. On 11 January 2013, the French Armed Forces intervened at the request of Sanogo's government, answering the urgent plea from the government of its former colony in West Africa. Mali needed help to blunt the sudden and aggressive advance into the center of the country by Islamist extremist militants. On January 30, the coordinated advance of the French and Malian troops claimed to have retaken the last remaining Islamist stronghold of Kidal, which was also the last of three northern provincial capitals. Simultaneously Britain has confirmed that it plans provide military assistance to French and African forces in Mali.[372]

In northern Mali, and especially in Bamako the capital, there is repression and intimidation. Hooded gunmen have abducted and beaten journalists at night. Soldiers who opposed the military junta have been tortured or forcibly "disappeared." Those who beat the country's elderly interim president have escaped without charges. Rather than taking on the Islamists who have seized northern Mali, the military in the south appears intent on striking back at rivals who carried out a failed counter-coup in

---

[372] "Mali" *New York Times*, 31 January 2013.

late April. Human Rights Watch accused the army of engaging in a campaign of "horrific" abuse against opposing soldiers at the junta's headquarters outside Bamako. One witness reported to the group that Captain Sanogo was seen kicking a detainee who has since disappeared. "Torture, sexual abuse and inhumane and degrading conditions" are reported by Amnesty International, at the base where Captain Sanogo has his headquarters, in a report to be released soon.

ICC chief prosecutor said she had launched a formal investigation into suspected war crimes in Mali, following rebels' seizure of large tracts of the West African state. "Since the beginning of the armed conflict in January 2012, the people of Northern Mali have been living in profound turmoil," ICC prosecutor Fatou Bensouda said in a statement. "At each stage during the conflict, different armed groups have caused havoc and human suffering through a range of alleged acts of extreme violence. I have determined that some of these deeds of brutality and destruction may constitute war crimes." Ms Bensouda said she would investigate a wide range of crimes including murder, mutilation, torture and rape, as well as executions that were implemented without a judgment from an established court. She said the investigation would also cover "intentionally directing attacks against protected objects."[373]

The chief prosecutor has also warned the Malian government following reports that its army may have committed abuses in the conflict-ridden west African country. "My office is aware of reports that Malian forces may have committed abuses in recent days, in central Mali," Fatou Bensouda said on Monday in a statement from the ICC's headquarters in The Hague. "I urge the Malian authorities to put an immediate stop to the alleged abuses and on the basis of the principle of complementarity, to investigate and prosecute those responsible for the alleged crimes," she said. The International Federation of Human Rights (FIDH) last week alleged that Malian soldiers have carried out multiple summary executions since the start earlier this month of a French-backed offensive against Islamist extremists in Mali. There is credible reports that Malian soldiers had carried out a string of executions at a military camp in the center of the country and that around 20 bodies had been dumped in wells or

[373]*New York Times*, 11 January 2013.

otherwise disposed of.

Bensouda on January 16 opened a war crimes probe in the war-torn west African nation, once one of the region's few democratic success stories. French and Malian troops have been fighting Islamist rebels since January 11 when it launched an offensive against the insurgents who have been occupying half of the country since April last year. French troops on Monday entered the historic city of Timbuktu, occupied for 10 months by Islamists who imposed a harsh form of Sharia. At least 144,500 refugees have fled from Mali to Mauritania, Niger, Burkina Faso and Algeria, U. N. humanitarian agencies have said, while another 230,000 are internally displaced. Bensouda in 2012 ordered a preliminary probe into reports of terrifying atrocities committed in Mali to see if the criteria for a fuller investigation were met.

At the time, Bensouda said the destruction of UNESCO-listed Muslim shrines in Timbuktu may also constitute war crimes. The Islamists who seized the ancient city considered the saints' tombs idolatrous. The Taliban is also accused of smashing traditional Sufi shrines in the ancient caravan town of Timbuktu [374]

Both Tuareg and Islamist groups have been guilty of gang rape, extrajudicial executions, and the use of child soldiers. On 3 April 2012, armed groups looted 2,354 tons of food from United Nation's warehouses in Kidal, Gao and Timbuktu, causing the U.N. to suspend its operations in northern Mali. Other targets of looting included hospitals, hotels, government offices, Oxfam offices and the offices and warehouses of other unnamed aid groups. The WFP also stated that 200,000 had so far fled the fighting, predicting that the number would rise. Islamist forces have reinstituted slavery and former slaves were the first targeted for punishment. With Taliban assistance former masters have used the violence to recapture ex-slave. When the Taliban fled Timbuktu it set fire to the Ahmed Baba Institute, destroying many of its priceless ancient manuscripts. Black Muslims have perpetrated outrages on Tuaregs and Arabs who lived in Bamako and elsewhere in southern Mali.[375]

---

[374] "ICC Prosecutor Warns Mali" *New York Times*, January 29, 2013

[375] "Fleeing Islamists burn priceless Timbuktu library" *New York Times*, 28 January 2013; "Human Rights Watch: Mali's Army Killing Civilians" *New York Times,* 19

The ICC investigation into alleged war crimes in Mali is placing a serious strain on an already over-stretched and cash-strapped institution. It is examining claims of murder, mutilation, torture, attacks on protected objects, executions, pillaging, and rape since January 2012 when insurgent groups began their campaign to take over northern Mali. French troops and the Malian army have been reclaiming captured towns this month, but ongoing fighting means ICC investigators are unlikely to be gathering evidence on the ground. Total court funding in 2013 is around US$144 million, with possible access to a contingency fund of up to $9.3 million, compared with $138 million in 2010. The prosecutor's office, which carries out the investigations, was this year allocated $37 million.[376]

Central African Republic

The Central African Republic has had a history of political instability and recurring armed conflict since its separation and independence from France. Once known as the Central African Empire, its emperor spent half of gross domestic product on his coronation. State authority is weak in many parts of the country, which are largely controlled by rebel groups and criminal armed groups. Coupled with ethnic tensions in the north, frequent armed incursions by rebel elements from neighboring countries and the continued presence of members of the armed Ugandan group known as the Lord's Resistance Army, all have added to insecurity and instability in CAR, which also has 170,000 people displaced internally. The members of the Security Council in late 2012 demanded that the armed groups immediately cease hostilities, withdraw from captured cities, cease any further advance towards the city of Bangui, return to peaceful activities, and respect the Libreville Comprehensive Peace Agreement. Signed in June 2008, the Libreville Comprehensive Peace Agreement helped bring an end to conflicts inside CAR, with the U.N. Integrated Peacebuilding Office in the CAR (BINUCA) playing a key role in encouraging the signing of the pact between the Government and three main rebel groups, as well as the holding in December that same year of the so-called Inclusive Political Dialogue between the Government,

---

January 2013.

376 "Cash Strapped ICC Takes on Mali" *New York Times*, 29 January 2013.

rebel groups, the political opposition, civil society and other relevant stakeholders. Security Council resolution 2031, adopted in 2011, demanded that all armed groups cooperate with the Government in the DDR process, with the latter being implemented in "a transparent and comprehensive manner."

The government of the Central African Republic (CAR) referred the situation in the CAR to the International Criminal Court (ICC) on 22 December 2004. "The ICC prosecutor's investigation opened on 22 May 2007, with former DRC vice-president Jean-Pierre Bemba Gombo the first person to face trial for alleged crimes committed in the CAR. On 7 January 2005, the CAR government referring to the prosecutor the crimes committed within the jurisdiction of the Court committed anywhere on the territory of the Central African Republic since 1 July 2002…." The prosecutor subsequently announced that he was carrying out a preliminary examination in order to determine whether to initiate an investigation. Only the ICC was able to try the most serious crimes committed in the CAR since 1 July 2002. CAR's highest court held that the CAR justice system was so disrupted that it was unable to carry out effective investigations and prosecutions. On 22 May 2007, the prosecutor announced the opening of the investigation into grave crimes allegedly committed in the CAR, with the peak of violence occurring in 2002 and 2003. The prosecutor's announcement highlighted in particular sexual violence, referring to hundreds of victims telling of rapes and other abuses committed "with particular cruelty." The prosecutor also explained that this was the first time he was "opening an investigation in which allegations of sexual crimes far outnumber alleged killings." The ICC Office of the Prosecutor had previously stated that it was waiting for the decision of the Cour de Cassation to decide whether to open an investigation in CAR, on the basis of the complementarity principle[377] contained in the Rome Statute. The trial opened on 22 November 2010 and is ongoing. No other cases are ongoing in the CAR situation and no other public arrest warrants have been issued.

---

[377] The complete description of a phenomenon requires the use of two distinct theories that are complementary to each other

Jean-Pierre Bemba Gombo was the first person on trial in the CAR case. He was the commander-in-chief of the Mouvement de Libération du Congo (MLC) and former vice-president of the Democratic Republic of Congo. Gombo was the son of a millionaire, he is one of the richest men in Africa. On 23 May 2008, ICC Pre-Trial Chamber III issued a sealed warrant of arrest for war crimes and crimes against humanity for Bemba, which was unsealed on 24 May 2008. On 24 May 2008, Belgium arrested Bemba and he was transferred to the custody of the ICC. The confirmation of charges hearing began on 12 January 2009. On 15 June 2009 PTC II confirmed two counts of crimes against humanity (rape and murder) and three counts of war crimes (rape, murder and pillaging) against Bemba, sending his case to trial. Reportedly, the MLC troops committed torture, rape, and attacks on human dignity, such as humiliating and degrading treatment. It is also alleged that the troops took part in looting, particularly in the cities of Mongoumba and Bossangoa and in a city denominated PK12. They are also allegedly responsible for attacks against the civilian population and torture and rape of a widespread and systematic nature. The crimes were allegedly committed in the CAR from 26 October 2002 to 15 March 2003.[378]

The defense for Bemba had sought permission to appeal the decision, arguing that judges had erroneously interpreted and applied Regulation 55 of the Regulations of the Court. This regulation states, among others, that when the possibility of a change to the legal characterization of the facts is envisaged at any time during trial, trial judges may suspend hearings in order to ensure that the participants have adequate time and facilities for effective preparation. In September 2012 judges notified parties to the trial that they might consider a re-characterization of the facts of the charges. Mr. Bemba is currently charged with failing to take action although *he knew* that his troops were committing rapes, murders, and pillaging during the 2002-2003 armed conflict in the Central African Republic (CAR). The proposed change would have the facts state that "owing to circumstances at the time, he should have known" that his troops were committing, or about to commit, those crimes. Thus the outcome of the trial depends upon the applicability

---

378 http://www.bembatrial.org/; http://www.coalitionfortheicc.org/?mod=bemba.

of the doctrine of leadership responsibility.[379]

[379]"The Doctrine of Command Responsibility in the Bemba Case" E2%80%9D-in-the-bemba-case; "Judges Reject Bemba Appeal" *Washington Post*, 18 January 2013.

8
Special Courts and Command Responsibility

The United Nations is free to create whatever courts, including ad hoc tribunals, that it wishes. Action would normally begin with the Security Council which would create the tribunal by resolution. Since the 1980s, states have been increasingly addressing human rights violations using multiple transitional justice mechanisms including domestic human rights trials. In the earlier period, scholars generally concluded that trials for past human rights violations were politically untenable and likely to undermine and weaken new democracies. These pessimistic claims of skeptics that human rights trials threaten democracy, increase human rights violations, and exacerbate conflict are not supported by any substantial evidence. If anything, the trials tend to show that the government is functioning and has taken the correct road to republican prosperity. The world has witnessed the emergence and dramatic growth of truth commissions and domestic human rights trials.

Our interest is in the behavior of executives and their supporters, both civilian and military. When we speak of command responsibility we focus on two items of behavior. Executives may issue orders that run contrary to basic human rights they must be stopped and then punished. When they learn of outrages perpetrated by those below they must act immediately and decisively to halt the acts and then punish the appropriate persons. We shall now examine several incidents of command irresponsibility and the consequent trials.

Genocide in Rwanda

In the 1990s Rwanda had a population of about seven million, composed of three ethnic groups: Hutu (approximately 85%), Tutsi (14%) and Twa (1%). In the early 1990s, Hutu extremists blamed the Tutsi minority population for the country's increasing social, economic, and political difficulties. Tutsi civilians were also accused of supporting a Tutsi-dominated rebel group, the Rwandan Patriotic Front (RPF).In 1992, President Habyarimana and his supporters began to emphasize the divisions that existed between Hutu and Tutsi by the end of 1992. They made certain that the Hutu remembered past years of oppressive Tutsi rule.[380]

On April 6, 1994, a plane carrying President Habyarimana, a Hutu, was shot down by unknown persons. Violence began almost immediately as the Hutu blamed the RPF. Hutu extremists launched their plans to destroy the entire Tutsi civilian population, in what became known as ethnic cleansing. Tutsi and people suspected of being Tutsi were killed in their homes and as they tried to flee at roadblocks set up across the country during the genocide. Entire families were killed at a time. Women were systematically and brutally raped. In the weeks following April 6, 1994, some 800,000 men, women, and children perished in the Rwandan genocide. That number represented as many as three-quarters of the Tutsi population. At the same time, thousands of Hutu were murdered because they opposed the killing campaign and the forces directing it.[381]

Humanitarian organizations estimated that some 200,000 people participated in the perpetration of the Rwandan genocide. It was thus obvious that war crimes trials could not possibly try and punish all, or even most, of the perpetrators of the mass murders. Still, the United Nations thought to punish some of those most responsible under the theory of leadership responsibility. It created the International Criminal Tribunal for

---

[380] For an overview see Morris, Virginia and Michael P. Scharf, *The International Criminal Tribunal of Rwanda*, 2 vols, Irvington-on-Hudson, N.Y.: Transnational Publishers, 1998.

[381] Richard Davies, "Issue: Proving the Nexus Between a Criminal Defendant and the Criminal Conduct of Subordinates and Associates in War Crimes Charges Pursuant to Article 4 of the ICTR -- Memorandum for the Office of the Prosecutor International Criminal Tribunal for Rwanda," New England School of Law, International War Crimes Project, May 2001. See also Rodney Dixon, "Prosecuting the Leaders: the Application of the Doctrine of Superior Responsibility before the United Nations International Criminal Tribunals for the former Yugoslavia and Rwanda in The Commander's Responsibility in Difficult Circumstances," in Netherlands Annual Review of Military Studies (1998), in Peter J. van Krieken, ed., *Refugee Law in Context: The Exclusion Clause*, The Hague : T.M.C. Asser Press, 1999 at pp. 109-130.

Rwanda (ICTR). The charge to the ICTR read, "The fact that any of the acts referred to in … the present Statute was committed by a subordinate does not relieve his or her superior of criminal responsibility if he or she knew or had reason to know that the subordinate was about to commit such acts or had done so and the superior failed to take the necessary and reasonable measures to prevent such acts or to punish the perpetrators thereof."

In 1998, at the ICTR the former Prime Minister of Rwanda, Jean Kambanda, pled guilty to six criminal counts, including genocide and crimes against humanity. Kambanda was Prime Minister of the interim government of Rwanda from 8 April until 17 July 1994. He exercised *de jure* and *de facto* authority and control over the members of his government, senior civil servants, senior officers in the military, and local government officials (préfets). He distributed weapons, incited others to commit massacres, and failed in his duty to ensure the security of the Rwandan population. He supported Radio Télévision Libre des Mille Collines which lauded the massacres and extermination of Tutsis and moderate Hutus. Kambanda was held criminally responsible because of his direct participation in the commission of massacres and because of his failure to stop or prevent them or to punish the perpetrators. Kamdana pled guilty to the six charges against him: genocide, conspiracy to commit genocide, direct and public incitement to commit genocide, complicity in genocide, crimes against humanity: murder and extermination. On 4 September 1998, Trial Chamber I of the International Criminal Tribunal for Rwanda found him guilty of all charges and sentenced him to life imprisonment.[382] He is currently serving that sentence for these crimes. The extension of leadership responsibility recognizes the important role which civilian officials and political leaders can play in the commission of atrocities.

The trial of Jean-Paul Akayesu was largely known for its establishment of genocide as a crime perpetrated by an individual. Akayesu had been appointed to a leadership position in the village of Taba, The Trial Chamber found that Akayesu was responsible for the maintenance of law and order in the village, including the protection of its

---

[382] The Hague Justice Portal "Jean Kambanda"

citizens. Additionally the tribunal found that he either knew, or had reason to have known, of the criminal acts taking place, particularly, near his own office and he did nothing to either prevent the crime or to punish the perpetrators.[383] Ultimately, the Trial Chamber did not find Akayesu guilty under Article 6(3) of the statute, and instead sentenced him on the grounds of *actus reus* [384] for his complicity in genocide by aiding, abetting, instigating, and procuring means.[385]

In 1999, Alfred Musema-Uwimana, a civilian in Rwanda, was prosecuted for his complicity in genocide. He owned of a tea factory in the Byumba Préfecture. As a non-military civilian, Musema-Uwimana was found guilty of criminal responsibility for his *de jure* as well as *de facto* control over his employees. He failed "to take any measure to prevent or punish the commission of these crimes," instead "aiding and abetting in their commission by his presence, and, in some cases, his participation"40 by helping transport armed rebels in a vehicle and with his presence during systematic attacks on Tutsi individuals.[386]

The man widely regarded as the architect of the 1994 Genocide against the Tutsi, Théoneste Bagosora, has been sent to Mali to serve his sentence. He was transferred to the conflict-ridden country together with three other high-profile convicts, namely; Yusuf Munyakazi, who was a businessman and commercial farmer in the former Cyangugu préfecture, Tharcise Renzaho, former Prefect of Kigali City, and Dominique Ntawukulilyayo, former Sub-Prefect of Gisagara, Butare. Bagosora, a former director of Cabinet in the Ministry of Defence, was given 35 years last December, following his appeal against a life sentence handed to him by the ICTR lower chamber. Ruled to have been de facto army chief in the first days of the Genocide, Bagosora was initially sentenced to life

[383] Williamson, Jamie Allan, "Command Responsibility in the Case Law of the International Criminal Tribunal for Rwanda," *Criminal Law Forum* 13 (2002) 3: 365-384.

[384] Latin, guilty act. As an element of criminal responsibility, the wrongful act or omission that comprises the physical components of a crime. Criminal statutes generally require proof of both *actus reus* and *mens rea* on the part of a defendant in order to establish criminal liability.

[385]Hendin, 248-52.

[386] *Prosecutor v. Musema*, Case No. ICTR 96-13-A, Judgment and Sentence, 57 (Trib. Pénal Int'l Pour Le Rwanda Jan. 27, 2000).

imprisonment in December 2008 on charges of genocide, crimes against humanity and war crimes.[387]

A case in May 1999 concerned Clement Kayishema and his role in genocide. The court held as in the trial of Akayesu, that Article 6(3) of the statute expresses a "clear duty upon those in authority, with the requisite means at their disposal, to prevent or punish the commission of a crime." It applied this statute to civilians exerting "requisite authority." A contentious subject due to the nature of the Rwandan conflict was the allusion by the Trial Chamber to the *de facto* power of a superior, notwithstanding the formality and/ or explicit definition of his or her power. The Tribunal also noted that the *mens rea* standard for non-military superiors with established *de facto* power would be held to a lower standard of 'had reason to know,' insofar as that it does not "demand a *prima facie* duty upon a nonmilitary commander to be seized of every activity of all persons under his or her control" The tribunal held that "In light of this incontestable control that Kayishema enjoyed, and his overarching duty as a Prefect to maintain public order, the Trial Chamber is of the opinion that a positive duty upon Kayishema existed to prevent the commission of the massacres. . . . No evidence was adduced that he attempted to prevent the atrocities that he knew were about to occur and which were within his power to prevent." The tribunal sentenced him to life imprisonment.[388]

It is apparent from the Musema, Kayishema and Akayesu cases that the ICTR did clearly define leadership responsibility and develop that concept in terms of its relevance to the unique national Rwandan conflict. In the Akayesu case, although the tribunal determined that he had exercised *de jure* control over his subordinates, it also deemed him to not have had effective or structural control. Therefore was not convicted on the *mens rea* standard of responsibility for the actions of his subordinates. The tribunal rejected the strict liability standard. But in the other two cases, the tribunal expanded both Kayishema's and Musema's convictions expanded the meaning of the leadership responsibility doctrine to

---

387 *New York Times*, 5 July 2012.

388 *Prosecutor vs. Clément Kayishema and Obed Ruzindana* (1999).

encompass civilian responsibility.[389] The Tribunal explicitly established that the *mens rea* standard, though less strict for non-military or *de jure* superiority, was nonetheless applicable to civilian superiors with structural control over their subordinates. It would thus appear as if the comprehension of leadership responsibility with relation to the *mens rea* standard has been well established by both Tribunals insofar as the negation of the standard of negligence. Further, both tribunals have seemingly distinguished more important topics incorporated into the Rome Statute, such as civilian versus military responsibility and the differences, if any, in standards of *mens rea*, as well as the 'had reason to know' versus 'should have known' arguments of customary international law.[390]

Special Tribunal for Jugoslavia

On May 25, 1993, United Nations Security Council Resolution 827 established the International Tribunal for the Former Yugoslavia (ICTY). Among its notable features was its limit in applying customary international law, interpreting the *mens rea* standard applicable to leadership responsibility as it existed in customary law at the time of commission of alleged offenses. The tribunal intended to specifically define leadership responsibility and the element of *mens rea*.[391] It held that act "committed by a subordinate do not relieve his superior of criminal responsibility if he knew or had reason to know that the subordinate was about to commit such acts or had done so and the superior failed to take such necessary and reasonable measures to prevent such acts or to punish the perpetrators thereto." There are two different levels of knowledge that are encompassed in the ICTY's definition of *mens rea.* First there is direct and 'actual' knowledge, the existence of which can be ascertained through testimony or through the compiling of circumstantial evidence. There is

[389] Roman Boed, "Current Developments in the Jurisprudence of the International Criminal Tribunal for Rwanda," *International Criminal Law Review* 2 (2002) 283-295

[390] Markham, Max, "The Evolution of Command Responsibility in International Humanitarian Law," *Penn State Journal of International Affairs* [2011] 51-57. http://psujia.files.wordpress.com/2012/04/

[391] Schabas, William A .,"*Mens Rea* and the International Criminal Tribunal for the Former Yugoslavia" *New England Law Review* 37 (2002-03) 1015-1036

also 'had reason to know' which was defined more strictly by the Appeals Chamber of the Celebici cases of the ICTY.[392]

In the Čelebići Prison Case the International Criminal Court alleged that war crimes had occurred and sought to try those responsible under the doctrine of leadership responsibility. The prosecutor wrote, "The power or authority to prevent or to punish does not solely arise from de jure authority conferred through official appointment. In many contemporary conflicts, there may be only de facto, self-proclaimed governments and therefore de facto armies and paramilitary groups subordinate thereto. Command structure, organized hastily, may well be in disorder and primitive. To enforce the law in these circumstances requires a determination of accountability not only of individual offenders but of their commanders or other superiors who were, based on evidence, in control of them without, however, a formal commission or appointment. A tribunal could find itself powerless to enforce humanitarian law against de facto superiors if it only accepted as proof of command authority a formal letter of authority, despite the fact that the superiors acted at the relevant time with all the powers that would attach to an officially appointed superior or commander."[393]

The Čelebići Prison camp was erected in the village of Čelebići in the central Bosnian municipality of Konjic and used during the Bosnian War. It was utilized principally by several units of the Bosnian Ministry of the Interior (MUP), Croatian Defence Council (HVO) and later the Territorial Defense Forces (TO). Here the Croats detained one hundred Serb prisoners of war. The Croats had detained these men during military operation designed to reopen the routes to Sarajevo and Mostar in May 1992. These routes had earlier been blocked by the Serb forces. Detainees at the camp were subjected to torture, sexual assaults, beatings and otherwise cruel and inhuman treatment. Certain prisoners were shot and killed or beaten to death.[394]

---

[392] Henquet, Thomas, "Convictions for Command Responsibility Under Articles7(1) and 7(3) of the Statute of the International Criminal Tribunal for the Former Yugoslavia," *Leiden Journal of International Law* 15 (2002) 805-834

[393] ICTY Judgment in *Prosecutor v. Delalic* et al. Case No. IT-96-21-A, 20 February 2001, at 195

[394] Fenrick, William J., "Some International Law Problems Related to Prosecution

During the conflict in the former Yugoslavia, Konjic municipality was of strategic importance as it contained important communication links from Sarajevo to southern Bosnia and Herzegovina. Furthermore, several important military facilities existed in Konjic, including the Igman arms and ammunition factory, the Yugoslavian National Army (JNA) Ljuta barracks, the Reserve Command Site of the JNA, the Zlatar communications and telecommunications center, and the Celebici barracks and warehouses. Serbs were not in majority in the Konjic municipality and the area did not form part of the so-called Serb autonomous regions, in March 1992. The Serbian Democratic Party (SDS), in co-operation with the JNA, had also been active in arming the Serb population of the municipality and in training paramilitary units and militias. The SDS distributed around 400 weapons to Serbs in the area. Konjic was also included in those areas claimed by Croatia in Bosnia and Herzegovina as part of the self-styled Croatian Community of Herzeg-Bosnia, despite the fact that the Croats did not constitute a majority of the population either. Thus, there were HVO units established and armed in the municipality by April 1992.[395]

Following the international recognition of the independent Bosnian state the SDS representatives from the Municipal Assembly boycotted the Assembly. They then created a War Assembly was formed to take charge of the defense of the municipality. Between 20 April and early May 1992 Bosnian government forces seized control over most of the strategic assets of the district along with some armaments. However, Serb forces controlled the main access points to the region, effectively cutting it off from outside supply. The Serbs expelled many Bosnian citizens. Many left for Serb-controlled villages following a decision that the Serb leadership promulgated.

Before the International Criminal Tribunal for the Former Yugoslavia," *Duke Journal of Comparative and International Law* 6 (1995-96) 103-125.

[395] Dixon, Rodney, "Prosecuting the Leaders: the Application of the Doctrine of Superior Responsibility before the United Nations International Criminal Tribunals for the former Yugoslavia and Rwanda in The Commander's Responsibility in Difficult Circumstances" in Peter J. van Krieken, ed., *Refugee Law in Context: The Exclusion Clause*, The Hague : T.M.C. Asser Press, 1999, at 109-1

On 4 May 1992, the Serb forced began shelling Konjic town. This shelling continued daily for over three years, until the signing of the Dayton Peace Agreement. Naturally the shelling inflicted substantial damage and resulted in the loss of many lives. Charitable organizations attempted to supply the local people with food and other essentials. On 20 May 1992 forces of the TO and HVO entered the area and Bosnian government soldiers moved through Viniste towards the villages of Cerići and Bjelovcina. Cerići.

Following the military operations the Bosnians arrested many Serbs and it was thus necessary to create a facility where they could be imprisoned. Sadly, the Serbs were also beaten, raped.[396] The majority of the prisoners who were detained between April and December 1992 were men, captured during and after the military operations at Bradina and Donje Selo and their surrounding areas. The Bosnians also created a military investigating commission, whose purpose was to establish the responsibility of these persons for any crimes. The Commission comprised representatives of both the police and the Croat Defence Council (HVO), as well as the Territorial Defense (TO). The Commission interviewed many of the Celebici inmates and took their statements. They also analyzed documents which had been collected to determine their role in the combat against the Konjic authorities as well as their possession of weapons.[397]

The commission placed Serbs in various categories and compiled a report recommending that certain persons be released. Some of the individuals in the lower priority categories were subsequently transferred to other camps. From May until December 1992, the Bosnians occasionally released individuals and groups from the Celebici prison camp. The International Red Cross visited the camp on two occasions in the first half of August. According to the *New York Times*, "The roughly 200 men held in the camp...were local Serbs who had been rounded up and disarmed," many of whom were elderly or infirm. According to human

---

[396] Swaak-Goldman, Olivia, "International Criminal Tribunal for the former Yugoslavia" American Journal *of International Law* 93 (1999) 514

[397] Crowe, Christopher N., "Command Responsibility in the Former Yugoslavia: The Chances for Successful Prosecution," *University of Richmond Law Review* (1994-95) 29: 191-233

rights investigators, the prisoners were fed rarely, on bread and water. They rarely bathed, slept on concrete floors without blankets, and many were forced to defecate on the floor. Serbian survivors said soldiers entered the base at night and beat prisoners with clubs, rifle butts, wooden planks, shovels and pieces of cable. Investigators say that in May and August, about 30 prisoners died from beatings and a few others were killed by the soldiers. Several of these victims were elderly.[398]

Among those tried were Zdravko Mucić, an ethnic Croat and commandant of the prison camp who was found guilty of torture and given 9 years imprisonment; Hazim Delić, Bosniak and deputy prison commander was found guilty of murder and torture and given 18 years in prison; and Esad Landzo, another Bosniak, a guard who found guilty of murder and given 15 years. In the case of Zejnil Delalić, the Court found that he did not have enough command control over the prison camp and the guards who worked there to allow a trial on the charge of criminal responsibility for their actions.[399]

From May to November 1992, Zdravko Mucić was commandant of the Čelebići prison camp. Zdravko Mucic, also known as "Pavo," born 31 August 1955, was commander of Celebici camp from approximately May 1992 to November 1992. In his position he possessed superior authority over the functioning of the prison-camp, with powers of control over its personnel, including the deputy commander and the guards. On 16 November 1998, the International Criminal Tribunal for the former Yugoslavia convicted Mucić of grave breaches of the Geneva Conventions and violations of the laws or customs of war. He was indicted with Esad Landžo, Hazim Delić, and Zejnil Delalić. Mucic was charged with responsibility as a superior for all of the offenses alleged in the Indictment. In addition to being charged as a participant for the creation of inhumane conditions, the unlawful confinement of civilians, the plunder of private property, with responsibility pursuant for acts of murder, acts of torture, acts causing great suffering or serious injury to body or health, inhumane

---

[398] Damaska, Mirjan R., "The Shadow Side of Command Responsibility" (2001). *Faculty Scholarship Series.* Paper 1574. http://digitalcommons.law.yale.edu/fss_papers/1574

[399] "Zdravko Mucić" Hague Portal.

acts, the subjection of detainees to inhumane conditions constituting the offenses of willfully causing great suffering or serious injury to body or health and cruel treatment. On 16 November 1998, Trial Chamber II sentenced Mucić to 7 years' imprisonment. On 9 October 2001, the Appeals Chamber increased his sentence to 9 years' imprisonment. On 18 July 2003, Mucić was granted early release having been given credit for the time he had spent in custody since 18 March 1996.[400]

In his position as deputy commander and subsequently commandant of the Čelebići camp, Hazim Delić was responsible for its overall administration. He also exercised hierarchical superiority over the camp guards as well as any others who were authorized to enter the camp. According to the indictment, Delić knew, should have known, or had reason to know, that those in a rank subordinate to him were abusing prisoners. He had failed to take all necessary and reasonable measures to ensure that these acts were not committed and to punish the offenders following the commission of such acts. He was also responsible for permitting the inhumane living conditions which had imposed on the prisoners. These failures included the deprivation of food and water, medical care, sleeping facilities and proper sanitation. Delić was accused not only of allowing these acts to be committed, but also of having himself actively participated in them. Later authorities of Bosnia-Herzegovina arrested Delić on May 2, 1996. He was transferred to the International Criminal Tribunal for the former Yugoslavia on 13 June 1996. He was sentenced to 20 years in prison on 16 November 1998, and the sentence was reduced to 18 years by the Appeals Chamber on 8 April 2003. He was granted early release 24 June 2008.[401]

The charges that the prosecution brought against Esad Landzo were of the most serious nature, including the willful killing and murder of Stepo Gotovac, Simo Jovanovi and Boko Samoukovi, the torture of Momir Kuljanin, Spasoje Miljevi, and Mirko, and willful causing of great suffering or serious injury to and cruel treatment of two other inmates. In addition to the specific acts in the Indictment which Landzo has been found to have committed, the Trial Chamber also notes that he contributed

---

[400] Case IT-96-21; *"Mucic, Zdravko"* Hague Justice Portal.

[401] "Hazim Delić" Hague Justice Portal.

substantially towards the atmosphere of terror prevailing in the Celebici prison camp through his brutal treatment of the detainees. The beatings and other forms of mistreatment which Landzo meted out to the prisoners detained in Hangar and elsewhere in the prison-camp were inflicted randomly and without any apparent provocation, in a manner exhibiting some imaginative cruelty as well as substantial ferocity. There \was no doubt as to the savagery with which Landzo beat to death Šcepo Gotovac, an elderly and defenseless man, and his potential for cruelty, exhibited by the pinning of a metal badge to Mr. Gotovac's head in addition to his beating. The Trial Chamber has also heard testimony that Mr. Landzo continued in his beating of Mr. Gotovac, impervious to the pleas for mercy of the victim. Many witnesses testified before the Trial Chamber about Landzo's apparent preference for inflicting serious burns upon detainees in the prison-camp.

With the Celebici case the courts found came a new identification of direct and indirect command responsibility, as well as a more definitive definition of the *mens rea* argument. The ICTY found that 'direct' responsibility was established as a result of a positive action, whereas 'indirect' responsibility would be established due to the omission or failure to undertake a necessary act.[402] Moreover, the Celebici Trial Chamber judgment took into account the issue of culpability of non-militarily involved superiors, commenting, "a superior may be exposed to culpability on the basis of *de facto* authority so long as the individual has the fundamental power to control the acts of subordinates."[403]

Radovan Karadžić was a former Bosnian Serb politician, self-styled president of Republika Srpska (1992-96) which he chose to add to Serbia. He was detained in the United Nations Detention Unit of Scheveningen, accused of war crimes committed against Bosnian Muslims and Bosnian Croats during the Siege of Sarajevo, as well as ordering the

[402] Commission of Experts in the former Yugoslavia, *Final Report of the Commission of Experts, Established Pursuant to Security Council Resolution 780 (1992)*, UN SCOR, Annex, UN Doc. S/1994/674

[403] Hendin, Stuart E. "Command Responsibility and Superior Orders in the Twentieth Century - A Century of Evolution." *Murdoch University in Perth Australia*. Mar. 2003. Web. 4 June 2011. http://www.murdoch.edu.au/ elaw/issues/v10n1/hendin101_text.html.

Srebrenica massacre. Radovan Karadžić moved to Sarajevo in 1960 to study psychiatry at the Sarajevo University School of Medicine. He studied neurotic disorders and depression at Næstved Hospital in Denmark in 1970, and during 1974-75 he received further medical training at Columbia University. Karadžić was co-founder of the Serbian Democratic Party in Bosnia and Herzegovina.

On 6 April 1992, Bosnia was recognized by the UN as an independent state, but a few months later Karadžić declared the independence of Republika Srpska from Croat and Muslim Bosnia. Karadžić became President of this Bosnian Serb administration in Pale about 13 May 1992 after the breakup of the Socialist Federal Republic of Yugoslavia. At the time he assumed *de jure* powers including command of the army of the Bosnian Serb administration. He had the authority to appoint, promote and discharge officers of the army. On 4 August 1995, with a massive Croatian military force poised to attack the Serb-held Krajina region in central Croatia, Karadžić announced he was removing General Ratko Mladić from his commandant post and assuming personal command himself. Karadžić had blamed Mladić for the loss of two key Serb towns in western Bosnia. Mladić ignored the insult and claimed to have the support of both the Bosnian Serb military and people at large. Karadžić denounced Mladić as a "madman," but Mladić's popular support forced Karadžić to rescind his order on 11 August. The main reason the courts were interested in Karadžić was the campaign of ethnic cleansing campaign that took place throughout areas controlled by the Army of the Republika Srpska during the 1992–1995 Bosnian War. ICTY judged that the 1995 Srebrenica massacre, known as "ethnic cleansing," was genocide and its instigator was Karadžić and that it constituted the worst case of genocide since World War II. He went into hiding in 1997 after a peace accord brokered by President Bill Clinton had brought the fighting in Bosnia to an end.[404]

Sought as a war criminal, Karadžić was a fugitive from 1996 until July 2008. The United States government offered a $5 million reward for his and Ratko Mladić's arrests. He had been indicted for war crimes by the International Criminal Tribunal for the former Yugoslavia [ICTY]. The

---

[404] *London Times*, 23 October, 2012; *The Guardian*, 16 October 2012.

principal charge in the indictment was genocide against Bosnian Muslim and Bosnian Croat civilians during the Bosnian War of 1992–1995. While a fugitive he worked at a private clinic in Belgrade specializing in alternative medicine and psychology under the alias Dr. Dragan David Dabić. Authorities missed arresting Karadžić in 1995, when he was an invitee of the United Nations. His ability to evade capture for over a decade made him a local hero among the Bosnian Serbs. During his visit to the United Nations in 1993, he was handed a service of process for a civil claim under the Alien Tort Act. American courts ruled that Karadžić was properly served and the trial was allowed to proceed in United States District Court. He was arrested in Belgrade on 21 July 2008 and brought before the War Crimes Court in Belgrade a few days later. That court extradited him to the Netherlands. He was sometimes referred to by Western media as the "Butcher of Bosnia, a sobriquet also applied to General Ratko Mladić."[405]

During the time the world was searching for Karadžić, on September 2006, the ICTY tried and found guilty former Bosnian Serb leader Momcilo Krajišnik. ICTY judged him guilty of multiple instances of crimes against humanity. However, while the ICTY judges found that there was evidence that the crimes committed in Bosnia constituted genocide (*actus reus*), they did not conclude that Krajišnik possessed genocidal intent, or was part of a criminal enterprise that had such an intent (*mens rea*).

Karadžić was accused by the ICTY of command responsibility for numerous war crimes committed against non-Serbs, in his several roles as Supreme Commander of the Bosnian Serb armed forces and President of the National Security Council of the Republika Srpska. He was accused by the same authority of being responsible for the deaths of more than 7500 Muslims. Under his direction and command, Bosnian Serb forces initiated the Siege of Sarajevo. He was accused by the ICTY of ordering the Srebrenica massacre in 1995, directing Bosnian Serb forces to "create an unbearable situation of total insecurity with no hope of further survival of life" in the UN safe area. In addition, he is accused by the ICTY of ordering that United Nations personnel be taken hostage in May–June

---

[405] *New York Times*, 25 January 2013.

1995.[406]

He was jointly indicted by the International Tribunal for the Former Yugoslavia in 1995, along with General Ratko Mladić. The indictment charges Karadžić on the basis of his individual criminal responsibility and superior criminal responsibility with: five counts of crimes against humanity, including extermination, murder, persecutions on political, racial and religious grounds, persecutions, inhumane acts, and forcible transfer of populations; three counts of violations of the laws of war including murder, unlawfully inflicting terror upon civilians, and the taking hostages; one count of breaches of the Geneva Conventions, i.e., willful killing; and the unlawful transfer of civilians because of religious or national identity.[407]

Goran Hadzic is the last of 161 suspects still alive and at large after the Yugoslav ethnic wars. He is accused of murder, torture and forcible deportation at the very outset of those wars. Prosecutors say Hadzic, president of the self-proclaimed Republic of Serbian Krajina from 1992-94, was responsible for killings and forced deportations of minority ethnic Croats from the region after Croatia broke away from Yugoslavia in 1991. Already sentenced in his absence to a total of 40 years in prison by Croatian courts in the mid-1990s, Hadzic was finally detained by Serbian authorities in 2011.[408]

Special Court for Sierra Leone

The Sierra Leone Civil War (1991–2002) began on 23 March 1991 when the Revolutionary United Front (RUF), with support from the special forces of Charles Taylor's National Patriotic Front of Liberia (NPFL), intervened in Sierra Leone in an attempt to overthrow the legitimate government headed by Joseph Momoh. Libyan dictator Muammar al-Gaddafi both trained and supported Charles Taylor and Foday Sankoh, the founder of RUF. Charles Taylor had also worked for The U. S. CIA in the 1980s. Viktor Bout, a Russian businessman, with close ties to the Soviet government, supplied Charles Taylor with arms for use in Sierra Leone

---

[406] "Radovan Karadzic denies Bosnia war crimes" BBC 16 October 2012
[407] guardian.co.uk, Tuesday 16 October 2012
[408] Reuters, 16 October 2012.

and also met with him about the various military operations. The resulting civil war lasted 11 years, enveloped the country, and left over 50,000 dead.

The RUF was initially quite successful militarily and during the first year of the war. It quickly took control of large areas in eastern and southern Sierra Leone, which were diamond rich. The initial rebellion could have easily been quelled in the first half of 1991, but the SLA's poor behavior and miserable record in battle made this outcome possible. The RUF was numerically inferior but by the end of the year controlled two-thirds of Sierra Leone. That and the disruption in diamond production precipitated a military *coup d'état* in April 1992. The coup was coordinated by the National Provisional Ruling Council (NPRC). By the end of 1993, the Sierra Leone Army (SLA) had succeeded in pushing the RUF back to the Liberian border, although the RUF recovered and fighting continued. In March 1995, the government of Sierra Leone hired Executive Outcomes (EO), a South African private military organization, to do battle with the RUF. Sierra Leone installed an elected civilian government in March 1996. The RUF then signed the Abidjan Peace Accord. Under great pressure from the United Nations, the government terminated its contract with EO before the accord could be implemented, and hostilities began anew.

In May 1997 a group of SLA officers who were frustrated by the continual but pointless war staged a coup and established the Armed Forces Revolutionary Council (AFRC). They announced that they were the new and sole legitimate government of Sierra Leone. The AFRC then joined with the RUF to continue the war. The coalition captured Freetown with little resistance. The AFRC, led by self-styled president Johnny Paul Koroma, declared that the war was now over. Instead, the AFRC initiated a wave of looting, rape, looting, and murder.

The Economic Community of West African States Monitoring Group [ECOMOG] sent troops which quickly retook Freetown for the legitimate government of Sierra Leone. Its troops found the outlying regions far more difficult to pacify.

In January 1999, various world leaders promoted negotiations between the RUF and the government of Sierra Leone. The resultant Lome Peace Accord was signed on 27 March 1999. The accord gave the RUF the national vice presidency as well as control of Sierra Leone's diamond mines in return for a cessation of the fighting. The United Nations sent a peacekeeping force to monitor disarmament and end all fighting. Known as the United Nations Mission in Sierra Leone (UNAMSIL) it was created by the U. N. Security Council in October 1999 and was active until 2005. UNAMSIL replaced a previous mission, the United Nations Observer Mission in Sierra Leone (UNOMSIL). The U.N. brought in a multi-national force commanded by General Vijay Jetley of India, later replaced by Lieutenant General Daniel Opande of Kenya in November 2000.

Government soldiers were indiscriminate in their search for rebels or rebel sympathizers among the civilian population. After retaking captured towns, the SLA would frequently transport citizens to concentration camps [called strategic hamlets] far from their homes in Eastern and Southern Sierra Leone. Supposedly the SLA was separating the population from the insurgents. In many cases this displacement was followed by much looting and theft after the villagers. SLA's brutal behavior led to the alienation of many civilians and caused some to join the rebel cause. A grassroots militia force, really *levees en masse*, the Kamajors, operated locally in familiar territory and soon became a significant impediment to both marauding government and RUF troops. The Kamajors clashed with both government and RUF forces and became instrumental in stopping the looting of villages.

On 18 January 2002, President Kabbah announced that the Sierra Leone Civil War was officially over. There had been many difficulties, most of which were overcome only with the assistance of foreign powers, notably India and Great Britain. The Security Council extended UNAMSIL's mandate until June 2005 and again until December 2005. UNAMSIL completed the withdrawal of all troops in December 2005.[409]

The Lome Peace Accord established of a Truth and Reconciliation Commission to provide a forum for both victims and perpetrators of human rights violations during the conflict to tell their stories and facilitate healing. Subsequently, the Sierra Leonean government asked the UN to help set up a Special Court for Sierra Leone (SCSL), which would try those who "bear the greatest responsibility for the commission of crimes

[409] "Sierra Leone" in Wikipedia

against humanity, war crimes and serious violations of international humanitarian law, as well as crimes under relevant Sierra Leonean law within the territory of Sierra Leone since 30 November 1996."[410] Both the Truth and Reconciliation Commission and the Special Court began operating in the summer of 2002.

In August 2003 President Kabbah testified before the Truth and Reconciliation Commission on his role during the civil war. In March, the Special Court for Sierra Leone issued its first indictments for war crimes during the civil war. Foday Sankoh (1937-2003) was already in custody. Accused of encouraging his troops to loot, rape, and commit mutilations, Sankoh died of complications arising from a stroke while awaiting trial.[411] RUF field commander Sam "Mosquito" Bockarie Koroma (1964-2003), a leading member of the RUF, was infamous during the Sierra Leone Civil War for his brutal tactics, which included looting, mutilation, and rape. On 3 March 2003, Sam Bockarie was indicted for crimes against humanity, and violations of international humanitarian law. He has been slated for trial by the SCSL, but was killed by Charles Taylor's agents. Taylor assumed that Bockarie would testify against him at the SCSL.[412] Samuel Hinga Norman (1940-2007) was arrested when the indictments were announced. was a Sierra Leonean politician from the Mende tribe. He was the founder and leader of the Kamajors. The Kamajors had supported the government of Ahmed Tejan Kabbah against the RUF. On 7 March 2003 Hinga Norman was indicted by the for war crimes and crimes against humanity. He died on 22 February 2007 in Dakar, Senegal, while undergoing medical treatment.[413] On 1 December 2003, Major General Tom Carew served in the SLA and was Chief of the Defense Staff of Sierra Leone from April 2000 to November 2003, at which point Sierra Leone President Ahmad Tejan Kabbah re-assigned him to non-military duties.[414]

---

[410] See records at http://www.sc-sl.org/scsl/Public/SCSL-04-16-PT-AFRC/SCSL-04-16-T-536/SCSL-04-16-T-536

[411] http://www.infoplease.com/spot/sankoh1.html

[412] "The Mysterious Death of a Fugitive" http://www.theperspective.org/fugitive bockarie.html

[413] "Samuel Hinga," ICC Justice Portal, http://www.haguejusticeportal.net/index.php?id=8328; See also the special report on Hinga at Reports/SamuelHingaNorman _SpecialReport.html

[414] http://www.ilhr.org/ilhr/regional/africa/kabala.html; "Tom Carew" on Wikipedia;

In June 2007, the Special Court found three of the eleven people indicted guilty of war crimes, including acts of terrorism, collective punishments, extermination, murder, rape, outrages upon personal dignity, conscripting or enlisting children under the age of 15 years into armed forces, enslavement, and pillage. Alex Tamba Brima (1971-), is a former Sierra Leonean military commander. He was one of a group of seventeen soldiers in the Sierra Leone Armed Forces who called themselves Armed Forces Revolutionary Council (AFRC) that successfully staged a coup that ousted president Ahmad Tejan Kabbah in May 1997. On 19 July 2007 he was convicted and sentenced to 50 years in prison for committing war crimes and crimes against humanity during the Sierra Leone Civil War.[415] Brima Bazzy Kamara (1968-) was a commander of the soldiers of the AFRC. Kamara was indicted on 7 March 2003, was arrested on 29 May 2003, and his trial before the SCSL began on 7 March 2005. He was tried along with Alex Tamba Brima and Santigie Borbor Kanu. Kamara was found guilty of crimes against humanity and war crimes on 20 June 2007, including counts of murder, rape, forced labor, and the use of child soldiers.[416] Santigie Borbor Kanu was a commander in the AFRC and was one of a group of 17 soldiers who successfully staged the *coup d'etat* that ousted president Ahmad Tejan Kabbah in May 1997. Kanu was indicted on 15 September 2003, was arrested on 16 September 2003, and his trial before the SCSL began on 7 March 2005. He found guilty of crimes against humanity and war crimes on 20 June 2007, including counts of murder, rape, forced labor, and the use of child soldiers.[417]

On 26 April 2012 Charles Taylor (1948-), former president of Liberia, was convicted of command responsibility for allowing his troops to commit serious international crimes during Sierra Leone's brutal armed

---

"Update on Carew" http://news.sl/drwebsite/publish/article_200519538.shtml

[415] sl.org/CASES/ProsecutorvsBrimaKamaraandKanuAFRCCase/tabid/106/Default.aspx; see also "Tamba Brima," in Wikipedia; also http://www.trial-ch.org/en/trial-watch/profile/db/facts/alex-tamba_brima_214.html

[416] "Brima Bazzy Kamara" Justice Portal, ICC. http://www.haguejusticeportal. net/index.php?id=8326; http://www.trial-ch.org/en/trial-watch/profile/db/facts/brima-bazzy_kamara_213.html

[417] "Santigie Borbor Kanu" in Wikipedia; "Santigie Borbor Kanu" ICC Justice Portal, http://www.haguejusticeportal.net/index.php?id=8327; http://www.sl.org/ CASES /Prosecutorvs BrimaKamaraandKanuAFRCCase/tabid/106/Default.aspx.

conflict. His trial lasted five years. Taylor was accused of backing rebels who killed tens of thousands of people in Sierra Leone's civil war. The SCSL convicted Taylor on 11 counts including terror, murder, and rape, but not guilty of ordering the crimes. Taylor was convicted of war crimes and crimes against humanity before the SCSL on charges that stemmed from his support for rebel groups there. He is the first former true head of state convicted by an international court since the Nuremberg military tribunal of Nazis after World War II. Chief prosecutor Brenda Hollis said it was "confirmation of what the people in Sierra Leone told us from the beginning of our investigations, and that is that Taylor was one of those who bore greatest responsibility for the crimes against them. Reading out the verdict in The Hague, Judge Richard Lussick said Taylor had been found guilty beyond reasonable doubt in connection with eleven counts of war crimes. He had sold diamonds and bought weapons on behalf of the RUF - and knew the rebels were committing atrocities."[418]

Special Court in Lebanon

The Lebanese government requested the assistance of the UN to investigate a series of assassinations and bombings that started in October 2004, which targeted prominent Lebanese figures and killed and injured many people. The Lebanese government requested that the UN create a tribunal of "international character" to try these cases. The U.N. Security Council by resolution 1757 on 30 May 2007 created the Special Tribunal for Lebanon (STL) to try those accused over the 2005 bombing that killed former prime minister Rafik al-Hariri and 21 others. Hariri on the Beirut waterfront in February 2005. He was killed along with 21 others when a massive truck bomb exploded on his motorcade. The court has a pre-trial judge, who can confirm indictments and issue arrest warrants. For considerations of justice and fairness, and also security reasons, the court is situated in the Netherlands. There are also three trial judges, five appeals judges and two alternative judges. Four judges are Lebanese. The maximum sentence the tribunal can impose is life imprisonment. It cannot impose the death penalty or forced labor, sentences which are possible under Lebanese law. Both the prosecution and defense have the right to

---

418 "Sierra Leone War Crimes Trial Verdict Welcomed" *New York Times*, 26 April 2012

present their case to the court, while victims have also been given the right to present their views. Trials in absentia are allowed. Some 51 percent of the court's budget is funded by voluntary contributions from states, while Lebanon's government is responsible for the other 49 percent. The tribunal employs 333 people from 62 countries, 50 of whom are Lebanese, and has a 2011 budget of $65.7 million. Hezbollah has demanded that Lebanon end all cooperation with the tribunal, withdraw funding and pull out the Lebanese judges.[419]

The Special Tribunal for Lebanon officially opened for business on March 1. The STL is the first tribunal of its kind to deal with terrorism as a distinct crime. The U. N. Security Council in resolution 1757 referred to terrorism as a "threat to international peace and security." The tribunal is applying the Lebanese legal definition of terrorism, an element of which is the use of a means "liable to create a public danger," such as explosive devices, inflammable materials, toxic or corrosive products and infectious or microbial agents. The STL appeals chamber ruled on 16 February 2011 that the list of means of attack is illustrative, rather than exhaustive. In the same ruling the appeals chamber defined terrorism as an international crime for the first time.

Victims who have suffered harm in the attacks may participate in the trial to present their views and concerns. The statute does not allow them to seek compensation at the STL, although once the case is over they are free to pursue their claims through national courts on the basis of a judgement by the STL. This is different from the Lebanese system which allows victims to claim damages from the criminal court during a trial. Victims can become involved in the STL once the investigation phase is over and the indictments have been confirmed. The STL statute aims to balance the rights of victims to participate in proceedings with the rights of the accused and the Office of the Prosecutor's strategy.[420]

The prosecutor of the international Lebanon tribunal issued draft indictments over the 2005 killing of former prime minister Rafik al-Hariri. The contents of the draft indictments, which were sent to pre-trial judge Daniel Fransen, were not initially revealed and details of the charge sheet

---

[419] "Special Tribunal for Lebanon" http://www.stl-tsl.org/

[420] "Unique Features of S T L" http://www.stl-tsl.org

may not emerge for some time, when Fransen is expected to decide whether there is enough evidence to proceed with a trial.

The indictment and accompanying arrest warrants were transmitted to the Lebanese authorities on 30 June 2011. The four individuals named in the indictment are: Salim Jamil Ayyash, Mustafa Amine Badreddine, Hussein Hassan Oneissi, Assad Hassan Sabra. El Sayed seeks the release to him of documents relating to his previous detention in Lebanon held by the Prosecutor. The pre-trial judge ordered that the tribunal's prosecutor release more than 270 documents to Jamil El Sayed. Three of the accused are residents of the Hezbollah stronghold of south Beirut, and the fourth is a resident of mainly Shiite south Lebanon. The statement did not mention Hezbollah, but it has been widely reported that the four men are affiliated with the militant group.

There is also the connected case of Hamadeh *et al.* The tribunal has established jurisdiction over three attacks relating to Marwan Hamadeh, George Hawi and Elias El-Murr. The pre-trial judge has also ordered that the Lebanese authorities provide the relevant files to the prosecutor. Among listed charges against them are conspiracy to commit a terrorist act and being an accomplice to the felony of premeditated homicide by using explosive materials While emphasis is on terrorism the principle of command responsibility is still in force. The STL is looking to convict those responsible for ordering the assassination of various officials in Lebanon.

The court's confirmation of the suspects' names marks another painful blow to Hezbollah, which is increasingly projecting an image of itself as heeding Iranian interests rather than being an Arab nationalist organization by proclaiming its undying support for Syria's embattled leader Bashar Assad, whose troops are engaged in a deadly crackdown on pro-democracy demonstrators. Hezbollah denounced the tribunal as a U.S. and Israeli conspiracy and has denied any involvement in the spectacular assassination of the ex-premier and others. Hezbollah Secretary-General Hassan Nasrallah has vowed to defy international authorities' demands to detain, arrest, and extradite any of the wanted men. Hezbollah has also vowed to hit hard at anyone trying to arrest the men, who have disappeared, possibly to Iran. Few, however, believe the men will ever be found and put before a court.[421]

[421] "Lebanon: Court Release Pictures" *New York Times*, 29 July 2011.

Bibliography

Allen, Thomas B. and Norman Polmar, *Code Name Downfall*. Simon & Schuster, 1995.

"A Hidden Chapter in History," *Bulletin of the Atomic Scientist* 37: 8 [October 1981]: 45–53.

Appel, J. M., "Is All Fair in Biological Warfare? The Controversy over Genetically Engineered Biological Weapons," *Journal of Medical Ethics,* 35 (2009) 7: 429–432.

Appleman, John A. *Military Tribunals and International Crimes.* Westport: Greenwood, 1971

Arthurs, Sean, "Comment and case Note: A Foolish Inconsistency: How Refusing to Review Ford v Garcia's Invited Error Demonstrates the 11th Circuit's Prioritization of Procedure over Justice" 72 *U. Cincinnati Law Review* [2004]

Banteka, Ilias. The Contemporary Law of Superior Responsibility, *American Journal of International Law*, 574 (1993).

Bassiouni, M. C., *Crimes against Humanity: Historical Evolution and Contemporary Application*. Cambridge: Cambridge University Press, 2011.

Bassiouni, M. C., "Perspectives on International Criminal Justice," *Virginia Journal of International Law* 5: 298.

Becker, Jean-Jacques. "Les procès de Leipzig." in *Les procès de Nuremberg et de Tokyo*, edited by Annette Wieviorka. Brussels, 1996.

Behr, Edward, *Hirohito: Behind the Myth*. Villard, 1989.

Birkhimer, William Edward, *Military Government and Martial Law.* New York: Hudson, 1914

Bix, Herbert P., *Hirohito and the Making of Modern Japan*. San Francisco: Harper Collins, 2001.

Bleszynski, Nick. *Shoot Straight You Bastards: The Truth Behind the Killing of Breaker Morant*. Green Earth Books, 1997.

Boister, N. & R. Cryer. *The Tokyo International Military Tribunal: A Reappraisal*. Oxford University Press, 2008.

Boot, Max, *The Savage Wars of Peace: Small Wars and the Rise of American Power*. Basic Books, 2003.

Brackman, Arnold C., *The Other Nuremberg*. New York: Morrow, 1987.

Brines, Russell, *MacArthur's Japan.* Lippincott, 1948.

Brooker, John W., "Ford v Garcia: A Puzzling Fusion of the Command Responsibility Doctrine with the Torture Victim Protection Act," 28 *N.C. Journal of International Law* [2003].

Brown, Bernard Edward. *American Conservatives: The Political Thought of Francis Lieber and John W. Burgess.* New York: AMS Press, 1967.

Burnett, Weston B., "Command Responsibility and A Case Study of the Criminal Responsibility of Israeli Military Commanders for the Pogrom at Shatila and Sabra," *Military Law Review* 107 (1985) 71.

Butow, Robert C. *Tōjō and the Coming of the War*. Stanford Univ. Press, 1961.

Carnegie Endowment for International Peace. *Violation of the Laws and Customs of War: Reports of Majority and Dissenting Reports of American and Japanese Members of the Commission of Responsibilities, Conference of Paris of 1919*. London , 1919.

Clapham, Andrew. "Issues of complexity, complicity and complementarity: from the Nuremberg Trials to the dawn of the International Criminal" in Philippe Sands, ed. *From Nuremberg to the Hague: the Future of International Criminal Justice*. Cambridge University Press, 2003.

Clark, John F. Clark and David Gardinier, eds. *Political Reform in Francophone Africa*, Boulder: Westview Press, 1997.

Cole, Hugh M. *The Ardennes: Battle of the Bulge*. U.S. Government Printing Office, 1955.

Conot, Robert E. Justice at Nuremberg. New York: Harper & Row, 1983.

Cowles, Willard B. "Trial of War Criminals by Military Tribunals" *American Bar Association Journal*, June 1944, 330-33.

Crowe, Christopher N., "Command Responsibility in the Former Yugoslavia: The Chances for Successful Prosecution," *University of Richmond Law Review* (1994-95) 29: 191-233.

Cryer, Robert, "Command Responsibility at the ICC and ICTY: In Two Minds on the Mental Element?" *European Journal of International Law,* July 20, 2009.

Damaska, Mirjan R., "The Shadow Side of Command Responsibility" (2001). *Faculty Scholarship Series.* Paper 1574. http://digitalcommons. law.yale. edu/ fss_papers/1574.

D'Amato, Anthony, "Superior Orders vs Command Responsibility" *American Journal of International Law*, 80: 3 (1986), 604-08.

Daws, Gavan, *Prisoners of the Japanese*. New York: Morrow, 1994.

Denhart, Jeff and Stanley Tilles, *By the Neck Until Dead: The Gallows of Nuremberg*. New York: Jona, 1999.

Denton, Kit, *The Breaker*. St. Martins, 1997; F. M. Cutlack, *Breaker Morant: A Horseman Who Made History*. Smith, 1980.

Dezalay, Yves and Bryant G. Garth, eds. *Global Prescriptions: The Production, Exportation, and Importation of a New Legal Orthodoxy*. University of Michigan Press, 2012.

Domingo, Pilar and Rachel Sieder, *Rule of Law in Latin America: The International Promotion of Judicial Reform*. University of London, 2012.

Doty, Joe and Chuck Doty, "Command Responsibility and Accountability," *Military Review*, (Jan.-Feb. 2012), 34-37.

Doty, Joe and Walt Sowden, "Competency vs. Character: It Must Be Both!" *Military Review* (Nov.-Dec, 2009).

Dower, John, *War Without Mercy: Race and Power in the Pacific War.* New York: Pantheon, 1985.

Dower, John W., *Embracing Defeat: Japan in the Wake of World War II*. New Yiek: Norton, 2000.

Engels, Émile, ed. *Ardennes, 1944-1945, Guide du champ de bataille*. Bruxelles: Racine, 1994.

Escoda, Jose M., *Warsaw of Asia: The Rape of Manila*, revised ed. Quezon City, Philippines: Giraffe Books, 2001.

Everett, Arthur et al. *Calley: The Full Compelling Story of a Case as Bitterly Controversial as the Vietnam War Itself*. Dell/Associated Press, 1971.

Falk, Richard, "Shimoda Case: A Legal Appraisal of the Atomic Attacks upon Hiroshima and Nagasaki," *American Journal of International Law*, 59: 4 [October 1965].

Falk, Richard A., Gabriel Kolko, and Robert J. Lifton, eds., *Crimes of War: A Legal, Political-Documentary and Psychological Inquiry into the Responsibility of Leaders, Citizens and Soldiers for Criminal Acts In War*. New York: Vintage Books, 1971.

Falk, Stanley, *Bataan: The March of Death*. New York: W. W. Norton, 1962.

Feldhaus, J. G. "The Trial of Yamashita," *Current Legal Thought*, 1946-47, 251.

Felshaus, J. Gordon, "The Trial of Yamashita," *South Dakota Bar Journal*, 15: 181-93 [1946].

Fenrick, William J., "Some International Law Problems Related to Prosecution Before the International Criminal Tribunal for the Former Yugoslavia," *Duke Journal of Comparative and International Law* 6 (1995-96) 103-125.

Fitz, David L., "Before the "Howling Wilderness:" "The Military Career of Jacob Hurd Smith, 1862-1902" *Military Affairs*, 43: 4 (December, 1979).

Foley, Charles, *Commando Extraordinary*. England: Arms & Armour, 1987.

Friedman, Leon, ed. *The Law of War: A Documentary History*. Abbey, 1977.

Ganoe, John, "The Yamashita Case and the Constitution" *Oregon Law Review*, April 1946, 143-58.

Gordon, Gregory, "The Trial of Peter von Hagenbach: Reconciling History, Historiography, and International Criminal Law." Electronic copy at http://ssrn.com/abstract=2006370.

Gordon, Gregory S., The Trial of Peter Von Hagenbach: Reconciling History, Historiography, and International Criminal Law (February 16, 2012). Available at SSRN: http://ssrn.com/abstract=2006370.

Green, Leslie,"Command Responsibility in International Humanitarian Law," *Transnational Law and Contemporary Problems* 5 (1995).

Green, Leslie, "Superior Orders and Command Responsibility" *Military Law Review* 75 (2003) 309.

Greene, Joshua. *Justice At Dachau: The Trials of an American Prosecutor*. New York: Broadway, 2003.

Greenhaw, Wayne, *The Making of a Hero: The Story of Lieut. William Calley, Jr*. Louisville: Tochstone, 1971.

Green, Leslie C., "War Crimes, Crimes against Humanity and Command Responsibility," file://A:\Green.htm.

Grotius, Hugo de Groot, *The Law of War and Peace* [*De Jure Belli ac Pacis*],

Louise Loomis, Trans., Walter Black, 1949.

Gutman, Roy and David Rieff, eds., *Crimes of War: What the Publ ic Should Know.* New York: Norton, 1999.

Guy, George, "The Defense of Yamashita," *Wyoming L. Jr.* 4: 153-80 (1950).

Handloff, Robert E. ed. *Ivory Coast: A Country Study*, Library of Congress Country Studies, Government Printing Office, 1991.

Hankel, Gerd. *The Leipzig Trials: German War Crimes and Their Legal Consequences after World War I.* Westport: Republic of Letters, 1982.

Harris, Sheldon H., *Factories of Death: Japanese Biological Warfare, 1932–1945, and the American Coverup.* New York; Rev. ed., Routledge, 1994.

Hart, Franklin A., "Yamashita, Nuremberg, and Vietnam: Command Responsibility Reappraised," *Naval War College Review* 25: 19-36 [1972].

Hastings, Max, *Retribution: The Battle for Japan, 1944-45*. Knopf, 2008.

Havers, R. P. W., *Reassessing the Japanese Prisoner of War Experience: The Changi POW Camp, Singapore, 1942–45.* London: Routledge Curzon, 2003.

Hendin, Stuart E., *Command Responsibility and Superior Orders in the Twentieth Century: A Century of Evolution*, 10 Murdoch U. Electronic Journal of Law 191-94 (2003).

Hébert, Valerie Geneviève. *Hitler's Generals on Trial: The Last War Crimes Tribunal at Nuremberg.* University Press of Kansas, 2010.

Henquet, Thomas, "Convictions for Command Responsibility Under Articles 7(1) and 7(3) of the Statute of the International Criminal Tribunal for the Former Yugoslavia," *Leiden Journal of International Law* 15 (2002) 805-834.

Heydecker, Joe J. and Leeb, Johannes. *Der Nürnberger Prozeß*. Köln: Kiepenheuer und Witsch, 1979; also Henkel, Matthias, ed. *Memoriam Nuernberger Prozesse.* Nuremberg: Museen der Stadt Nuernberg, 2011.

Hicks, George, *Comfort Women: Japan's Brutal Regime of Enforced Prostitution in the Second World War.* New York: Norton, 1997.

Hoffman, Stanley, "War Crimes: Political and Legal Issues," *Dissent*, 18: 530-34 (1971).

Huntington, Samuel P. *The Third Wave: Democratization in the Late 20th Century.* U. Oklahoma Press, 1991.

James, D. C., *The Years of MacArthur*. New York: Houghton Mifflin, 1985.

Japanese Prisoners of War, eds. Philip Towle et al. London: Hambledon and London, 2000.

"Japanese Use the Chinese as 'Guinea Pigs' to Test Germ Warfare," *Rocky Mountain Medical Journal* 39: 8 [August 1942].

Keith, Kirsten M., "The *Mens Rea* of Superior Responsibility as Developed by ICTY Jurisprudence" *Leiden Journal of International law* 14 [2001]: 617 at 631.

Kerr, E. B., *Surrender and Survival: The Experience of American POWs in the Pacific, 1941–1945*. New York: Morrow, 1985.

Kershaw, Alex. The Longest Winter: *The Battle of the Bulge And the Epic Story of World War II's Most Decorated Platoon*. Da Capo Press, 2005.

Kirk, John Foster, *History of Charles the Bold.* Philadelphia: Lippincott, 1864.

Knox, Donald, *Death March: The Survivors of Bataan.* New York: Harcourt Brace Jovanovich, 1981.

Kramer, Alan, "The First Wave of International Trials: Istanbul and Leipzig" *European Review*, 14: 4 [Oct. 2006].

Kratoska, Paul H. *Asian Labor in the Wartime Japanese Empire.* Aemonk, NY: Sharpe, 2005.

Kratoska, Paul, ed., *Southeast Asian Minorities in the Wartime Japanese Empire.* London: Routledge Curzon, 2002.

Kuhn, Arthur, "International Law and National Legislation in the Trial of War Criminals" *American Journal of International Law*, July 1950, 559-62.

Lael, Richard L., *The Yamashita Precedent.* Wilmington, DE: Scholarly Resources, 1982, 59-64.

Landas, Marc, *The Fallen: A True Story of American POWs and Japanese Wartime Atrocities.* Wiley, 2004.

Li, Peter, *Japanese War Crimes*. Transaction Publications, 2013.

Lippman, Matthew, "The Evolution and Scope of Command Responsibility" *Leiden Journal of International Law* 13 (2000).

Lippman, Matthew, "Conundrum of Armed Conflict: Criminal Defenses to Violations of the Humanitarian Law of War," *Dickinson Jr of Int. Law* 1 (1996).

MacDonnell, John and Coleman Phillipson, *International Law and the Great War* (1915). Nabu Press reprint, 2012,

Maga, Timothy P., *Judgment at Tokyo: The Japanese War Crimes Trials.* University of Kentucky, 2001.

Maguire, Jill C., "Rape under the Alien Tort Statute" *George Mason Law Review*, 13: 956.

Manning, Paul, *Hirihito: The War Years*. New York: Dodd Mead, 1986.

Markham, Max, "The Evolution of Command Responsibility in International Humanitarian Law," *Penn State Journal of International Affairs* (2011) 51-57. http://psujia.files.wordpress.com/2012/04/

Materials on the Trial of Former Servicemen of the Japanese Army,Charged with Manufacturing and Employing Bacteriological Weapons. Moscow: Foreign Languages Publishing House, 1950.

Meloni, Chantal, *Command Responsibility in International Criminal Law.* Cambridge University Press, 2010.

Meron, Theodor, *Henry's Wars and Shakespeare's Laws*, Oxford, England: Oxford University Press, 1994.

Mettraux, Guénaël, *The Law of Command Responsibility*. Oxford, England: Oxford University Press, 2009.

Miller, Stuart Creighton, *Benevolent Assimilation: The American Conquest of the Philippines, 1899–1903*, Yale University Press, 1982

Minear, Richard R., *Victors' Justice: The Tokyo War Crimes Trials*. University of Michigan Press, 1971, 71-72.

Moloto, Bakone, "Command Responsibility in International Criminal Tribunals" *Berkeley Journal of International Law*, 3: (2009).

Morris, Virginia and Michael P. Scharf, *The International Criminal Tribunal of Rwanda*, 2 vols, Irvington-on-Hudson, N.Y.: Transnational Publishers, 1998.

Muñoz, Heraldo, *The Dictator's Shadow: Life under Augusto Pinochet*. New York: Basic Books, 2008.

Mullins, Claude. *The Leipzig Trials: An Account of the War Criminals' Trials and Study of German Mentality*. London: Witherby, 1921.

Nerlinger, Charles, *Peter von Hagenbach and the Burgundian Domination*. Persee, 1890.

Nmaju, Mba Chidi, "Violence in Kenya: Any Role for the ICC in the Quest for Accountability?" 3 *African Journal of Legal Studies* (2009) 78-95.

Oppenheim, Lassa J, *International Law: War and Neutrality.* New York, 1921. Reprint by Frankin Classics, 2018.

Page, James Madison. *The True Story of Andersonville Prison: A Defense of Major Henry Wirz.* Digital Scanning, 1999.

Parks, William H., "Command Responsibility for War Crimes" *Military Law Review*, 28 (1973).

Powell, John W., "Japan's Germ Warfare: The U.S. Cover-up of a War Crime," *Bulletin of Concerned Asian Scholars* 12: 4 (Oct-Dec 1980): 2–17.

Raimondo, Tony: "The My Lai Massacre: A Case Study, " Human Rights Program, School of the Americas, Fort Benning, Georgia.

Ryan, Allan A., *Yamashita's Ghost: War Crimes, MacArthur's Justice, and Command Accountability*. University Press of Kansas, 2012.

Simpson, Gerry J., "Conceptualizing Violence: Present and Future Developments in International Law" *Alabama Law Review* 60 (1997)

Piccigallo, Philip R., *The Japanese on Trial: Allied War Crimes Operations in the East, 1945-51*. University of Texas, 1979.

Priemel, Kim C. and Stiller, Alexa, eds. *Reassessing the Nuremberg Military Tribunals: Transitional Justice, Trial Narratives, and Historiography.* Berghahn Books, 2012.

Reginbogin, Herbert R. and Christoph J. M. Safferling: *The Nuremberg Trials: International Criminal Law Since 1945*. De Gruyter, 2006.

Reel, A. Frank, *The Case of General Yamashita,* New York: Octagon Books, 1971.

Roht-Arriaza, Naomi, *The Pinochet Effect: Transnational Justice in the Age of Human Rights*. University of Pennsylvania Press, 2005.

Rummel, R.J., *Genocide and Mass Murder Since 1900*. Charlottesville, VA: School of Law, University of Virginia, 1997.

Rutherford, Mildred L. *Facts and Figures versus Myths and Misrepresentations: Henry Wirz and the Andersonville Prison.* 1921; reprint Pranava, 2018.

Russell, Lord Russell of Liverpool, *The Knights of Bushido: A Short History of Japanese War Crimes*. Berkeley Books, 1961.

Schabas, William A ., "*Mens Rea* and the International Criminal Tribunal for the Former Yugoslavia" *New England Law Review* 37 (2002-03) 1015-1036.

Schabas, William A., *An Introduction to the International Criminal Court.* 2nd ed.; Cambridge University Press, 2004.

Schmidt, David Andrew, *Ianfu–The Comfort Women of the Japanese Imperial*

Army of the Pacific War: Broken Silence. Lewiston, NY: Edwin Mellen, 2000.

Scholtz, Leopold. *Why the Boers Lost the War*. Basingstoke: Palgrave-Macmillan, 2005.

Schwarzenberger, George, "A Forerunner of Nuremberg: The Breisach War Crime Trial of 1474" *Manchester Guardian*, 28 September 1946.

Sikkink, Kathryn and Carrie Booth Walling, "The Impact of Human Rights Trials in Latin America." *Journal of Peace Research*, 44 (2007) 4: 427-45.

Slack, John, *Lieutenant Calley: His Own Story*. Tempo Books, 1971.

Solis, Gary D. (1999). "Obedience of Orders and the Law of War: Judicial Application in American Forums." *American University International Law Review.* 15: 481–526.

Stryszak, Michael, "Command Responsibility" *U.S.A.F. Academy Journal of Legal Studies* 11 (2022) 27: 29-30.

Sun Tzu, *The Art of War.* Trans. and annotation by Samuel B. Griffith. Oxford University Press, 1963.

Swaak-Goldman, Olivia, "International Criminal Tribunal for the former Yugoslavia" American Journal *of International Law* 93 (1999) 514.

Tanaka, Yuki, *Japan's Comfort Women: Sexual Slavery and Prostitution During World War II and the U.S. Occupation.* London: Routledge, 2001.

Tanaka, Yuki, "The Atomic Bombing, The Tokyo War Crimes Tribunal" *Asia-Pacific Journal* (2 November 2009).

Tanaka, Yuki, *Hidden Horrors: Japanese War Crimes in World II.* Boulder: Westview Press, 1996.

Thurman, M. J., *War Crimes: Japan's World War II Atrocities*. Turner, 2001.

van Krieken, Peter J., ed., *Refugee Law in Context: The Exclusion Clause*, The Hague : T.M.C. Asser Press, 1999.

Van Schaack, *Beth,* "*Romagoza v. García*: Proving Command Responsibility under the Alien Tort Claims Act and the Torture Victim Protection Act." Center for Human Rights and Humanitarian Law in conjunction with the Washington College of Law at American University.

Vaughan, Richard, *Philip the Good.* Woodbridge: Boydell Press, 2002

Wakabayashi, Bob Tadashi, "The Nanking 100-Man Killing Contest Debate: War Guilt Amid Fabricated Illusions," *Journal of Japanese Studies* 26: 2, [Summer 2000)].

Wallach, Evan and Maxine Marcus "Command Responsibility" in Cherif Bassouni, ed. *International Criminal Law*. 3rd ed., 2008.

Wallach, Evan and Maxine Marcus "Command Responsibility" in Cherif Bassouni, ed. *International Criminal Law*. 3rd ed., 2008.

Weingartner, James J. *Crossroads of Death: The Story of the Malmedy Massacre and Trial.* University of California Press, 1979.

Whiting, Charles, *Skorzeny: "The Most Dangerous Man in Europe,"* DaCapo Press, 1998.

Whiting, Charles. *Massacre at Malmedy.* Stein & Day, 1984.

Wilcox, Craig, *Australia's Boer War: The War in South Africa 1899-1902*. Oxford

University Press , 2002.

Williams, Peter and David Wallace, *Unit 731: Japan's Secret Biological Warfare in World War II* New York: Free Press, 1989.

Williamson, Jamie A., "Some Considerations on Command Responsibility and Criminal Liability" 90 *International Review of the Red Cross* [2008].

Williamson, Jamie Allan, "Command Responsibility in the Case Law of the International Criminal Tribunal for Rwanda," *Criminal Law Forum* 13 (2002) 3: 365-384.

Willis, James F. *Prologue to Nuremberg: The Politics and Diplomacy of Punishing War Criminals of the First World War*. Westport, 2014.

Witt, John Fabian. *Lincoln's Code: The Laws of War in American History*. New York: Free Press, 2012.

Witton, Edward, *Scapegoats of the Empire: The True Story of Breaker Mo rant's Bushveldt Carbineers*. Clock & Rose Press, 2003 reprint.

Womack, Brandy "The Development and Recent Applications of the Doctrine of Command Responsibility: With Particular Reference to the *Mens Rea* Requirement" *International Crime and Punishment, Selected Issues* 1 (2003) 101.

Yamamoto, Masahiro, *Nanking: Anatomy of an Atrocity.* Westport, CT: Praeger, 2000.

Yang, Daqing, "Documentary Evidence and the Studies of Japanese War Crimes: An Interim Assessment" in *Researching Japanese War Crimes Trials*. Interagency Working Group, 2006.

Index

N

O

P

R

S

Y

www.ingramcontent.com/pod-product-compliance
Lightning Source LLC
LaVergne TN
LVHW010718210926
848485LV00008B/1443/J
* 9 7 8 1 6 8 0 5 3 1 3 3 6 *